Understanding and Sharing

Understanding and Sharing
An Introduction to Speech Communication

Judy C. Pearson
Iowa State University

Paul E. Nelson
Iowa State University

wcb

Wm. C. Brown Company Publishers

Dubuque, Iowa

Acknowledgments

The authors and publishers of this book would like to thank all
sources for the use of reprinted material.

Acknowledgments to authors and publishers for permission to
reprint from copyright material is made at the end of the chapter in
which the material appears.

Credit lines for photographs and cartoons appear below and on the
extension of the copyright page at the end of this book.

Chapter 1

Page 4   Photograph by Rick Smolan
Page 7   Photograph by Chuck Isaacs
(continued on page 338)

Dedicated to our parents:
Sophia and J. D.
Ferne and H. B.

Contents

Elements of the
Communication
Process
1

Intrapersonal and
Interpersonal
Communication
81

Public Communication
171

     *An Application of the Principles of Public
     Communication*   288

The Purposes of Persuasive Speeches   290
     Adoption/Discontinuance
Relating the Persuasive Speech to the Audience   291
Categories of Persuasive Strategies   293
     *The Rhetoric of Reason/The Rhetoric of Refutation/The
     Rhetoric of Emotion*
Evaluating the Persuasive Speech: A List of Inquiries
304
Summary   305

                                        Glossary   309
                                        References   321
                                        Topics for Activities   331
                                        Name Index   333
                                        Subject Index   335

Preface

As experienced teachers of speech fundamentals we
are familiar with the problems faced in assessing a
textbook. A textbook must fit the goals of the
course, the background and experience of the
teacher, and the abilities of the students.
Understanding and Sharing is an appropriate text
for a beginning course in speech fundamentals that
emphasizes interpersonal communication and public
speaking. In the area of interpersonal
communication, the book focuses on dyadic
communication as it occurs in information-seeking
or job interviews and on small group communication
in problem-solving. In public speaking, the main
emphasis is on the informative and the persuasive
speech, but the material on public communication is
adaptable to a wide variety of speech purposes.

   Understanding and Sharing uses a skills
approach to help students learn effective
communication behavior in interpersonal and public
situations. The book attempts to combine speech
heritage with the results of recent experimental
studies, pedagogy, and classroom experience.
Understanding and Sharing can help a student
discover the kinds of questions to ask in an
interview; the characteristics of the leader in a small
group; and the functions of an introduction, body,
and conclusion in a public speech; but it is the
teacher who can help the student apply on a
practical level the skills that are described. The
book, the teacher, and the students become partners
in a creative transaction that results in learning
communication skills through practical application.

Audience

Understanding and Sharing is for both the
experienced teacher who can richly supplement any
textbook with personal knowledge and the graduate
teaching assistant who is in the classroom for the
first time.

   It is intended for students in their first speech
course at a community college, technical school,
four-year liberal arts college, or university, and it
was designed to appeal to their interests and written
in their own level of vocabulary. The authors have

tried to make speech communication concepts
palatable by defining them when they are
introduced, by listing new terms as a review at the
end of each chapter and by assembling them
alphabetically in the glossary.

Organization

Understanding and Sharing is divided into three
major parts, each of which focuses on
communication skills.

   Part 1, "Elements of the Communication
Process," begins with "The Nature of
Communication," in which communication is
defined and related to the self, and relates
perception to communication in chapter 2,
"Perception: The Process of Understanding."
Chapter 3, "Verbal Codes: A Tool of Sharing,"
focuses on language and how it can both help and
hinder communication. The last chapter in Part 1,
"Nonverbal Codes: A Tool of Sharing,"
concentrates on the nonverbal aspects of human
communication.

   Part 2, "Intrapersonal and Interpersonal
Communication," opens with "Understanding
Yourself," a chapter on self-awareness, self-
concept, and journal writing as an exercise in
understanding intrapersonal communication. The
second chapter, "Sharing Yourself," emphasizes
self-disclosure, how it operates in interpersonal
communication, when it is appropriate and when it
is inappropriate. "Understanding Another" focuses
on active listening and empathy, and the last chapter
consists of practical application of interpersonal
communication skills in the interview and the small
group discussion.

   Public communication is the subject of Part 3.
It begins with a chapter on audience analysis and
adaptation, examines source credibility in chapter
10, covers topic selection, research, and evidence in
chapter 11, speech organization in chapter 12, and
delivery in chapter 13. The last two chapters are
practical applications that examine in detail the two
most commonly delivered speeches in the basic

speech course: the informative speech and the persuasive speech.

All of the chapters emphasize application of speech concepts; all of them concentrate on skills that can be employed in interpersonal and public communication.

Special Features

Each chapter begins with objectives that state specifically what students should be able to do when they have completed the chapter. For example, ''A student should be able to name three kinds of secondary evidence and their uses.'' Educational research indicates that students learn better if they know specifically what is expected of them. The chapter is previewed in the introduction, and throughout the chapter application exercises are strategically placed so that students can test ideas for themselves immediately after learning about them. Contemporary cartoons, photos, and line drawings illustrate concepts effectively for visually oriented students of the television generation. Chapter 8 on the interview and small groups, chapter 14 on the informative speech, and chapter 15 on the persuasive speech can be especially helpful to students in implementing their knowledge through practical application. Subject matter is summarized and annotated sources for further reading are listed at the end of each chapter.

Instructor's Resource Manual

Understanding and Sharing and the *Instructor's Resource Manual* that accompanies it are our answer to the problems in selecting a text we encountered over the years. Because many textbooks were too theoretical for our pragmatic students, we wrote a skills-oriented book with ideas for everyday application. Because some books were good for public speaking and others were good in interpersonal communication but few were good in both areas, we tried to write an effective book in both areas of speech communication. Because we found the development of good classroom activities to be a problem, we have provided a *Resource Manual* filled with them. Finally, because we found exam questions difficult to develop and resource materials time consuming to find the *Resource Manual* provides them in every chapter.

Each chapter of the *Resource Manual* includes ten true-and-false examination questions, ten multiple-choice and ten essay questions; an annotated list of films, records, and slides that reinforce concepts; and an annotated list of additional readings. Beginning teachers will find especially helpful the manual's quarter and semester schedules for a course based on *Understanding and Sharing*. All teachers can be helped by the manual's resource material and by the activities, from which they can select those that best fit their own teaching style and the objectives of their course. These classroom-tested exercises include explanations of what usually occurs when students do the exercises, what the students are supposed to learn, and what implications of the exercise the teacher should emphasize.

The Authors

Because the textbook is an impersonal entity—the reader does not see the writer and, even worse, the writer cannot see the reader—we self-disclose to reduce the distance between us and the persons who read *Understanding and Sharing*:

Judy C. Pearson is first and foremost a teacher. She earned her doctorate at Indiana University and served as basic course director at Bradley University, Indiana University-Purdue University at Fort Wayne, and at Iowa State University. Paul E. Nelson earned his Ph. D. at the University of Minnesota and was the basic course director at the University of Missouri and chairman of the Speech Department at Iowa State University.

We have taught speech fundamentals all of our professional lives. More importantly, fundamentals is what we like best. We both were honored to win the Central States Speech Association's

Outstanding Young Teacher Award, and both of us attribute much of our abiding interest in fundamentals to the enthusiastic support of our colleagues in the Midwest Basic Speech Director's Conference.

Don Yoder is particularly well qualified as co-author of the instructor's manual because he is a sensitive teacher and because he knows first-hand and recently the needs of a beginning teacher. He served as a graduate teaching assistant at the University of Nebraska where he earned his Master's degree. At Iowa State University he was assistant director of the Basic Speech Program and an instructor in public speaking and interpersonal communication. Don, presently a Ph. D. student at The Ohio State University, assembled and developed many of the activities in the *Instructor's Resource Manual*, collected and developed examination questions, and wrote the objectives for each of its chapters.

Acknowledgments

Understanding and Sharing is a cumulative effort by publishers, editors, critic-evaluators, students, fellow teachers, and the authors. Encouraged by Iowa's harsh winters and hot summers to stay inside to write, we typed our own material, criticized each other's writing, and—because we are husband and wife—encouraged each other lovingly to the completion of the book.

Our graduate professors at Indiana University and the University of Minnesota, our colleagues at many colleges and universities who share our affection for speech fundamentals, and our five children, who can blame us in later years for ignoring them to write a book, deserve our special thanks. The people at Wm. C. Brown Company Publishers have earned our grateful appreciation. We are also grateful for the helpful suggestions from college and university faculty members who evaluated the manuscript at several stages of development: Paul Batty, Parkland Community College; John Crawford, University of Wyoming; Sandra Davis, El Paso Community College; Dennis

Fus, University of Nebraska; M'liss Stewart
Hindman, Tyler Junior College; Loretta Malandro,
Arizona State University; Michael Moore,
University of Maryland; Kathryn Ott, Suffolk
County Community College; Lynn Phelps, Miami
University at Oxford; Edd Sewell, Virginia
Technical Institute; and Edgar B. Wycoff, Florida
Technological University. Finally, we were granted
time occasionally by the Iowa State University
Department of Speech to work on this book. For
that too we are thankful.

Judy C. Pearson
Paul E. Nelson

Understanding and Sharing

Elements of the Communication Process

Communication is the process of understanding and sharing meaning. In this first section of the text, the elements of the communication process are considered. Among the topics discussed are perception, verbal codes, and nonverbal codes. Chapter 1, "The Nature of Communication," includes a consideration of the definition of communication, the function of communication, and problems involved in communication. Chapter 2, "Perception: The Process of Understanding," contains an explanation of the role of perception in the communication process, why differences occur in perception, the activities involved in perception, and methods by which we can validate our perceptions. Chapter 3, "Verbal Codes: A Tool of Sharing," contains an examination of how words create a major obstacle to communication, but also describes methods by which verbal skills can be improved. Chapter 4, "Nonverbal Codes: A Tool of Sharing," includes descriptive material on various nonverbal codes such as bodily movement and facial expression, space, touching, vocal cues, and clothing and other artifacts.

1

The Nature of Communication

Objectives
After study of this chapter you should be able to do the following:

1. Define communication and the relationship between understanding and sharing
2. Differentiate among intrapersonal, interpersonal, and public communication
3. Explain and give examples illustrating Barnlund's concept of the "six persons" involved in interpersonal communication
4. Discuss why communication is centered in the self
5. Discuss and give examples of verbal and nonverbal codes
6. Differentiate between the encoding and decoding processes and discuss the relationship between them
7. Differentiate among action, interaction, and transaction views of communication and discuss the perspective each of these views gives to the study of communication
8. Discuss the ways in which communication is used for survival of the individual and society in today's world
9. Identify three factors which can create barriers to communication and relate these factors to specific personal experiences
10. Describe a personal experience in which you perceived the presence of a hidden agenda and describe the effects of the hidden agenda on your communication

*"I tried to explain to my father why I wanted to go to college, but I just can't
communicate with him."*

*"The woman who sits behind me in comp is really something. I'd like to get to
know her better, but every time I try to talk to her, I freeze up."*

*"I don't know how she does it! I don't think I could ever stand up in front of the
whole congregation and explain why the church needs more money for its youth
program."*

All of us have heard remarks like these, and most of us have expressed similar
sentiments at one time or another. A number of studies have shown that we
spend more time in verbal communication than in any other single activity.[1]
Nonetheless, according to a recent study, Americans reported that their greatest
fear was the fear of speaking in front of a group.[2] Communication pervades the
social atmosphere in which we live—in a sense, it is as essential to people as the
ocean is necessary for the survival of sealife—still, many of us do not feel confident even about our ability to speak to others.

This text is designed to help you to improve your ability to communicate
with other people. Included in this consideration are intrapersonal communication, interpersonal communication, and public communication. Among the forms
of communication discussed are the journal, the interview, the small group discussion, the informative speech, and the persuasive speech. As you read the
text, and as you participate in the suggested activities and exercises, you should
become more able to communicate with others.

Definition of Communication

Communication Is the Process of Understanding and Sharing Meaning

The word *communication* is used in a variety of ways. Before the term is used
further, a common understanding of the word should be established. *Communicate* comes from the Latin *communicare*, which means *to make common*. Originally, communication suggested that some thought, some meaning, or some
message was held in common. Contemporary definitions suggest the manner in
which these are shared: we "exchange thoughts," we "discuss meaning," and
we "transmit messages."

We shall define communication as *the process of understanding and sharing
meaning*. Communication is defined as a process because we recognize that it is
an activity that is characterized by action, change, exchange, and movement.
We cannot stop the process of communication, nor does it have a beginning and
an end.

Communication involves understanding. Persons involved in communication must understand what they are saying and hearing. All of us have been in
situations where we could repeat another person's message but could not understand it. Communication does not occur unless understanding exists.

Communication requires sharing. Consider the popular use of the word
sharing. We share a meal, we share an event, we share a sunset. Sharing is a gift
that people exchange. We can also share with ourselves—when we allow ourselves time to relax and daydream, time to consider who we really are and what
our goals truly are. We share with ourselves in intrapersonal communication; we
share with others in interpersonal and public communication. Regardless of the
situation, communication requires sharing.

In the process of communication, what we understand and share is
meaning. Earlier definitions of communication have identified messages or
thoughts as the objects of sharing. Neither of these terms is as accurate as
meaning however. The term *message* is not sufficient, because it does not imply
any level of understanding. If I repeat an Iranian phrase to a student from Iran,
that only shows that I have heard the phrase and can repeat it. No communication has occurred, even though we shared a particular message. *Thought* is also
a troublesome term. It is very difficult to define thoughts, and even more difficult to determine when our thoughts are the same as another person's. The term
meaning refers to that which is felt to be the significance of something, and is a
more accurate and useful descriptor of the object of communication.

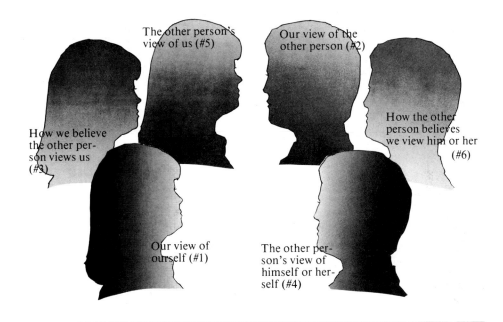

The other person's
view of us (#5)

Our view of the
other person (#2)

How the other
person believes
we view him or her
(#6)

How we believe
the other per-
son views us
(#3)

Our view of
ourself (#1)

The other per-
son's view of
himself or her-
self (#4)

Figure 1.1   Barnlund's "six people"
involved in every two-person
communication. Adapted from Dean C.
Barnlund, "A Transactional Model of
Communication," in *Foundations of
Communication Theory.*

Communication Begins with the Self

Communication requires that we understand and share, but we need to emphasize that communication begins with oneself. All communication is viewed from
the perspective of self.

Dean Barnlund, a communication scholar, introduced the notion that communication is viewed from one's own perspective in his discussion of the "six
persons" involved in every two-person communication situation.[3] These six
persons emerge first from the way in which you view yourself; second, the way
in which you view the other person; third, how you believe the other person
views you; fourth, how the other person views himself or herself; fifth, how the
other person views you; and sixth, how the other person believes you view him
or her. Barnlund believes that we "construct" ourselves, as well as other persons, through the relationships that we have, wish to have, or perceive ourselves
as having. He encourages us to consider the various perspectives that are involved in communication and to recognize the centrality of the self in communication.

All of our perceptions of communication are tied to ourselves. In our descriptions, explanations, and evaluations of communication, we reflect a great deal of ourselves. As participants in communication, we are limited by our own view of the situation. For example, a woman might describe a heated conversation with her spouse as "Nothing at all. He made a mountain out of a molehill." The husband, on the other hand, might conclude that "She never really has understood me."

Communication Occurs in a Variety of Situations

We can communicate with ourselves, with another person, or with a number of other people. Communication scholars discuss the various situations in which communication can occur and distinguish among them on the basis of the number of people involved or on the purpose of the communication. They also use such criteria as the degree of formality or intimacy, the opportunities for feedback, the need for prestructuring messages, and the degree of stability of the roles of speaker and listener.

For our purposes, we distinguish among the various situations in which communication occurs on the basis of our definition of communication, which is that it is the process of understanding and sharing meaning.

Intrapersonal communication, thus, is a process of sharing and understanding that occurs within a person. It is internal communication. Intrapersonal communication includes internal problem solving, resolution of internal conflict, planning for the future, emotional catharsis, and evaluations of oneself, others, and relationships between oneself and others. Intrapersonal communication involves only the self, and it must be clearly understood by the self because it constitutes the basis for all other communication.

We are engaged in intrapersonal communication almost continually. We might more easily become absorbed in "talking to ourselves" when we are alone —walking to class, driving to work, taking a shower—but most of us are involved in this form of communication in the most crowded circumstances as well —during a lecture, at a party, or visiting friends. Think about the last time you looked at yourself in a mirror. What were your thoughts? Intrapersonal communication is almost continuous, and yet we seldom focus on our communication with ourselves.

Interpersonal communication is the process of understanding and sharing meaning between oneself and at least one other person. Interpersonal, like intrapersonal, communication occurs for a variety of reasons: to solve problems, to resolve conflicts, to share information, to improve our perception of ourselves, or to fulfill such social needs as the need to belong or to be loved. Interpersonal communication includes interviews with an employer or teacher, talks with a parent, spouse, or child, and small group communication in clubs or in small civic, social, and church groups.

HIDDEN AGENDA –

The addition of another person complicates communication greatly. Although each of us holds conflicting perceptions, beliefs, values, and attitudes (indeed a great deal of our intrapersonal communication concerns these conflicts), the differences between two people are generally far greater than those within an individual. In addition, we all have different ways of expressing what we feel. Consequently, the possibility of successful communication decreases.

Next to intrapersonal, interpersonal communication is generally considered the most influential form of communication, and the most satisfying to the individuals involved in it. Interpersonal communication typically occurs in an informal setting and includes face-to-face verbal and nonverbal exchanges, a sharing of the roles of speaker and listener, and minimal planning.

Public communication is the process of understanding and sharing meaning with a large number of other people. It is recognized by its formality, structure, and planning. One person speaks, the others listen. We are frequently the listeners in public communication: as students in lecture classes, at convocations, and in church. Sometimes we are speakers, as when we speak before a group, when we try to convince other voters of the merits of a particular candidate for office, or when we introduce a guest speaker to a large audience. Public communication most often has the purpose of informing or persuading, but it also may have the purpose of entertaining, introducing, announcing, welcoming, or paying tribute.

FORMAL PREPLANNED.

Communication Involves Codes

All communication is coded. We typically use the word *code* to describe the secret language that children use or to refer to specialized, stylized, or shortened
languages, such as Morse Code. For our purposes, however, a *code* is any systematic arrangement or comprehensive collection of symbols, letters, or words,
that has an arbitrary meaning and is used for communication. *we assign meaning*

We can distinguish between two major kinds of codes that are used in communication: verbal codes and nonverbal codes. *Verbal codes* consist of words
and their grammatical arrangement. It is easier to think of the German language
as a code, or to consider French as "some kind of code," than it is to realize
that our own language is a code. All languages are codes. The English symbols,
letters, and words we use are arbitrary. We have no more reason to call a heavy
outer garment by the word *overcoat,* than a German does to call it *der mantel.*
Nature does not provide a rationale for any particular language.

Nonverbal codes consist of all symbols that are not words, including our
bodily movements, our use of space and time, our clothing and other adornments, and sounds other than words. Nonverbal codes should not be confused
with nonoral codes. All nonoral codes—such as bodily movement—are nonverbal codes, but nonverbal codes also include pitch, duration, and rate of
speech, as well as sounds like *eh* and *ah,* all of which are decidedly oral. Nonverbal codes refer to *all* codes that do not consist of words.

Communication Consists of Encoding and Decoding

If communication involves the use of codes, the process of communicating can
be viewed as one of encoding and decoding. *Encoding* is defined as the act of
putting a message or thought into a code. *Decoding* is assigning meaning to that
message. The relationship between encoding and decoding is unclear. Three
views have been popularized by researchers: (1) encoding and decoding are separate functions in persons; (2) encoding and decoding are successive phases of a
single ongoing process; and (3) encoding and decoding are the same operation
viewed from opposite ends of the system.

These three views of the relationship between encoding and decoding influence the way we view communication. In the past, people believed that communication could be viewed as *action,* that is, one person sends a message (encoding) and another person receives it (decoding). This view is depicted in figure
1.2.

A second view evolved. Communication is viewed as *interaction:* one
person sends a message to a second person who receives it and, in turn, responds with another message. The communicators take turns encoding and decoding messages. This point of view is pictured in figure 1.3.

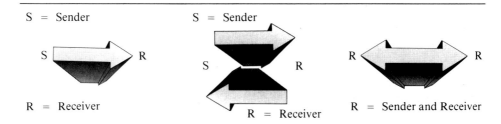

Figure 1.2
Communication as action.

Figure 1.3
Communication as
interaction.

Figure 1.4
Communication as
transaction.

The most recent view is that communication is a *transaction* in which the communicators simultaneously encode and decode (fig. 1.4). Encoding and decoding are thus not separate activities, nor do they occur one at a time. According to the transactional view, people are continually sending and receiving messages. They cannot avoid communication. This most recent view of communication is accepted in this text.

Any factor that intervenes between encoding and decoding is known as *noise*. Noise is generally thought of as static—stimuli that are external to the person or persons engaged in communication. But it also includes interference that is internal to one or both of the communicators. External noise includes loud banging, confusing lights, a strong and unpleasant odor and so forth. Internal noise may result from worries, daydreams, or a negative reaction to a particular word.

To recapitulate, we have defined communication as the process of understanding and sharing meaning that begins with oneself, occurs in a variety of situations, involves codes, and consists of encoding and decoding. Communication is one of our most basic activities. Let us examine its functions.

The Case of Sharon Black

Sharon Black, a freshman at an extension university, worked thirty hours a week at a local department store—a very busy schedule. Sharon wanted to spend more time with her co-workers, but her college work interfered. The other workers usually ate lunch together, but Sharon had a class that started at 12:30 four days a week. She usually couldn't attend parties because she had homework to do.

Sharon became increasingly quiet at work and felt more alienated as time

passed. Her co-workers began to suspect that "the college girl" was avoiding them because she felt superior. They began to plan activities that would exclude Sharon.

Sharon's work was exemplary and she became eligible for promotion to supervisor. Her boss told her that a lot depended on whether the other workers would accept her leadership and co-operate with her. But Sharon's co-workers were resentful of the possible promotion of a person who had so little

experience at the store. They also felt that
she was being "pushed ahead" because
she was a college student. At lunch that
day, they decided that Sharon would not
get the promotion if they had anything to
say about it. One of the women offered to
tell the boss how they felt.

    Sharon was called into the office two
days later. Her boss said "Sorry." Sharon
didn't seem to be getting along well with
the others, and it did not look like they
would cooperate with her. Sharon broke
into tears and ran from the office.

1. Does communication begin with self in
   this example? If so, how does it begin
   with self?
2. Identify the communication situations
   that are involved in this case.
3. Does this case illustrate
   communication as action, interaction,
   or transaction? How?
4. Discuss the "noise" in the
   communication between Sharon and
   her co-workers.
5. What conclusions can be drawn about
   this breakdown in communication?

Functions of Communication

The two general functions of communication are (1) the survival of the self and
(2) the survival of the society. The term *survival* may seem a bit unusual and
perhaps too strong. We generally associate survival with prehistoric cave people
or with the taming of the Wild West. That is because we use the word *survival* to
refer to physical survival. Communication continues to help us to survive physically. We can scream for help when we need it, and it allows our society to deal
with questions of war, pollution, and unequal distribution of natural resources. It
also assists us to survive in less obvious ways.

Survival of Self

When we consider the survival of the self, we can identify four separate goals
that are aided by communication. Physical safety is one, but in order to have a
full and complete existence, we desire also to (2) increase our personal awareness, (3) present ourselves to others, and (4) achieve our personal ambitions. We
increase our personal awareness or discover who we are through communication. Other people tell us—verbally and nonverbally—important information
about ourselves. They tell us that they respect us when they ask for, and listen
to, our opinions. They tell us that they enjoy our company when they seek opportunities to spend time with us. They tell us that we have a well-developed
sense of humor when they encourage us to relate humorous anecdotes.

    It is also by communicating that we present ourselves to others. As other
people communicate to us who they believe we are, we can communicate to
them who we believe we are. Our behavior is influenced by the impressions that
others have of us, but we also influence those impressions. We communicate
who we are verbally—"I try to be patient with my husband and children," "I

think I really did a good job!''—and nonverbally, by the clothing we wear, the expression on our faces, the posture we assume, and the way we touch other people.

Finally, we communicate to achieve personal ambitions. We communicate in committee work, in discussions with our supervisors, instructors, and parents, and in larger groups to gain specific ends. We attempt to convince others— through information, compelling arguments, and exemplary behavior—that they should agree with us or act on our behalf.

Survival of Society

In addition to serving the function of allowing the self to survive, communication serves in the survival of the society. We communicate to improve social relationships and to enhance the continued existence of a society. Few people would choose the hermit-like existence that Howard Hughes maintained during his last years. Most of us are socially oriented. We seek out and enjoy the company of others. We communicate to help establish, maintain, and improve the relationships that are the foundation of our society.

We also communicate to enhance the continued existence of our society. The theorist Kenneth Burke describes the American society in very bleak terms. He maintains that our society is on the brink of extinction and warns people that they should not forget that we build our cultures by ''huddling together.''[4] While Burke was speaking abstractly, he was emphasizing the point that a society can exist only to the extent that people are able and willing to communicate with each other.

Leaders

Contemporary examples of the importance of communication to the survival of the society are abundant: they include the communication of Israel's Begin, Egypt's Sadat, America's Kissinger, and countless others on the international scene who have demonstrated the use of political and diplomatic communication to prevent violence, war, and even the total destruction of nations. Society could not survive without such communication.

RIGHTS Domestic examples of the importance of communication are also readily apparent. The mass media have, because of recent events, focused on our judicial system, our right to protest, freedom of the press, Watergate, and our right to know. These issues point up how desperately society depends upon communication for survival.

Communication, as we have seen, is essential to the survival of the self and the survival of the society. It allows and encourages the survival of the self by promoting our physical safety, increasing our personal awareness, providing a means for presenting ourselves to others, and assisting in our personal achievements. It aids the survival and enhancement of society by improving social and diplomatic relationships and by promoting understanding. But communication is beset by problems.

Problems in Communication

Communication is one of our most basic activities. It serves us in our most basic need—the need to survive. We therefore spend a great deal of our time communicating and trying to improve our ability to communicate. Nonetheless, all of us have problems communicating. We can name three essential causes for these problems: (1) lack of interest; (2) lack of understanding; and (3) lack of common goals and assumptions.

Lack of Interest

Communication cannot occur if one person has no interest or desire to understand or to share. While Beetle Bailey is correct when he claims the right to say what he thinks, communication is made impossible by his sergeant's obvious lack of interest.

BEETLE BAILEY

There are reasons for a lack of interest. People are sometimes not motivated to understand certain things or to show interest in certain people. The various subcultures in contemporary America provide numerous examples of persons or groups who blithely ignore other persons or groups. The small-town business owner in northern Minnesota may be motivated to understand the difficulties of Indians on reservations but may have no interest in the plight of inner-city blacks. Similarly, the husband whose wife cheerfully stays home may not be motivated to understand the liberated woman who is his professional colleague.

Moreover, people are sometimes suspicious, defensive, and distrustful, as well as just uninterested. The reasons for their suspicions and distrust may be complex, but the result is disastrous to effective communication. As we shall see in chapter 6, the quality of being open to others is essential to successful communication.

Lack of Understanding

Sometimes we sincerely wish to communicate with others but are unable to do so because, for one or another reason, we cannot understand them. There may be a language barrier. The barrier is obvious when one person is speaking English and the other person is speaking Spanish. It may be less obvious when one person is speaking black English and the other is speaking white English.

Even when two people share a common language and dialect, misunderstandings can still result. More subtle differences in the use of language also af-

BEETLE BAILEY

fect understanding. One person may use a word or phrase figuratively, only to have another interpret it literally. An example of the difference in usage is illustrated in the cartoon. The lieutenant takes the general's figurative suggestion literally.

Among the more subtle differences are also differences in our nonverbal language: one person may employ an elaborate and extensive set of nonverbal symbols in communicating with another person who is not sensitive to nonverbal communication.

Communication Breakdown

You are the supervisor in an office of moderate size. Your boss phones to say that he wants the weekly report today, a day early because he is going out of town.

Annie, who generally types the report, is absent. You explain the job to John, who interrupts, protesting that it is Annie's job. You counter by telling him that you need the report today and that Annie will not return until tomorrow. After you give John all of the figures and a copy of last week's report you ask, "You do understand, don't you?" John indicates that he does and types the report.

Three hours later, John places the report on your desk. You find that, because John forgot to consider the holiday in the preceding week, all of the figures are one column out of place. When you show him his mistake, he emphatically states that he did exactly what he was told.

Sufficient time remains for John to retype the report.

1. How would you manage to have the report completed?
2. Should you take further action?
3. What problems in communication occurred?

Lack of Common Goals and Assumptions

Although we are interested in understanding another person and do, in fact, understand what he or she has to say, we may still find that we have a communication problem with that person. A third problem in communication is that we do not share the other person's goals and assumptions. All of us have heard arguments in which one person concluded, "Well, you just don't understand me," and the other person replied, "No, I understand you perfectly well, I just don't agree with you." It is difficult to recognize a problem in communication that arises because people do not share the same goals and assumptions.

Differences in goals and expectations can show themselves in different ways. We can have a situation in which one person is clear about the differences but refuses to state them. For example, your goal in visiting a professor might be to gain information about tomorrow's exam. Instead of stating your goal, however, you tell her that you "just dropped in to talk." Your professor attempts to be responsive to your stated needs by discussing something of general interest. You become frustrated because the conversation does not get around to the exam. The professor becomes irritated because you do not appear interested in the conversation, even though you were the person who initiated it. When you leave the office, both of you feel dissatisfied.

When we have specific goals in mind but do not state them or share them with the person with whom we are communicating, problems occur. The term *hidden agenda* refers to an unstated goal or motive. In the example cited, your hidden agenda was to gain information about the exam. Hidden agendas are generally destructive to open and effective communication.

We also have situations in which the people involved are not clear about their differences and thus do not state them. No one has any intention of subverting the communication, but difficulties ensue just the same. For instance, if you value your college education and your parents do not share this value, you may have countless arguments and disagreements without ever discovering the reason. If you live at home, your parents might feel you should continue to join them on family outings, as you did when you were in high school, but you might want more time to study or to spend with people in your classes. You will argue about a dozen similar matters, but you are really arguing about an unrecognized and unstated difference in values and assumptions.

Summary

In this chapter, the concept of communication was introduced. Communication was defined as the process of understanding and sharing meaning. Communication begins with the self. It has a variety of forms, including intrapersonal communication, which is the understanding and sharing that occurs within a person; interpersonal communication, which is the process of understanding and sharing that occurs between oneself and at least one other person; and public communication, which is the process of understanding and sharing that occurs between oneself and a large number of other people. Communication involves codes, both verbal and nonverbal, and it consists of encoding and decoding, which occur simultaneously. Interference in the encoding and decoding process is known as noise.

The function of communication is to allow people to survive and to allow society to survive. Communication helps us to survive physically, increase our personal awareness, present ourself to others, and achieve personal goals. Three common causes of problems in communication are a lack of interest, a lack of understanding, and a lack of common goals and assumptions.

We spend a large proportion of our time communicating, and yet many Americans report that their greatest fear is the fear of public speaking. This text is designed to help you to become more familiar with communication and to communicate more competently. We now turn to a consideration of perception, which is central to an understanding of communication.

New Terms

Communication
Understanding
Sharing
Meaning
Messages
Thought
Barnlund's "six persons"
Intrapersonal communication

Interpersonal communication
Public communication
Codes
Verbal codes
Nonverbal codes
Encoding
Decoding
Action

Interaction
Transaction
Noise
Survival of self
Survival of society
Hidden agenda

Additional Readings

Barnlund, Dean C. "Toward a Meaning Centered Philosophy of Communication." *Journal of Communication* 12 (1962): 198–202.
A presentation and discussion of several axioms of communication; communication is a circular, unrepeatable, and irreversible process involving the total personality. An examination of why people communicate and the nature of their communication.

Dyer, Wayne. *Your Erroneous Zones.* New York: Avon Books, 1976.
Concerned with the centrality of self in communication, Dyer argues that we must develop self-awareness and self-acceptance in order to take charge of our own lives and challenges us to come to

grips with our goals and values so that we can base our decisions on our own desires.

Morris, Desmond. *The Naked Ape.* New York: Dell Publishing Co., Inc., 1967.
This easy-to-understand book traces the evolution of the human. Morris focuses primarily on the importance of nonverbal communication–clothing, appearance, touching, and eye contact–to human survival.

Mortensen, C. David. "Communication Postulates." In *Messages,* edited by Jean Civikly. 2d ed. New York: Random House, Inc., 1977.
Mortensen develops five principles to explain the nature of communication. A

good fundamental overview of the
communication process, including
bibliography for further reading.

Schramm, Wilbur. "How Communication
Works." In *The Processes & Effects of
Mass Communication*, edited by Wilbur
Schramm. Urbana, Ill.: University of
Illinois Press, 1971.
*A discussion of several variables that
affect the communication process,
offering a model of communication
based on those variables. Includes an
explanation of messages, feedback,
fields of experience, signals, and
encoding and decoding.*

*Smith, Raymond G. *Speech
Communication: Theory and Models*.
New York: Harper & Row, Publishers,
1970.
*A scholarly discussion of models and
their development. Smith presents
several different models of*

communication and examines their
limitations and their strengths. He also
explores the nature of models in general
and their uses in understanding human
communication.

Wenburg, John R., and Wilmot, William.
The Personal Communication Process.
New York: John Wiley & Sons, Inc.,
1973. Chapters 1, 2, and 3.
*Chapter 1 is a discussion of six axioms of
communication. A story illustrates
communication as a process. Chapter 2
is an examination of the contexts of
intrapersonal, interpersonal, small
group, public, and mass communication,
and a discussion of how each of these
arenas of communication differs. In
chapter 3, the nature of models is
explained, and the strengths and
weaknesses of several basic
communication models are discussed.*

*Indicates more advanced readings.

Notes

1. See, for example, Paul T. Rankin,
"Measurement of the Ability to
Understand the Spoken Language" (Ph.D.
diss. University of Michigan, 1926), cited
in *Dissertation Abstracts* 12 (1926): 847;
Paul T. Rankin, "Listening Ability: Its
Importance, Measurement, and
Development," *Chicago Schools Journal*
12 (1930): 177; and J. Donald Weinrauch
and John R. Swanda, Jr., "Examining the
Significance of Listening: An Exploratory
Study of Contemporary Management,"
Journal of Business Communication 13
(Fall 1975): 25–32.

2. "What Are Americans Afraid Of?"
Bruskin Report 53 (1973).

3. Dean C. Barnlund, "A Transactional
Model of Communication," in
Foundations of Communication Theory,
ed. Kenneth K. Sereno and C. David
Mortensen (New York: Harper & Row,
Publishers, 1970), pp. 98–101.

4. Kenneth Burke, *Permanence and Change*
(Los Altos, Calif.: Hermes Publications,
1954), pp. 234–36.

2 Perception: The Process of Understanding

Objectives

After study of this chapter you should be able to do the following:

1. Specify the physiological characteristics that affect your own perception

2. State the differences between the view of perception as passive and the view of perception as active; describe a situation that illustrates creative meaning as opposed to inherent meaning

3. Discuss the processes of selection, organization, and interpretation as they apply to the perception of others

4. Give examples of experiences in which you used consensual validation, repetitive validation, multisensory validation, and comparative validation

5. Discuss the relationship between perception and intrapersonal communication and between perception and interpersonal communication

6. Describe an experience in which you and another person had different perceptions of the same stimuli and discuss the reasons for those differences

7. Identify the cultural roles that you play and explain the effect of those roles on your behavior

8. Relate an experience in which your expectation of another's behavior was based on a cultural or subcultural role

9. Discuss the processes of selective attention and selective retention as they occur in the speech classroom

10. Give examples that illustrate the processes of organization: figure and ground, proximity, closure, similarity, and perceptual constancy

"At 8:07 P.M. on March 7, 1979, a late-model blue sedan was involved in a collision with a lightweight ten-speed bicycle at 2200 College Drive. No one was injured, but the bicycle was damaged."

Police report

"Did you hear what happened last night? I didn't get all the details, but some teacher ran into a student on a bicycle. Seems like these guys have it in for us all the time."

College student

"I am sorry to report that an unfortunate accident occurred last evening. As a result of our inadequate street lighting, an automobile driven by a student was hit in the rear bumper by a faculty member on a bicycle. Luckily, no one was injured, but the front fender on the bicycle was bent."

Dean of college

These are three descriptions of the same accident. They can be recognized as descriptions of a similar event, but they vary in all other details. The first description, from the police report, is objective, disinterested, and dry. The second, from a student, is embellished and more interesting. The dean offers an explanation for the accident, and gives more details.

In none of the descriptions does the speaker claim to have witnessed the accident. But eye-witness accounts also vary greatly. Accident reports are filled with conflicting evidence. People who have seen an automobile accident, for example, will disagree about who was at fault, the number of people involved, the year, the make, and even the color of the vehicles.

Differences in *perception,* in the way people see, hear, smell, taste, or feel a specific stimulus, are common. Whether we are describing an event (say, an automobile accident), an idea (how communication occurs), or something about ourselves (how we feel about our own bodies), we encounter differences in perception. Individual experiences are not identical. Neither are individual perceptions, even of the same event.

Communication occurs only to the extent that we share perceptions. In the last chapter, we stated that communication involves two activities—understanding and sharing. In this chapter, we will consider the first of these two activities, understanding.

How Does Communication Involve Perception?

Perception is the process by which we come to understand ourselves and others. Understanding is necessary to communication. In order to make the connection more concrete, let us delineate two specific ways in which perception is related to communication.

The Process by Which We Come to Understand Ourselves

First, perception is essential to the study of communication because it is the process by which we come to understand ourselves. Communication begins with self, as we stated in chapter 1. In chapters 5 and 6, we will explore the role of self in communication further. At this point, it is necessary only to realize that our self-concept consists of our perceptions of ourselves. In other words, self-concept is what we understand about ourselves.

Our perceptions of ourselves affect our communication. If a person believes himself or herself shy, that person tends to avoid communicating; if another person believes that he or she is aggressive, that person may tend to dominate conversations and be loud and boisterous. We sometimes draw inferences about other people's self-concepts from the way they speak.

The Process by Which We Come to Understand Others

Second, perception is the process by which we come to understand others. Most communication involves other people. In chapter 7, we shall consider further how we understand others. At this time, we need only recognize that perception is the process by which we understand them.

We make judgments and draw conclusions about other people within a few seconds of meeting them. We use the nonverbal cues available, including the

person's facial expression, vocal patterns, body language, clothes, jewelry, as well as what the person says. Our perception of the other person, including the way that person looks, sounds, and smells, provides immediate information.

The perceptions that we have of others affect our communication with them. A number of minority group people—blacks, Mexican Americans, and handicapped persons—have related their experiences with others. Frequently, the early portion of a conversation will focus on their uniqueness—their race, their nationality, or their particular handicap. People who talk with them tend to be limited in their early perceptions. Often, the topic of conversation does not shift until these persons have known each other for some time.

What Is Perception?

In the past, people believed that perception was nothing more than sensing stimuli. It was commonly believed that people were merely cameras that recorded the events that occurred around them. The implication was that people were passive. Sights, sounds, smells, and other stimuli were sent to them. A second implication was that people were objective. In other words, no one added or subtracted from the stimuli. This point of view also implied that meaning was inherent in the object being perceived. No room for interpretation existed because the stimulus contained all of the meaning.

The contemporary view of perception is that perception is subjective, active, and creative. People do add and subtract from the stimuli to which they are exposed. They blend the external stimuli and their internal states. In the contemporary view, when we perceive something, we are really "doing our own thing."

Consider the last time you were driving in the country. As you drove between the fields on the two-lane highway, your attention shifted from one stimuli to another. You did not passively absorb all of the stimuli in the environment, but you actively chose to focus on the sports car that zoomed past you and to ignore the family sedan that you followed for a number of miles. When a large van came into your vision in your rear-view mirror, you did not objectively perceive the vehicle, but instead you began to think about your truck-driver friend and you subjectively thought about the truck as a means of income. When you looked at the fields planted with corn and barley, you did not identify an inherent meaning in the plants that others would easily share, but you recognized, in your creative way, that the plants were different from those with which you are familiar, and taller.

In order to understand how the contemporary view of perception affects communication, try to remember the last week of final exams. Perhaps, as you were rushing to the exam, you noticed one of your friends coming toward you. You singled out your friend from a number of other people on the sidewalk. When you noticed him, you did not drop your glance, but you maintained eye

contact to signal that you wanted to talk for a moment or two. As you began the conversation, you noticed that the rain was very cold. You began to feel uncomfortable and wondered why your friend continued to talk. Your thoughts shifted back to the exam. Your friend remarked that you seemed touchy. As he walked away, he told himself, "That's what happens when you lend people money—they try to ignore you!"

If you assumed that the older view of perception was accurate, this conversation would be difficult to interpret and understand. If you take into consideration that perception is active, subjective, and creative, your friend's misunderstanding can be explained. Barnlund's notion that every two-way communication involves six persons is also helpful in understanding this particular situation. Instead of holding that there is a single, objective view of this encounter, we recognize that at least two perspectives are possible: the way the other person views the situation and the way you view it. True, you both reacted to the same external stimuli—the sight of each other, the extended glance, and the cold rain. But your inner state, including anxiety over the upcoming exam, and your friend's inner state, including his concern about money he had lent you, produced a unique communication that could be viewed from a variety of perspectives.

Why Do Differences in Perception Occur?

We have just demonstrated a common phenomenon: Different people perceive the same event in different ways. Moreover, perception is subjective, active, and creative. We now turn our attention to the factors that account for differences in perception.

Differences occur in perception for several related reasons. There are physiological reasons. There are differences due to past experience. There are differences in mood, and there are different circumstances. Let us consider these reasons in more detail.

Physiological Factors

None of us are physiologically identical. We vary in height, weight, body type, and in our senses. People can be tall or short, have less than perfect vision, and suffer from impaired hearing. Such differences in physiology alter perception. The cartoon on page 24 illustrates a simple physiological difference with which most of us are familiar. Anyone who has attempted to "get back into shape" can understand the runner's perception of the distance he ran.

An unfortunate experience will illustrate this point. Two small boys set out on a three-block walk to the neighborhood drugstore. As they approached their destination, they were stopped by two bigger boys who blocked their way and threatened them with a knife. The two little boys were asked if they had any money. When the bigger boys found out that they had practically no money, they ran off, leaving two frightened little boys.

Back at home, the two little boys were asked by a detective to describe the bigger boys. One boy maintained that one of the aggressors was about sixteen and the other about twenty. He thought one was about 5'6", the other about 5'10". His friend was questioned in another room. He told the detective that the two bigger boys were twenty and twenty-seven years old. He guessed their heights at 5'10" and 6'2". The detective was disappointed because the two descriptions were not the same.

A student of perception would have understood the differences in point of view. One boy was a large nine-year-old who is five feet tall. His smaller and younger friend was only six years old and just over four feet tall. Knowing this removes some of the mystery. The smaller and younger boy saw his assailants as larger and older, but even the taller boy probably exaggerated their size and age.

A second example of how physiological differences influence perception comes from Michigan State University and a 23-year-old student named James M. Renuk. Renuk suffers from cerebral palsy, and his speech is not understandable to most people. To write, he has to position himself on the floor and balance a pen against his leg. Renuk is hopeful that the artificial language department at Michigan State will perfect a group of portable machines equipped with microcomputers that will allow him and others with similar difficulties to communicate through voice synthesizers and small television screens. Although there can be no doubt that Renuk has different perceptions than other people, one of the most interesting differences is the language he uses to refer to people who are not handicapped. He and his other activist friends at M.S.U. call the rest of us TABs, Temporarily Able-Bodied. The assumption that Renuk makes in this choice of words is that we do not know how long we will be able-bodied. It is a far different assumption that we make when we refer to ourselves as "normal."[1]

Past Experience

All of us tend to pay attention to those aspects of our environment that we expect or anticipate. We also tend to expect or anticipate that which is familiar to us. A common example of this tendency occurs to most of you almost daily. You are sitting in a classroom waiting for class to begin, or you are busy doing some work. Conversations are going on around you, but you do not hear anything until someone mentions your name. At the sound of your name, you suddenly perk up and pay attention to the conversation. It really seems to make no difference if someone was talking about you or about someone else with the same name; you pay attention to one of the most familiar words you know—your name.

Differences in perception, then, are affected by physiology and also by past experience. They are also affected by cultural roles, cultural differences, and subcultural differences. Each of these factors helps explain differences in the perceptions of various groups of people.

Cultural Roles   People have different perceptions, and are perceived differently, because of their cultural roles, that is, the parts that they play within a particular society. Flo Capp demonstrates, in the cartoon, that she is aware of the differences in our perception created by cultural roles. The roles that we play in our culture, including student, worker, and son or daughter, affect our perceptions of the events around us.

One of the evolving cultural roles in the United States is that of the professional or career woman. We can gain an understanding of the effect of a difference in cultural role by using the example of Dr. Elizabeth Fish, a chemist, and comparing her to Mrs. John Anderson, a homemaker. To Dr. Fish, shopping is a routine task that she shares with her husband and her teenage children. In Mrs. Anderson's life, shopping takes center stage. A great deal of time, attention, and energy goes into marketing. She spends time planning meals, writing out grocery lists, clipping coupons from magazines, checking the newspaper for specials and sales, selecting the best time and day to do the shopping, and then spends time discussing the bargains she has found or deploring the high prices. Dr. Fish perceives shopping as a necessary but relatively unimportant task;

ANDY CAPP

Mrs. Anderson perceives it as central to her workweek. The differences in the cultural roles of these two women accounts for differences in their perception of shopping.

Cultural Differences   Another factor that accounts for differences in perception is our culture. In our shrinking world, we have become more aware of cultural differences. As the Middle East, for example, has become more visible to us, we have been especially cognizant of the differences between ourselves and people from that part of the world. Until recently, one excellent example of differences in perception between ourselves and nomadic Arabs, for example, has been the mode of transportation. Many Americans can describe automobiles in great detail—they can distinguish among makes, models, and years of cars; they discuss horsepower and gas mileage; they know a fine car from a poor one. Many Arabs, on the other hand, were knowledgeable about camels. They could distinguish among various species; predict life span and ability to work; and recognize a superior camel from an inferior one. While Arabs had a small vocabulary for automobiles, Americans could barely distinguish beyond one hump and two when it came to camels. The cultural difference accounted for the differences in perception of cars and camels.

Subcultural Differences   Still another factor that helps explain why people perceive the same stimuli in different ways is subcultural differences. Such differences occur within a particular culture. Men see some things differently from women, blacks from whites, old people from young people, and so forth.

Two scholars recently found that the subcultural difference between rural and urban people had an effect on how these persons perceived communication. In their study, they found that country children are more likely to become apprehensive about communicating. Urban children have a much more positive attitude toward communication.[2]

One subcultural difference with which you are probably very familiar is the so-called generation gap. The difference in age between yourself and your parents, instructors, or classmates may significantly affect your perception of them and, consequently, your communication with them. Consider rock music, and such events as President Kennedy's assassination, the Viet Nam War, and the impeachment of Richard M. Nixon. A difference in age can affect how you hear music and perceive events, what you say about them, and the meanings that are evoked when they are mentioned in a conversation. Subcultural differences affect our perception and, thereby, our communication.

Present Feelings and Circumstances

Differences in perception also arise from different feelings and circumstances. A headache, backache, or toothache can cause us to perceive a critical comment

CROCK   by **Rechin & Parker**

when a friendly one is being offered. We sometimes don't see a stop sign if our thoughts are elsewhere. One of the prisoners in the cartoon feels a draft at 140° because the usual temperature is 150°. Our perceptions alter: they can become more acute, less acute, or changed by our present feelings and circumstances.

If you have ever spent a night alone in a large house, a deserted dormitory, or an unfamiliar residence, you probably understand that perceptions are altered by circumstances. Most people experience a remarkable change in their hearing. Creaking, whining, breaking, scraping, cracking sounds are heard, although none were heard in the daytime. The lack of other stimuli—including light, other sounds, and the lack of people with whom to talk—coupled with a small feeling of anxiety, provides the circumstances which result in more acute hearing.

Similar circumstances may account, in part, for the mirages seen by lonely travelers. Commander Robert Peary encountered massive snowy pinnacles that appeared to rise thousands of feet above the plain of solid ice deep inside the Arctic Circle in 1906. Seven years later, Donald MacMillan, another explorer, verified his discovery. However, when MacMillan asked his Eskimo guide to choose a course toward the peaks, the guide explained that the spectacle was only *poo-jok* (mist). Meteorologists have explained the existence of such mirages, but have hastened to add that they are "reported infrequently because people aren't looking for them."[3] The variance in the feelings and circumstances of the many explorers may account for the difference between sighting and not sighting specific illusions.

What Occurs in Perception?

According to the most recent information, people appear to engage in three separate activities in perception. None of us is aware of these separate processes because they occur quickly and almost simultaneously. Nonetheless, each activity is involved in our perceptions. The three activities include *selection* (we neglect some of the stimuli in our environment and focus on a few), organization (we group the stimuli in our environment into units or wholes), and interpretation (we give particular meanings to stimuli). Let us consider each of these activities in more detail.

Selection

None of us perceives all the stimuli in our environment. As an illustration of this principle, if you drove to school today, you were bombarded with sights, sounds, smells, and other sensations during your ride. At the time, you elected to perceive some of the stimuli and you chose to disregard others. Now, you can recall some of the stimuli you perceived but you have forgotten others. In the future, you will also expose yourself to some sensations and ignore others.

Our selectivity is of three types. First, we are selective in the stimuli to which we attend. *Selective attention* means that we focus on certain cues and ignore others. On our way to school, we check our timing with the bank clock, but we fail to notice the couple walking in front of the bank.

Second, we select which stimuli we will recall or remember. *Selective retention* means that we categorize, store, and retrieve certain information, but discard other information. If you played the car radio on your way to school, try to remember one of the songs you heard, or one of the commercials, or one of the public-service announcements. Although your attention may have been drawn to a particular song or message this morning, you may find that you cannot remember anything you heard. Your mind has discarded the sounds you heard from your radio.

Third, we are selective in the stimuli to which we allow ourselves to be exposed. *Selective exposure* means that we perceive stimuli that we wish to perceive and disregard stimuli that we do not wish to perceive. If we have a tendency to drive slightly over the limit, we might selectively perceive other fast drivers. Selective exposure allows us to disregard many other cars that are moving more slowly.

The relationship between selection and communication can be clarified by the concept of stereotyping. *Stereotyping* is the process of placing people and things into established categories, or of basing judgments about people or things upon the categories in which they fit, rather than on their individual characteristics. All of us stereotype to a certain extent, but particular stereotypes vary from person to person. Stereotyping involves selective attention, selective retention, and selective exposure.

A specific example will illustrate the relationship among these concepts. Suppose you perceive women to be emotional and men to be logical. In order to maintain this stereotype, you selectively attend to women who behave emotionally, and ignore those who are unemotional. Similarly, you selectively attend to men who are logical, rather than to those who seem unpredictable. When you try to recall the significant men and women in your life, you find that the women were either moderately or extremely emotional and that the men were fairly rational. You have selectively retained the memory of those who fit your stereotype. Finally, as you interact with others, you find that the women you meet tend to be emotional and that the men you encounter tend to be logical. You carefully expose yourself only to those persons who fit the stereotype that you have established. Selective exposure allows you to perceive only emotional women and logical men. Selectivity in perception affects stereotyping, and stereotyping is a process by which we categorize in order that we can communicate with others. We will consider the processes of stereotyping, abstracting, and categorizing further, in the next chapter, when we consider verbal codes and words that we have developed and used.

Organization

All of us have a tendency to organize the stimuli in our environment. The unorganized figure 2.1, on page 30, is difficult for us to describe if we only glance at it for a minute. When we attempt to describe it, we do so by organizing the lines we see. We might say that it consists of straight and squiggly lines, or that it has a rectangle, a triangle, and a square, or we may categorize the stimuli in some other way. The important point is that we attempt to organize the figure as we describe it.

Gestalt psychology (the German word *gestalt* means "whole") clarified the importance of organization to perception. A fundamental principle of Gestalt psychology is that the many elements that are presented to a particular sense are perceptually organized into a whole structure. Gestaltists maintain that the structures or holistic pictures that we perceive are always the simplest possible under the conditions.

Figure 2.1   The unorganized figure.

Figure 2.2   An example of
figure and ground: a vase
or twins?

Figure 2.3   An example of
figure and ground: ink
blobs or a bearded man?

Figure 2.4   An example of
closure: ink blobs or a cat?

Figure 2.5   An example of
closure: triangle or straight
lines?

Figure 2.6   An example of
closure: circle or straight
lines?

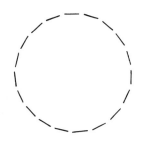

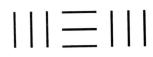

Figure 2.7   An example of
proximity: three groups of
lines or nine separate
lines?

We organize stimuli in a number of ways. One method of organizing is to distinguish between *figure and ground*. In figure 2.2, some people perceive a vase while others perceive twins facing each other. People who see a vase identify the center of the drawing as the figure, and the area on the right and left as the ground, or background. Conversely, people who see twins facing each other see the center as the background and the area on the right and left as the figure.

Figure 2.3 is another illustration of the principle of figure and ground. As we first glance at the drawing we perceive nothing but ink blobs—nothing is clearly distinguishable as either the figure or the background. If we continue to look at the drawing, however, we perceive the face of Christ or of a bearded man at the top center of the picture. When we see the face, it becomes the figure; the rest of the drawing becomes the ground.

Another way of organizing stimuli was described by the Gestaltists as *closure*. We engage in closure every time we fill in things that do not exist. If someone showed us figure 2.4 and asked us what we perceive, we would probably say that it is a picture of a cat. But, as we can clearly see, the figure is incomplete. We can see a cat only if we are willing to fill in the blank areas. Additional examples of closure are given in figures 2.5 and 2.6. Most of us would identify figure 2.5 as a triangle and figure 2.6 as a circle, rather than claiming that both are simply short lines.

We also organize stimuli according to their *proximity*. The principle of proximity or nearness operates whenever we group two or more things that simply happen to be close to each other. When we group according to proximity, our assumption is that "birds of a feather flock together," even though we know that this is not always true. In figure 2.7, we tend to perceive three groups of lines of three lines each rather than nine separate lines, because of the principle of proximity or nearness.

Similarity also helps us to organize stimuli. We sometimes group elements together because they resemble each other in size, color, shape, or other attributes. For example, we tend to believe that people who like the music we do will enjoy the same movies as we do. We assume that a suit that looks like one of our own is probably within the same price range. We perceive squares and circles, rather than a group of geometric shapes, in figure 2.8 on page 32 because of the principle of similarity.

A final method that we use in organizing stimuli is known as *perceptual constancy*. According to the principle of perceptual constancy, we rarely change our perceptions of something once we have established a particular image of it. We are able to "see" the objects in our bedroom—even when the light burns out and the room is dark. All of us have a tendency to view things as stable and unchanging after we have formed a point of view.

In order to understand the relationship between the organizing of stimuli and communication, let us consider a typical party. When you arrive at a party,

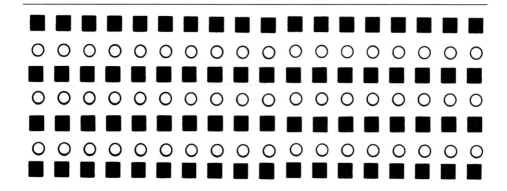

Figure 2.8   An example of similarity:
squares and circles or a group of
geometric figures?

you immediately begin to organize the stimuli—the people there—into groups.
You focus first on your friends and acquaintances—who serve as *figure*—and
largely ignore the strangers present, who serve as *ground*. Those friends who are
standing closest to you will talk with you first, because of their *proximity*. The
people with whom you will spend most time are those who you perceive to be
similar to you. The persons whom you will avoid are those whom you have previously determined to be boring, dull, or perhaps threatening. You assume that
they will behave in the same way tonight because of *perceptual constancy*. Finally, you notice that two married friends, separated for a number of months and
considering divorce, arrive together. As the evening progresses, they tend to
stand together and to talk in an intimate way. You achieve *closure* by assuming
that they have reconciled their differences. When you approach them, your
mood is light and your conversation is spirited. This example illustrates how
organizing stimuli—one activity of perception—affects communication. It helps
to determine with whom we speak, how we speak, what we speak about, how
long we speak, and the tone of voice that we use.

Interpretation

Each of us interprets the stimuli we perceive. The more ambiguous the stimuli,
the more room we have for interpretation. The basis for the well-known inkblot
test lies in the principle of interpretation of stimuli. Figure 2.9 is an inkblot that
a psychologist might ask you to interpret. The ambiguity of the figure is typical.

In our interpretation of stimuli, we frequently rely on the context in which
we perceive the stimuli, or we compare it to others. Sometimes these are helpful
clues. For example, the letters and numbers are useful to us as we attempt to

Figure 2.9   An example of interpretation:
the inkblot.

Figure 2.10   An example of the
usefulness of context in the interpretation
of stimuli.

Figure 2.12   An example
of interpretation: Is the
width of the holder the
same length as the candle?

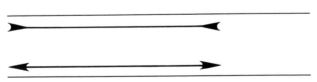

Figure 2.11   An example of
interpretation: Which line is longer?

interpret the middle figure in figure 2.10. The context tells us it is two number
1's, rather than one H.

Nonetheless, comparisons and the use of context can be confusing. All of
us are familiar with figures like 2.11 and 2.12. In these figures, we perceive differences in the lengths of the lines, and in the height of the candle and the width
of the candleholder, although they do not exist.

The relationship between the interpretation of stimuli and communication
can be demonstrated in a situation that may be familiar to you. Women who
work in large businesses or corporations more frequently serve in secretarial or
clerical positions than in executive or managerial jobs. As a result, a person who
is unfamiliar with a particular office may mistakenly request a cup of coffee from

the lawyer instead of her secretary. The stereotype leads the visitor to an inaccurate assumption, an incorrect interpretation, which in turn leads to difficulty in communication.

How Can We Validate Our Perceptions?

Although perception is the process by which we come to understand ourselves and others, we have seen that perceptions vary. But communication can occur only to the extent that we can share perceptions. We have investigated why people have different perceptions of the same phenomenon. We need now to identify some ways of validating our own perceptions so that we can establish common perceptions.

Consensual Validation

An obvious way to validate our perceptions is to check with other people. We can simply ask them if they share our perceptions, and we thus gain *consensus* or agreement. Examples of consensual validation include questions like, "Isn't it warm in here?" "Did you see that sports car speed by us?" "Can you hear what the speaker is saying?"

Repetitive Validation

Another way of validating our perceptions is to *repeat* our observations. This method involves checking with ourselves rather than others. In order to validate our perceptions through repetition, we simply look, listen, smell, taste, or touch again. If the soup tastes flat, we might taste it again before salting it. Similarly, if we see something unexpected, we will probably turn around and look at it again.

Multisensory Validation

The third way we can check our perceptions is through the use of our *other senses*. If something looks strange to us, we may touch it. If a gallon of milk smells spoiled, we may taste it. In this method, we again check with ourselves rather than with someone else.

The most common examples of multisensory validation occur when people are in altered states of consciousness—due to drugs or alcoholic beverages. It is not unusual to see someone who has had a sufficient amount of a drug or liquor to "feel" his or her way into a room, rather than to rely on sight alone. A number of people report that they also need the assurance of a foot on the floor when they go to bed after such an experience: the foot assures them that the room is really not spinning around, as their eyes are telling them.

Comparative Validation

We can also check our perceptions by comparative validation. Again, we check with ourselves and consider similar past experiences. One professor begins her speech course with a lecture on perception. She darkens the room, uses a candle for light, and burns incense. Some students are reluctant to enter. When asked about their hesitation, they may respond, "I've never seen a class like this before," or "I've been to another university, and it certainly wasn't like this!" These students were validating their perceptions by considering similar experiences. They are reluctant to enter the room because the situation is not similar to their past experience. They think that maybe it isn't their classroom.

Jack can see he sees
   what he can see Jill can't see
and he can see
   that Jill can't see that she can't see
but he can't see WHY
   Jill can't see that Jill can't see. . . .
Jill can see Jack can't see,
   and can't see he can't see.
Jill can see WHY
   Jack can't see,
but Jill cannot see WHY
   Jack can't see he can't see. . . .
Jack can't see he can't see
and can't see
   Jill can't see Jill can't see it,
and vice versa.[4]

R. D. Laing includes this poem in his collection *Knots.* The poem captures the complexity of perception and the difficulty of establishing common perceptions.

Discuss an experience in which you and another person attempted to reach an agreement, but could not. Identify the differences in perception, suggest reasons for those differences, and enumerate the methods you attempted to use to validate your perceptions.

Summary

Perception was discussed in this chapter. Perception is the process by which we come to understand ourselves and others, and understanding is an activity basic to communication. Perception, in the contemporary view, is considered active, subjective, and creative. Differences in perceptions result from physiology, cultural and subcultural factors, differences in past experiences, and differences in present feelings and circumstances. Perception involves selection, organization, and interpretation. We validate our perceptions through consensual validation, repetitive validation, multisensory validation, and comparative validation.

GESTALT - (whole) -

New Terms

Perception

Passive perception

Objective perception

Inherent meaning

Subjective perception

Creative perception

Active perception

Cultural roles

Cultural differences

Subcultural differences

Organization

Interpretation

Selective attention

Selective retention

Selective exposure

Figure and ground

Closure *FINISH UNFINISH*

Proximity *group cause closeness*

Similarity

Perceptual constancy

Consensual validation *FEED BACK*

Repetitive validation *Double Take*

Multisensory validation *See so TASTE*

Comparative validation *PAST*

Stereotyping

Additional Readings

*Allport, Gordon W. *The Nature of Prejudice.* Garden City, New York: Doubleday & Co., Inc., 1958. Chapters 10 and 12.
A thorough treatment of the relationship between perceptual processes and prejudice. Allport discusses specific stereotypes of Jews and Negroes as well as the effect of the mass media on the formation of stereotypes.

Carney, Clarke G., and McMahon, Sarah L. *Exploring Contemporary Male/ Female Roles.* La Jolla, Calif.: University Associates, Inc., 1977.
Stereotypes are based on our perceptual processes. This book is an examination of one of the most basic stereotypes today—male and female roles. A close look at the stereotypes reveals the social patterns that foster them, the problems they cause, and ways to create a different perception of the sexes.

Edwards, David C. *General Psychology.* 2d ed. New York: Macmillan, Inc., 1972. Chapters 4 and 5.
Chapter 4 is a description of the psychological basis and mechanisms of perception, including organization, depth perception, and color perception. In chapter 5 Edwards discusses attention as it relates to perception, as well as the variables that affect our attention in hearing, seeing, and thinking about stimuli.

Haney, William V. *Communication and Organizational Behavior.* Homewood, Ill.: Richard D. Irwin, Inc., 1967. Pages 51–77.
Haney devotes a chapter to perception as it relates to communication, examines the problems that can be created by misperceptions and different fields of experience, and makes it easy to understand by using analogies and models.

Hastorf, Albert H.; Schneider, David J.; and Polefka, Judith. *Person Perception.* Reading, Mass.: Addison-Wesley Publishing Co., Inc., 1970.
The creative view of perception. A discussion of the factors that influence our attitudes and behavior toward other people. Granting that our perceptions are inherently subjective, the authors offer suggestions for communicating them to others.

*Korten, Frances F. "The Influence of Culture on the Perception of Persons." *International Journal of Psychology* 9 (1974): 31–44.
An investigation of the influence of various cultures on the categorization of people into groups. Korten argues that cultural needs affect the use of categories in perceiving others. The study is explained in detail and offers

*Indicates more advanced readings.

several possible reasons for the
differences in cultural perceptions.

Rubin, Zick. "The Rise and Fall of First
Impressions." In *Interpersonal
Communication In Action,* edited by
Bobby R. Patton and Kim Giffin. 2d ed.,
pp. 149–67. New York: Harper & Row,
Publishers, 1977.
An interestingly written discussion of the
factors that affect our impressions of
others. Many good examples from
sports, teaching, and politics, and a
summary of some important studies of
the formation and influence of first
impressions.

*Triandis, Harry C. "Cultural Influences
upon Perception." In *Intercultural
Communication: A Reader,* edited by
Larry A. Samovar and Richard E.
Porter. 2d ed., pp. 119–23. Belmont,
Calif.: Wadsworth Publishing Company,
1976.
Triandis presents research that suggests
a connection between culture and
retention, recognition, emotions, and the
perception of space. Different societies
interpret the same stimuli differently. A
technical treatment of the topic.

Notes

1. James M. Renuk, "A Medium for His
   Message," *Washington Post,* 1977.

2. V. P. Richmond and D. Robertson,
   "Communication Apprehension as a
   Function of being Raised in an Urban or
   Rural Environment" (Monograph, West
   Virginia Northern Community College,
   1976).

3. Alistair B. Fraser, "Fata Morgana—The
   Grand Illusion," *Psychology Today* 9
   (January 1976): 22.

4. R. D. Laing, *Knots* (New York: Pantheon
   Books, Inc., 1971), pp. 75–76.

Self Image — How Others see us | Parents
Feed Back
How I see thing or Do | Teachers
Things · Selecti | Friends
on

Choice
Organize
Define

3
Verbal Codes: A Tool of Sharing

Objectives

After study of this chapter you should be able to do the following:

1. Explain what is meant by *symbol* and identify its relationship to reality
2. Discuss the relationship among words, codes, encoding, and decoding
3. Discuss ways in which verbal codes can become barriers to communication and illustrate each type of barrier with examples
4. Give examples of how our verbal symbol system (English) gives us a different perception of reality than other verbal symbol systems (e.g., French, Hopi, Russian, Eskimo)
5. Discuss the relative importance of denotative and connotative meanings in our communication of ideas and feelings
6. Give examples of how meanings differ among cultures and subcultures; individuals; situations and contexts
7. Discuss three ways in which we can improve our verbal skills
8. Describe an experience in which the operational definition of a word or words helped to clarify the message
9. Discuss someone's appearance using evaluative words; using descriptive words; discuss the effect of these two types of encoding on the relationship between you and the other person
10. Differentiate between paraphrasing the content and paraphrasing the intent of a message
11. Explain how paraphrasing can increase the understanding of a message
12. Define and give examples of dating and indexing as ways of increasing concreteness
13. Discuss the relationship between the use of euphemisms and clichés and the skills of concreteness and descriptiveness

Comedian Will Rogers said of President Calvin Coolidge: "He don't say much –but when he does–he don't say much."

"A conservative is defined as a liberal who was mugged yesterday."

"An X-rated film that I enjoy is provocative, *one that you enjoy is* tasteless, *and one that someone else enjoys is* pornographic.*"*

These three comments demonstrate various facets of the words that we use. Words—verbal symbols—and sets of words—verbal codes—are basic to communication. However, misconceptions about words may cause them to serve as barriers, rather than as bridges, to communication.

Before we consider why words sometimes become obstacles to communication, we need to clarify some essential terminology. We define *words* as verbal symbols. *Verbal* refers to anything that is associated with or pertains to words. A *symbol* is something that stands for, or represents something else, either by association, resemblance, or convention.

Figure 3.1   Figure 3.2a

A word is a symbol in the same sense that a wedding ring is a symbol for marriage, a flag is a symbol for a particular country, and long hair—just a decade ago—was considered a symbol of defiance by many people. Words symbolize events, people, and ideas by agreement among the people who use them, and through conventional use. They do not resemble the thing they represent; they are arbitrary representations of them. Statements like, ''The word is not the thing,'' and ''Words don't mean, people do,'' allude to this arbitrary nature of words.

Sets of words are verbal codes. You will recall that we defined *code* in chapter 1 as any systematic arrangement or comprehensive collection of symbols, letters, or words that are given arbitrary meaning and are used for communication. When we use verbal language to communicate, as senders we *encode*, or put the message or thought into a verbal code, and as receivers we *decode*, or assign meaning to the verbal code that we receive.

Words Can Be a Major Obstacle to Communication

We can support the argument that there are more than three billion different languages in the world. Each of us talks, listens, and thinks in a unique language (and sometimes we have several) that contains slight variations of agreed-upon meanings and that may change each minute. Our personal language is shaped by our culture, country, neighborhood, job, personality, attitudes, values, and mood. The possibility that even a few of us will share all of these ingredients in the same way at the same time is really quite remote.

Two experiments were used to illustrate the differences in our personal language. The photograph reproduced in figure 3.1 was shown to three people: a sophomore enrolled in a speech communication course, a Ph.D. in speech com-

Figure 3.2b   Figure 3.2c

munication, and a veterinarian. Each person was asked to define or describe the picture. Their descriptions follow:

> It is a deer-like animal with a white belly and horns. The ears appear relatively large and the rump is higher than the shoulders.
>
> *Student*

> A four-legged mammal of indeterminate size with hooves, variegated horns, large ears, elongated neck, and a two-toned torso. The rear legs are larger than the front legs as if the animal were designed for running. Its relatively large eyes are on the sides of the animal's face, so it is probably among the grazing hunted animals rather than the carnivorous hunters.
>
> *Speech communication professor*

> Gazella dorcas.
>
> *Veterinarian*

In the second experiment, the following definition of a gazelle was given to three people, who were then asked to draw the figure: "A hoofed mammal of Africa and Asia characteristically having a slender neck and ringed, lyrate horns." The drawings in figures 3.2a, 3.2b, and 3.2c were made by a nine-year-old boy, a woman, and a man. These experiments demonstrate something that occurs every day to each of us. Our personal verbal systems provide a barrier to communication when the messages we encode to others are decoded differently. You might try similar experiments to demonstrate this phenomenon.

There are three reasons why words and language often hamper effective communication. People sometimes intentionally use language to distort. People also frequently assume that words have an inherent, intrinsic meaning that is universally understood. And people often behave as though their language is "real" in some sense. Let us consider each of these reasons in more detail.

There is probably little doubt that Jimmy Carter wished he could have withdrawn some of the comments he made to a *Playboy* interviewer while campaigning for the presidency of the United States in 1976. Carter was apparently attempting to counter the criticism that he was "holier-than-thou."

After he had used the generally unobjectionable terms *fornicate* and *sexual intercourse,* Carter demonstrated his lack of puritanism by switching to the term *shack up.* The slang synonym surprised and shocked many voters. Carter's error was two-fold: He failed to stay with the abstract terms or vague phrases that could have been interpreted to the voter's liking; and he used slang that is not used by most people in public statements.

We Intentionally Use Language to Distort or Alter Our Meaning

The lawyer in the cartoon expresses the concern of many of us who attempt to confuse ourselves and others with language. We all do it. For example, a friend asks, "How do I look?" and we respond with a compliment rather than with an honest response. People sometimes press us to state a point of view before we have had time to think it through. If pressed too hard, we may make a vague response in order to gain more time to consider the issue. We also sometimes hedge when someone asks for information that we do not have. Through ambiguity, we attempt to convey the idea that we really know more than we do.

Politicians provide abundant examples of language intentionally used to obstruct communication. People running for political office often use abstract terms and vague phrases in order to say nothing or everything. They recognize that specific and concrete terms will offend one group or another, so they seek the safety of empty and meaningless language.

Advertisers, too, often intentionally use language to confuse the consumer. Words like *better, improved, new,* and phrases like *revolutionary change, a taste worth smoking, a real taste, real satisfaction, more than just low tar, this is ultra-low tar,* and *We're Number One* are typical. Such words and phrases, like the sign in the cartoon that advertises a *100-foot pool,* do not convey a clear message.

Politicians and advertisers are skilled in using confusing language but they by no means have exclusive rights to this practice. Each of us uses *euphemisms,*

THE WIZARD OF ID   by Brant parker and Johnny hart

INN
100-FOOT
POOL

VACANCY

I THOUGHT
YOU SAID YOU
HAD A *100*-
FOOT POOL?

TRY TO
TOUCH
BOTTOM

substitute words that are considered inoffensive instead of words that are thought to be offensive, and *clichés*, words or phrases that are overused and that have lost their effectiveness because of overuse. Euphemistically, we say *rest room* for *toilet*, *senior citizens* for *old people*, and *lower socioeconomic status* for *poor*. Among some of the more frequently heard clichés are *as good as gold*, *absence makes the heart grow fonder*, *take it with a grain of salt*, *all wool and a yard wide*, *give them an inch, they'll take a mile*, and *you will get out of it only as much as you put into it*.

Lyle the Lion can take some comfort in Dodo Bird's use of a cliché to criticize Lyle's speech. Each of us uses a variety of clichés and euphemisms. Try to list at least five clichés and five euphemisms you use. If you have difficulty identifying clichés and euphemisms in your own language, use someone else's expressions. It is sometimes easier to identify clichés and euphemisms in other people's communication.

Clichés

1. _____
2. _____
3. _____
4. _____
5. _____

Euphemisms

1. _____
2. _____
3. _____
4. _____
5. _____

ANIMAL CRACKERS

DODO, WOULD YOU MIND READING OVER THIS SPEECH THAT I'VE WRITTEN?

GAD, LYLE! IT'S FULL OF CLICHÉS!

I'M AFRAID IT ISN'T WORTH THE PAPER THAT IT'S WRITTEN ON!

Why do we use euphemisms and clichés? We use them to protect ourselves: to establish a healthy self-concept or to maintain a distorted self-concept; or to deny self-awareness or to gain time in order to develop self-awareness. We also use euphemisms and clichés to protect others: to help them maintain a selective view of reality or to help them distort their world; or to help them acknowledge successes or deny difficulties. A *late bloomer* does not have to admit being a decade or two older than the other students; an *underachiever* can't really expect high grades. The existence of a *word processing center* allows us to alter our perception of jobs in a typing pool. A discussion of *low rent housing* denies the real situation in the inner-city slums.

In general, the use of euphemisms, clichés, and other language to distort meaning or confuse ourselves and others should be avoided. We can establish destructive patterns of talking that minimize our ability to gain self-awareness, that distort an appropriate and positive self-concept. We can easily fall into the habit of using language that prevents us from seeing social problems and weakens our sensitive perception of joy and sorrow.

Sometimes the use of language to distort is not harmful. When there is social agreement, euphemisms may be used without negative effects. Asking for directions to the *rest room* instead of the *toilet,* telling a friend that a new suit is

not as good-looking as it might be instead of just plain *ugly,* and reporting that a student is *below average* rather than *stupid* may sometimes be preferable. The situation, the other people involved, and your intent must all be considered when you choose intentionally or deliberately to alter your message by the words that you choose.

We Assume That Words Have an Inherent, Intrinsic Meaning That Is Universally Understood

Words Vary in Meaning Among Cultures A family we know spent a summer in Europe a couple of years ago. As they traveled from country to country—sometimes crossing two or three borders in a single day—the wife noticed a striking similarity in the behavior of the Europeans they met. Although her husband is fluent in a number of European languages, the children and she are not. After successfully communicating with the husband, the European would turn to the wife and attempt to make small talk or social conversation. She would shrug her shoulders to indicate that she did not understand. The European would repeat the remark, but a bit more loudly. She would again try to say she could not understand the language. The other person would stand closer to her, use more gestures, and repeat the message very loudly. Generally, the husband intervened at this point, and explained that she really did not understand the language.

This happened everywhere the family went. People in the Netherlands, France, Germany, Spain, Italy, and other countries all shared the assumption

that speaking more loudly and more enthusiastically would result in understanding. This European experience is similar to experiences that all of us have
had in this country: people often assume that their words have an inherent, intrinsic meaning that is universally understood. Unfortunately they do not.

Words Vary in Meaning Among Subcultures   Differences in language seem
obvious when we consider different cultures and different countries. The examples are more subtle within a culture. Consider differences in our own country
between poor and wealthy people, older and younger people, black and white
Americans, and women and men. Too often, we assume that if we ''just talk
louder'' people from other subcultures will understand us, but *bad* means bad
unless it means ''very good,'' regardless of how loudly we talk.

Two children provided a clear example of differences in subcultural usage at
a dinner party not long ago. A number of adults were enjoying an after-dinner
conversation in the living room while the children were supposedly asleep. In
the middle of the conversation, the young boy announced, as he came down the
stairs, that his sister had said five "bad" words. The dinner guests were de-
lighted with the boy's precociousness. One of the men in the room asked the boy
if he could share what his sister had said. The boy grinned, said, "Sure," and
then repeated, "Lady, lady, lady, lady, and lady." He went off to bed, pleased
with his joke.

In this particular home, the parents had attempted to "desex" the language
and to exercise care with words that might have a degrading or negative meaning
for males and females. The children knew that their parents thought that the
word *lady* means a woman who is proper, who expects privileges because of her
sex and her station in life, and who never commits wrong acts but may condemn
others. They also knew, however, that other people use the word to show respect for women. The parents had explained to the children that some people
believe that the word *lady* is tied up with the current class struggle between men
and women, and that the usage of the word can cause the same reaction that the
traditional "four-letter words" have caused. Thus they were able to play a safe
joke on the grown-ups, based on the adults' different interpretations of a word.

Definitions

To Plato, the human was a "biped without
feathers." To Aristotle, "a political
animal." To Seneca, "a social animal."
To Shakespeare, "a poor, bare, forked
animal." To Byron, "half dust, half
deity." To Emerson, "a god playing the
fool." To Huxley, "an intelligence in
servitude to his organs." To Mark Twain,
"the only animal that blushes. Or needs
to."

Each of these definitions embodies a
unique way of looking at men and women,
and each represents considerable thought.

Ways of viewing the word *lady* were
just explained. Identify at least three
words for which you have special
definitions. Explain each definition in at
least one page, suggesting the origin of
your relationship with the word.
Examples may include *mother, love,
abortion, baby, war, poverty, philosophy,
communication, education, ecology,
money,* and *Caucasian.*

Words Vary in Meaning Among Individuals   We can demonstrate again
that words do not have an inherent meaning by considering the differences
among individuals within the same subculture. If, for example, you find yourself
in conflict with the idea that *lady* is a sexist term, you are demonstrating a difference among individuals within a subculture. You might find yourself arguing,
"But I am a woman, and I don't feel that way," or "I consider myself a feminist, and I don't think that," or "I'm proud to be known as a lady." All these

statements point up the different meanings that a word can have, and the idea that words vary in meaning from person to person.

A distinction is frequently made between the denotative and connotative meaning of words. *Denotative meaning* refers to an agreed upon meaning; *connotative meaning* refers to an individualized or personalized meaning. Denotative meanings are understood and shared by a large number of people. Connotative meanings are limited to a single person or to a very small number of persons.

In general, people use the denotative meaning as the real meaning of a word. In addition, most of us use a dictionary, thesaurus, or other reference books to determine a word's meaning. This provides no problem for us unless we forget two principles: the meaning of words is constantly undergoing change, and the meaning printed in an old dictionary may not represent the current usage; and the connotative meaning of the word, which may well be the meaning that another person intended, is not in the dictionary.

Words Vary in Meaning Depending on the Situation and Context   Not only does the meaning of words vary in different cultures, subcultures, and to different individuals, it also varies with the same person, depending upon the situation and the context. A dictionary frequently provides us with a number of denotative meanings for a word. The *Oxford English Dictionary* provides us with twenty or thirty meanings for a number of different words. For example, the word *close* has twenty-one separate definitions and many more subtypes; the word *clear* has twenty-seven definitions and many subtypes; the word *head* has sixty-six definitions with about two to four subtypes of each; and the word *come* has sixty-nine definitions, but nearly two hundred definitions when all the subdefinitions are counted.

We gain a clue about the particular denotative meaning a person has in mind from the context in which the word is used. For example, if someone asks us for bread, we would probably hand them something to eat if we were sitting at the dinner table, but a small amount of cash if we are standing in the parking lot.

An additional problem with spoken English, not as great in written English, is the number of words that sound the same, but have distinctive spellings and meanings. The "Wizard of Id" cartoon illustrates *hair* and *hare,* and the "Pea-

THE WIZARD OF ID   **by Brant parker and Johnny hart**

nuts'' strip calls to mind *tail* and *tale*. Unless we are sensitive to the context and the situation, we can easily receive the unintended word.

Words vary in meaning with cultures, subcultures, individuals, and context. They also vary as a result of factors like our work, our neighborhoods, and other subgroups to which we belong. They do not have an inherent, intrinsic meaning that is universally understood. Unless we keep this principle in mind, words can become an obstacle to communication.

In *Through the Looking Glass,* Humpty Dumpty and Alice become involved in an argument about language and meaning:

"I don't know what you mean by 'glory'," Alice said.
Humpty Dumpty smiled contemptuously. "Of course you don't—till I tell you. I meant there's a nice knock-down argument for you!"
"But 'glory' doesn't mean 'a nice knock-down argument'," Alice objected.
"When I use a word," Humpty Dumpty said, in a rather scornful tone, "it means just what I chose it to mean—neither more nor less."
"The question is," said Alice, "whether you can make words mean so many different things."
"The question is," said "Humpty Dumpty, "which is to be master—that's all."[1]

Consider the arguments you have had during the last week or two. Select one that was caused by difference in definitions. For example, you may have argued with a professor about the amount of homework in a course (definitional difference concerning the *appropriate* amount of work for a three-credit college course), you argued with your husband about who should do the laundry (definitional difference about what *wife* or *husband* means); or you may have argued with a friend about dieting (definitional difference about *overweight*).

Write a two-page paper or give a short talk identifying the difference in definition, the arguments each of you gave in favor of your way of defining the term, and how you resolved the argument. Did you realize that the difficulty between you was definitional?

We Behave as if the Reality We Create Through Language Is Real

We name or label things in our environment by observing them, identifying certain characteristics or qualities about them, and by classifying them into one group or another. For example, if you are shopping for furniture and you spot a roll-top desk in the corner of a furniture store to which you want to draw your companion's attention, you would probably say, "Look at that desk over

there,'' and gesture toward it. You named it *desk* after observing it and determining that it had the essential characteristics that you associate with desks.

Language provides an important function in this regard. It allows us to
order all of the stimuli that bombard us into meaningful groups or classes. If we
did not have the word *desk,* for example, you might have to say to your friend,
''Look at that wooden object that has four legs, six drawers, a tabletop surface
on which to write, about twenty or thirty small pigeonholes in which to file papers and other materials and that is about five feet wide, four feet high, and two
feet deep.''

When we classify objects, persons, or situations, we are stating, in effect,
that they have characteristics that are similar to other members of a particular
group. We determine that the roll-top desk has sufficient essential characteristics
to call it *desk* instead of *chest,* or *buffet,* or *table.* In doing so, we neglect the differences between the object—the roll-top desk, in this instance—and other
members of the class, other desks. By naming the piece of furniture *desk* we fail
to take into account the pigeonholes, the size, and other unusual features.

Classifications are neither right nor wrong. Instead, the classifications we
make reveal to others the criteria we are using in naming the person, object, or
situation. All of us have had the experience of trying to point out a particular
person to someone and of having them fail to locate the person we are describing. A conversation, as you are waiting for class to begin, might go something like this:

"Look at that woman!"
"Do you mean the blonde?"
"No, the short woman over on the right."
"Do you mean the one with the blue eyes?"
"No, she has brown eyes."
"Is it the one in the red t-shirt?"
"It looks like orange to me."
"Is she heavy?"
"I wouldn't call her heavy at all."
"Now she's moving to the front of the room."
"Why didn't you say it was the instructor!"
"I guess I never thought about it."

Both of the communicators used a variety of classes into which to place the
person they were discussing—sex, hair color, eye color, weight, clothing, position in the room, and, finally, occupation. This example is a particular favorite
because it illustrates a phenomenon that has been experienced a number of
times. Students—regardless of their age or sex—tend to classify instructors as
instructors, rather than by sex, attractiveness, or other physical features.

language DETERMINES Reality
UNIVERSE SpliT DIFFERENTly – everyone is RIGHT.

In the conversation between the two students about the female instructor, the first student was unable to help his fellow student "see" the person to whom he was referring. The classification system, or language, of the two caused differences in perception. This intimate relationship between language and perception no longer seems as remarkable as it did when it was first proposed by Edward Sapir, a linguist, and Benjamin Lee Whorf, a fire-insurance expert. The Sapir-Whorf hypothesis, as it has become known, states that our perception of reality is determined by our thought processes and that our thought processes are limited by our language; therefore, our perception of reality is dependent upon our language.[2] To understand how the Sapir-Whorf hypothesis works, we can consider the difference in perception and language when an optometrist examines our eyes and when we look at our own eyes in the mirror. Whereas we may see our eyes only as "nice," or "bloodshot," the optometrist might note the dilation of the pupil, the lack of perceptual acuity, the apparent distortion of the eyeball, and the accuracy of depth perception.

One of the most bizarre examples of the relationship between language and reality was contained in the story of the Charles Manson murders in the late 1960s. Manson found justification for his actions in the Bible and in the Beatles' *White Album*. Vincent Bugliosi, prosecutor in the Manson case, explains Manson's interpretation of the ninth chapter of Revelation in *Helter Skelter: The True Story of the Manson Murders*, reprinted on pages 52 to 54.

As we stated earlier, classification is neither right nor wrong, it merely reflects differences in our perception. As long as we recognize that other people may classify differently and, consequently, perceive the world differently, we have no problem. Unfortunately, most of us make the error, from time to time, of assuming that our view of reality is the only possible one. We fail to understand why someone from a different culture, subculture, or group does not use the same language as we do and does not perceive the same reality. When we behave as though the reality we create through our use of language is real, we allow language to become a barrier to effective communication.

Improvement of Verbal Skills

We have seen that language can become a major obstacle to our communication with others. Each of us has a unique language. Sometimes we intentionally distort meaning or attempt to confuse others. At other times, we mistakenly assume that words have an inherent, intrinsic meaning that others understand. Finally, we occasionally behave as though the reality that we have created through our use of language is real and is shared by others.

We can alter the situation so that words are not obstacles to communication. Three changes can be made in our verbal usage that will help us become

Helter Skelter
The True Story of the Manson Murders

The "four angels" were the Beatles, whom Manson considered "leaders, spokesmen, prophets," . . . The line "And he opened the bottomless pit . . . And there came out of the smoke locusts upon the earth; and unto them was given power . . ." was still another reference to the English group, . . . Locusts—Beatles—one and the same. "Their faces were as the faces of men," yet "they had hair as the hair of women." An obvious reference to the long-haired musicians. Out of the mouths of the four angels "issued fire and brimstone." . . . "This referred to the spoken words, the lyrics of the Beatles' songs, the power that came out of their mouths."

Their "breastplates of fire," were their electric guitars. Their shapes "like unto horses prepared unto battle" were the dune buggies. The "horsemen who numbered two hundred thousand thousand" and who would roam the earth spreading destruction, were the motorcyclists.

"And it was commanded them that they should not hurt the grass of the earth, neither any green thing, neither any tree; but only those men which have not the seal of God in their foreheads." I wondered about that seal on the forehead. How did Manson interpret that? . . .

"It was all subjective," Manson said, "There would be a mark on people." Charlie Manson had never told him exactly what the mark would be, only that he, Charlie "would be able to tell, he would know" and that "the mark would designate whether they were with him or against him."

One verse spoke of worshiping demons and idols of gold and silver and bronze. Manson said that referred to the material worship of the establishment: of automobiles, houses, money.

"Directing your attention to Verse 15, which reads: 'And the four angels were loosed, which

were prepared for an hour, and a day, and a month, and a year, for to slay the third part of men.' Did he say what that meant?''

"He said that those were the people who would die in Helter Skelter one third of mankind . . . the white race.''

The Beatles White Album *is a two-record set that was issued by Capitol records in 1968. Most people would describe it as consisting of thirty songs ranging from tender love ballads to pop songs to electronic noise. Manson felt it was prophecy. Bugliosi explains:*

Almost every song in the album had a hidden meaning, which Manson interpreted for his followers. To Charlie "Rocky Raccoon" meant "coon" or the black man. While to everyone except Manson and the Family it was obvious that the lyrics of "Happiness Is a Warm Gun" had sexual connotations, Charlie interpreted the song to mean that the Beatles were telling blackie to get guns and fight whitey.

According to Poston and Watkins, the Family played five songs in the *White Album* more than all the others. They were: "Blackbird," "Piggies," "Revolution I," "Revolution 9," and "Helter Skelter."

"Blackbird singing in the dead of night / Take these broken wings and learn to fly / All your life / You were only waiting for this moment to arise," went the lyrics of "Blackbird." According to Jakobson, "Charlie believed that the moment was now and that the black man was going to arise, overthrow the white man, and take his turn." According to Watkins, in this song Charlie "figured the Beatles were programming the black people to get it up, get on it, start doing it." . . .

(Continued)

... ''Revolution 9'' is easily the weirdest. . . . It
is a montage of noises—whispers, shouts, snatches
of dialogue from the BBC, bits of classical music,
mortars exploding, babies crying, church hymns,
car horns, and football yells—which, together with
the oft reiterated refrain ''Number 9, Number 9,
Number 9,'' build to a climax of machine-gun fire
and screams . . .

It was the Beatles' way of telling people what
was going to happen; it was their way of making
prophecy; it directly paralleled the Bible's
Revelation 9.

It was also the battle of Armageddon, the
coming black-white revolution portrayed in sound,
Manson claimed.

more effective communicators: we can avoid the intentional use of words to distort or confuse; we can become increasingly descriptive in our communication; and we can become increasingly concrete as we communicate with others.

Avoid Intentional Confusion

Some of the verbal patterns that we fall into have become so habitual that we no longer feel that we are intentionally confusing; rather, we believe that "everyone" speaks the way we do. We take comfort in our clichés. Edwin Newman, television news personality, talks about his own use of clichés in two recent books. Newman stated his specific motivation for writing the two books, *Strictly Speaking* and *A Civil Tongue:*

> One thing that happened to me, as a reporter on the air, was that I realized I was
> pushing along ideas that had no substance. I was taking phrases and using them as if
> they had substance, and they didn't.[3]

We should strive to become increasingly sensitive to our own use of empty language, ambiguities, clichés, and euphemisms. It is often helpful to have someone else monitor our statements and point out the problem areas. After someone else has sensitized us to our confusing phraseology, we can "take the reins in our own hands." (Er, that is, do the job ourselves!) Our goal, at all times, is to keep it simple.

Confusion can also arise when we use unusual terms or if we use a word in a special way. If we suspect that someone might not understand the terminology that we are using, it is essential to define the term. We need to be careful not to offend the other person, on the one hand, and to offer a definition that is clearer than the term itself, on the other.

Operational definitions, or definitions that point to the behavior, action, or properties that a word signifies, are sometimes very useful. When Alice asked the Dodo, in *Alice's Adventures in Wonderland,* what he meant by a Caucus-race, he wisely replied by offering an operational definition: "Why, the best way to explain it is to do it."[4] We use operational definitions when we explain, "For me, a good day is any day I don't have to go to classes or go to work," or when we explain outlining to a friend by writing a partial outline.

Descriptiveness

Descriptiveness is the practice of describing observable behavior or phenomenon instead of offering personal reactions or judgments. You are being descriptive if you state, "The food in the cafeteria tends to be high in cholesterol," but you are showing a lack of descriptiveness if you say, "I think that cook is trying to kill us." Teachers are being descriptive when they say something like

"You've been absent from my class six times this term," but not when they say, "I know you hate this speech communication class."

We can be descriptive in different ways. We can describe shared experiences. In order to communicate effectively with another person, it is important to have a common understanding of an event that has occurred, or the definition of a particular phenomenon. We can check on our shared experiences by perceptual checks or consensual validation and by separating inferences from observations.

We discussed perceptual checks of various kinds in chapter 2. Consensual validation, you will recall, is checking with another person to determine if their perceptions are the same as your own. We ask another person, "Do you feel a draft?" or "Don't you get tired, studying and working at a full-time job?" Many disagreements occur because people do not stop to make these simple checks of their perception.

Each of us confuses inferences—the drawing of a conclusion from or about things that we have observed—with observations. One of the most obvious times we do this is when we walk through a dark room at night. We cannot see the furniture or other obstacles, but we conclude they are still where they were, and we walk around them without turning on the light. We have no problem with this kind of simple exchange of an inference for an observation—unless someone moved the furniture, or someone placed a new object in the room, or our memory is not accurate. Even simple inferences can be errors. Many shins have been bruised because someone relied on inference rather than observation.

Problems in communication occur when people draw different inferences from similar observations. Researchers have been known to perform the same experiment and conclude entirely different things. Lawyers have lost cases in the courtroom because none of the witnesses could agree upon critical details. Spouses face marital discord when they reach different inferences from the same observations.

Difficulties in communication can also ensue when persons fail to separate their inferences from their observations. Obviously, we have to make some assumptions when we make statements about observable data. If we walk into a classroom and observe a person who appears to be about twenty-five years old, male, and Caucasian, standing at the front of the room behind a podium, we draw a number of conclusions. Most of us would assume that the living being was human, male, of an approximate age, and of a particular race. Some of us might also conclude that he is the instructor. A few people might decide that he is a graduate assistant, a boring lecturer, too formal, poor, unaware of current clothing styles, or has a host of other characteristics. All of these conclusions are inferences, but they are not all verifiable by observation to the same degree. All of the conclusions rely on assumptions. We assume that a person with relatively short hair and who is wearing a three-piece suit is a man. We assume that persons who are blond and blue-eyed are Caucasian. We assume that a certain stance, body position, and lack of wrinkles indicates a certain age. These assumptions are generally shared, and we usually agree that persons who display these characteristics are of a specific sex, age bracket, and race.

As the number of assumptions that we make increases, the likelihood that we are accurate decreases. In addition, as we move from generally agreed-upon assumptions to more questionable ones, we move from the area of observation to the area of inference. Sometimes we fail to recognize that we are drawing inferences based on many questionable assumptions and believe that we are simply stating observations that are shared by others. If you observed the person described above and concluded that he dressed in an outdated style, you might feel uncomfortable when the student sitting next to you told you how good you would look if you bought a similar suit. Agreement between you might not be possible until you both recognize that your statements reflect individual inferences based upon your separate perceptions, attitudes, values, and beliefs.

A second way that we can be descriptive is to utilize descriptive feedback. *Descriptive feedback* consists of nonevaluative, nonthreatening statements about our observations of the other person and his or her communication with us. It is essential that these comments be free of evaluation and judgment. Examples of descriptive feedback include statements like, ''You appear to be preoccupied and unable to concentrate on what I'm discussing with you,'' ''I perceive an edginess in your voice,'' and ''You seem enthusiastic when you talk about him.'' Statements like ''You're a real slob,'' ''I don't like the way you talk to me,'' and ''You sure could improve your relationship with your boyfriend, if you wanted to'' are not appropriate descriptive feedback because of their evaluative, threatening, judgmental nature.

Descriptive feedback provides a method of indicating to the other person what we do, and what we do not, understand from their message. It allows the other person the opportunity to validate accurate perceptions, and to correct misunderstandings. Paraphrasing—one form of descriptive feedback—allows increased understanding between two people. Simply stated, *paraphrasing* is the restatement of the other person's message. It is not merely repetition, however, since repetition only shows that you have received the words, not that you have really understood the message.

Suppose a student says, ''I don't understand descriptiveness.'' The teacher can respond by repeating, ''I hear you say that you don't understand descriptiveness,'' or ''Do you mean my explanation of that skill wasn't clear?'' or ''Do you mean that you would like me to explain the skill further to you?'' In the first case, the teacher is merely repeating the message and has only shown that the words were heard. The second reply shows that the content of the student's message has been understood. The third reply shows the intent of the message has been understood. The first response is mere repetition; the second and third are two levels of paraphrasing. The exercises in paraphrasing on pages 58 and 59 illustrate these levels of response.

Paraphrasing

For each of the following dialogues,
identify the response as repetition,
paraphrasing of content, or paraphrasing
of intent.

1. Question or statement: If you had to do it over again would you do the same thing?
   Response: Do you mean, would I state my disagreement to my employer?

2. Question or statement: Will your wife move to the new location with you if you secure this promotion?
   Response: Are you asking if my wife will move with me to the new location if I get the job?

3. Question or statement: I'm always afraid I'm going to make a mistake!
   Response: What do you mean, you feel like you're going to make a mistake?

4. Question or statement: I've lived here for three months, but I still don't know my way around the city.
   Response: Would you like me to show you some of the principal landmarks and the main streets?

5. Question or statement: I really appreciate the time you have spent talking to me.
   Response: I would like to encourage you to come in and see me whenever you have a problem—I understand how important it is to be able to talk to your supervisor.

Concreteness

Concreteness is specificity of expression. A person who is concrete uses statements that are specific, rather than abstract or vague. "You have interrupted me three times when I have begun to talk; I feel as though you do not consider my point of view as important as yours" is specific; "You should consider my viewpoint, too," is not.

Concreteness is any form of more specific expression. Two of the more interesting subtypes are dating and indexing. *Dating* refers to the idea that everything is subject to change. Often we view things as remaining the same. We form a judgment or point of view about a person, an idea, or a phenomenon, and we maintain that view, even though the person, idea, or phenomenon has changed. Dating is a method of avoiding this kind of frozen judgment. Instead of saying that something is always or universally a certain way, we state when we made our judgment and state that our perception was based on that experience.

Repetition	Paraphrasing of Content	Paraphrasing of Intent
———————————	———————————	———————————
———————————	———————————	———————————
———————————	———————————	———————————
———————————	———————————	———————————
———————————	———————————	———————————

For example, if you had a course with a particular instructor four or five years ago, it is essential that your judgment about the course and instructor be qualified as to time. You may tell someone, "English 100 with Professor Jones is a snap course," but it may no longer be true. Or, suppose you went out with a man two years ago and now your best friend is looking forward to her first evening with him. You might say that he is quiet and withdrawn, but it may no longer be accurate: the time that has passed, the person he was with, and the situation have all changed. Statements like "English 100 with Professor Jones was a snap course for me in 1975," and "Joe seemed quiet and withdrawn when I dated him two or three years ago," will create fewer communication problems.

Indexing is using the idea that all members of a subset do not share all of the characteristics of the other members of that subset. Earlier in the chapter we discussed the importance of being able to generalize and classify. Nonetheless, problems can arise when we generalize and classify. We sometimes have a tendency to assume that the characteristics of one member of a class apply to all of the members of the class. For example, you may incorrectly generalize that since your Volvo takes very little gas, all Volvos take little gas. Or you may incorrectly believe that since your older brother is more responsible than you, that all first-born children are more responsible than their siblings.

A second problem occurs when we assume that a characteristic of one member of a group is true of another member of the same group. If you delegated the characteristics of your Volvo to your friend's Volvo, you would be making this error. Or, if you assume that somebody else's older brother is responsible because your older brother is, you would be running the risk of generalizing incorrectly.

Indexing assists us in avoiding these pitfalls. Indexing is simply recognizing differences among the various members of a group. Instead of grouping all automobiles together and assuming that a characteristic that one car has is shared by all of the others, we recognize that the car we own could be unique. Instead of assuming that all older children are alike, we exhibit openness and an inquiring attitude about older children, other than the one we know.

We are indexing when we make statements like "I have a Volvo which uses very little gas. How does your Volvo do on gas mileage?" or "My older brother is far more responsible than I. Is the same true of your older brother?" We lack an ability to index when we state, "Volvos get good gas mileage—I know, I own one," or "Older children are more responsible than their younger brothers and sisters."

Concreteness

To determine if you can identify statements that are concrete from those which are not, mark the following statements *NC*, not concrete; *D*, dating; and *I*, indexing.

1. That TV program is out of date! _____

2. She never listens to anyone. _____

3. My mom is always crabby. _____

4. The President seemed so warm and friendly when he was running for office. _____

5. Have you seen Tom lately—he has seemed so jumpy the last two weeks. _____

6. Have you met the new woman in chem class? She's really stuck up—but students from the northern part of the state are all that way. _____

7. Who's the guy with Sue? Knowing her, he will be looking around for someone new to date soon!
_____

8. Why do you want this job, Ms. Paris? You know that women just get married and quit. _____

9. When my mother died, my dad was depressed for nearly two years—he just sat in his chair night after night. _____

10. I was really disappointed to have a woman for my introduction to marketing course, after I had such a bad experience with the woman lecturer in geography. I decided not to prejudge her, though. Because one woman instructor doesn't work out, doesn't mean that all female college instructors are incompetent. _____

Summary

In this chapter we have discussed verbal codes. We defined words as verbal symbols and languages as verbal codes. We use verbal language in communication by encoding, putting our messages or thoughts into a code, and by decoding, assigning meaning to the codes that we receive.

Words become a major obstacle to communication for several related reasons: we sometimes intentionally use language to distort and confuse; we often assume that words have an inherent, intrinsic meaning that is universally understood; and we frequently behave as though the reality we create through our language is real in some objective sense.

We can improve our use of language through three practices. We can avoid intentional confusion by defining the terminology we use and by avoiding euphemisms and clichés. Second, we can share experiences more effectively by becoming increasingly descriptive. Third, we can gain understanding through our ability to be concrete.

New Terms

Words ~VERBAL SYMBOL~	Clichés	Sapir-Whorf hypothesis *LANGUAGE PRECEIVES REALITY*
Verbal ~SETS OF WORD~	Culture and subculture	Operational definitions
~WE ASSIGN MEANING~ Symbol ~REPRESENTS SOMETHING ELSE.~	Denotative meaning	Descriptiveness
Code	Connotative meaning	Consensual validation
Encode ~PUT INTO CODE a MESSAGE~	Public code	Inferences
Decode	Private code	Paraphrasing
Personal language	Intrinsic meaning	Concreteness
(3) Language distortion ~DELEBRATE AMBIGUOUS~	Arbitrary meaning	Dating
Euphemisms	Classifications	Indexing

Additional Readings

Hayakawa, S. I. *Language in Thought and Action.* 3d ed. New York: Harcourt Brace Jovanovich, Inc., 1972.
An easily understood examination of the nature of language and the uses of symbols. Includes a discussion of verbal styles, figures of speech, language construction, inference making, and the socio-political uses of language.

*Hertzler, Joyce O. *A Sociology of Language.* New York: Random House, Inc., 1965.
Scholarly treatment of cultural and subcultural influences on language, embracing the characteristics of language, differences between languages, how languages change, and how society reflects change in its language system.

*Johnson, Wendell. *People in Quandaries.* New York: Harper & Row, Publishers, 1946.
An introduction to the principles of general semantics. Johnson shows how words can cause problems and gives suggestions about using words effectively. A classic scholarly work about verbal symbol systems.

Kramer, Cheris. "Folk-Linguistics: Wishy-Washy Mommy Talk." *Psychology Today,* June 1974, pp. 82–85.
A brief look at the differences between male and female language, including the use of adjectives, taboo words, and frequency of talking. Kramer describes some original research that indicates men talk differently than women.

Laird, Charlton. *The Miracle of Language.* Greenwich, Conn: Fawcett Publications, 1953.
Laird traces the development of language from caveman to the present in a vivid and stimulating manner. Discusses some of the quirks of our language and the fallacies of the ways we teach and learn to speak and write our native tongue.

*Lee, Irving J. *How to Talk With People.* New York: Harper & Row, Publishers, 1952.
On the basis of several years of observation of people in various contexts, Lee theorizes about how language can cause misunderstandings and offers suggestions for improving the effectiveness and clarity of our use of verbal symbols. Excellent application of verbal principles to human interaction.

*Morton, John, ed. *Biological and Social Factors in Psycholinguistics.* Urbana, Ill.: University of Illinois Press, 1970.
A collection of readings explore various elements of language behavior. Grammar, syntax, word usage, and universals of language are examined. Excellent bibliography for further study is included.

Newman, Edwin. *A Civil Tongue.* Indianapolis: Bobbs-Merrill Co., Inc., 1976.
A humorous, tongue-in-cheek look at the uses and misuses of language. Newman warns that we are constantly bombarded with incorrect language usage by TV, radio, advertisements, political bureaucracy, and schools. He argues that the ideas we present are no stronger than the words we use to express them.

Pei, Mario. *The Story of Language.* New York: New American Library of World Literature, 1949.
Pei advances and explains several hypotheses about the origin of language, discusses the elements of language, and compares several different languages in terms of grammar, syntax, and construction. The social implications of language are also explored.

*Indicates more advanced readings.

Notes

1. Lewis Carroll, *Through the Looking Glass* (New York: Random House, Inc., 1965), p. 94.

2. Benjamin Lee Whorf, "Science and Linguistics," in *Language, Thought and Reality,* ed. John B. Carroll (Cambridge, Mass.: M.I.T. Press, 1956), pp. 207–19.

3. John Barbour, "Edwin Newman Talks to Himself, but for a Good Reason," *Des Moines Sunday Register,* June 5, 1977.

4. Lewis Carroll, *Alice's Adventures in Wonderland* (New York: Random House, Inc., 1965), pp. 27–28.

4 Nonverbal Codes: A Tool of Sharing

Objectives
After study of this chapter you should be able to do the following:

1. Discuss the relative importance of verbal and nonverbal codes in expressing ideas and feelings
2. Discuss the validity of interpreting similar movements in the same way; explain the factors that influence our interpretation of movement
3. Draw some conclusions about people that can usually be based on their body orientation and position
4. Discuss your own use of personal space and explain why it differs when you are with a close friend, a stranger, at home, or at a party
5. Differentiate between personal space and territoriality
6. Discuss the relationship between touch and personal space
7. Identify the factors that influence the meaning and use of touch
8. Define six characteristics of paralinguistics that can affect the meaning of a message
9. Specify the information that paralanguage can give us about another person
10. Discuss your own use of objects in communication and discuss the meaning that you think they convey
11. Identify the factors that make it difficult to interpret nonverbal behavior accurately
12. Name some guidelines that can help you interpret nonverbal behavior more accurately
13. Discuss ways in which you can increase the accuracy of other people's interpretations of your nonverbal behavior

"The look of love is in your eyes."

Burt Bacharach

"There is a space between us which we cross to touch each other softly and so make up our loss."

Carole King and Toni Stern

"And when I touch you I feel happy inside."

John Lennon and Paul McCartney

These three excerpts from songs that were popular in the 1960s and 1970s illustrate the importance of nonverbal communication. The first lyric emphasizes facial expression; the second is about the use of space in human communication; the last concerns the key role of touch in human communication. Each of these songs is about communication that does not require words.

Importance of Nonverbal Codes in Communication

The little boy in the cartoon is well aware of the importance of nonverbal communication. Although his sister may scoff, his conclusion is borne out in research on nonverbal communication. A number of researchers have investigated the percentage of a message that is transmitted nonverbally, as opposed to verbally. Birdwhistell determined that only 35 percent of the meaning in a situation is transmitted verbally and that 65 percent is transmitted nonverbally.[1] Another student of nonverbal communication, Mehrabian, also analyzed message transmission and found that only 7 percent of the meaning is transmitted verbally. The 93 percent of the message that is transmitted nonverbally is divided between 38 percent vocal cues and 55 percent facial cues.[2] Although the findings vary, we can conclude that nonverbal cues are probably more important than verbal cues to the sharing of meaning. The statement, "*What* you say is less important than *how* you say it," appears valid.

Nonverbal Meeting

In order to understand the importance of the nonverbal in your communication, try the following:

1. Spend thirty minutes with a good friend, spouse or child without using any written or spoken words. Instead, use bodily movement, the space between you, gestures, facial expression, and other nonverbal cues to communicate.
2. Spend fifteen minutes with an acquaintance without using any words. Again, communicate only with nonverbal cues.
3. Spend ten minutes with a person you have spoken to before, but restrict your communication to nonverbal cues.

In a short paper, discuss your reactions and conclusions. Did you find that communicating nonverbally was easier or more difficult than you predicted? Did you find it easier to communicate nonverbally with someone you knew well, or with a relative stranger? Why? Do you think the other person understood the message you were trying to communicate nonverbally? Do you believe that communication would have been hindered or helped if you could also have used words? How?

Definition and Identification of Nonverbal Codes

Nonverbal codes were defined in chapter 1 as codes of communication that consist of symbols that are not words. Bodily movements, facial expression, use of space, touching, vocalized sounds other than words, clothing, and artifacts are all nonverbal codes. Let us consider each of these systematic arrangements of symbols that have been given arbitrary meaning and that are used in communication.

Bodily Movement and Facial Expression

Kinesics is the term that means the study of people's bodily movements. Kinesics includes the study of posture, gestures, and facial expression. We communicate many of our feelings or emotions in these nonverbal ways. Ekman and Friesen determined that our faces give others information about *how* we feel and that our bodies suggest the *intensity* of the particular emotion.[3]

A number of best sellers in the 1960s and 1970s, among them *Body Talk, Body Language,* and *How to Read a Person Like a Book,* have conveyed the importance of kinesics to the average person. These popular books familiarized the public with the importance of bodily movement in communication, but they also suggested that bodily movement is relatively easy to understand. Serious students of nonverbal communication know that this is not true. Assigning meaning to human movement is actually complicated. Alterations in the meaning of a person's movement may be due to characteristics of that person, characteristics of the observer, and characteristics of the environment.

In order to make an accurate assessment of the meaning of another person's movements, we need to take into account the person's particular characteristics. We may be grimacing because we have just left the dentist. Our quick pace may be due to lateness rather than habit. A lack of gestures and hand movement

might result from fatigue. The physical, psychological, and emotional characteristics of the person being observed must all be taken into account.

Our own particular characteristics must also be considered when we are
observing another person. When we interpret another person's movements as
unfriendly, we need to consider our own expectations. Are we expecting that
person to be unfriendly, and thus perceiving what we want to perceive? If
someone appears nervous to us, is it because we are feeling tension and pro-
jecting our feelings onto someone else? Our own attitudes, values, and beliefs,
coupled with our current needs and goals, must be taken into account when we
assign meaning to another person's movements.

Finally, we need to consider the particular characteristics of the environment. A person standing with arms crossed may feel cold. Someone who is
moving around slowly might be sensitive to another person's headache and
might be trying to avoid making noise. A clerk who is darting in and out of the
storeroom may be waiting on customers who are hard to please. Environmental
factors must be considered when we try to understand bodily movement.

Mehrabian took these variables into consideration in the research he completed in 1971. He was interested in a person's body position and orientation—
the degree to which one's shoulders and legs were turned toward another
person. Mehrabian found that he could draw some general conclusions about
this by considering three variables: (1) liking; (2) power or status; and (3) vitality
or responsiveness. He found that liking was often expressed by leaning forward,
a direct body orientation, greater closeness, increased touching, a relaxed posture, open arms and body, positive facial expression, and more eye contact.
Consider your own body orientation and movement when you are with persons
you like. You tend to sit closer to them, lean toward them, touch them more,
relax physically, smile at them more, and look at them more. When you are with
persons whom you do not know or do not like, you tend to sit farther away from
them, you seldom touch them, you are physically tense or at least not relaxed,
you smile less, and you establish only minimum eye contact.

Mehrabian found that power or status was communicated by expansive gestures, relaxed posture, and less eye contact. When you consider persons in authority whom you know, you probably can recall their large gestures, the relaxed
posture of their body, and their tendency to look at you less often. Supervisors,
teachers, employers, and parents exhibit such behavior.

Mehrabian also found that responsiveness or involvement with other people
is shown by movement toward other people, spontaneous gestures, a shifting of
posture and position, and facial expressiveness.[4] Consider those persons whom
you consider highly responsive. They move a great deal, they are spontaneous in
their gestures and movements, and their faces are very expressive. If we keep in
mind the particular characteristics of the person we are observing, our own particular characteristics, and the particular aspects of the environment, we can use
Mehrabian's findings to help us interpret the movements of other people.

Space

Edward T. Hall introduced the importance of *proxemics,* the human use of space, in 1966, in his book *The Hidden Dimension.* Robert Sommer analyzed the topic further in 1969, in *Personal Space: The Behavioral Basis of Design.* These researchers and others that have followed have demonstrated the role that space plays in human communication.

Two concepts that have been considered essential to the study of the use of space are territoriality and personal space. *Territoriality* is our need to establish and maintain certain spaces of our own. Territoriality has been studied more in animals than in humans, but it is recognized as a human need. People stake out their territory in various ways. Students leave coats or books on a library table while they search the stacks. Faculty members arrange their offices so their own chairs are identifiable. We all use fences, "no trespassing" signs, wedding rings, and other symbols that indicate our territory. We can purchase bumper stickers that read "If you can read this, you're too close"; hotels and motels provide us with "Do not disturb" signs, and airlines offer us cards that state, "Sorry, this seat is occupied." Territoriality refers to territory that is generally immovable and typically separate from a person.

Personal space, on the other hand, is the area surrounding a person that moves with the person. Personal space is the amount of physical distance you

maintain between yourself and other people. We seldom think about personal
space until someone invades it, but such an invasion may create stress or evoke
defensive behavior.

Personal space varies from person to person and from situation to situation.
Among the variables that determine personal space are (1) the characteristics of
the individuals; (2) the relationship between them; (3) the physical setting; and
(4) their cultural background. Two relevant characteristics of individuals are
their size and sex. People who are larger require a greater amount of personal
space, and people who are smaller—including children—require a smaller
amount of space.[5] Women show the least discomfort when the space around
them is small, and tend to interact at closer range.[6]

The relationship between the people who are interacting is also important.
Generally, we stand closer to friends and farther away from enemies.[7] We also
stand away from strangers, authority figures, people of higher status, physically
handicapped people, and individuals from a different racial group.

The physical setting can alter our personal space. People tend to stand
closer in large rooms and farther apart in small rooms.[8] In addition, physical
obstacles and furniture arrangements can affect personal space.

The cultural background of the people involved must be considered. Edward T. Hall was among the first to recognize the importance of cultural background. In 1963, he was training American service personnel for service over-
seas and began to recognize the importance of cultural differences in his work.
Hall writes:

> Americans overseas were confronted with a variety of difficulties because of cultural
> differences in the handling of space. People stood ''too close'' during conversations,
> and when the Americans backed away to a comfortable conversational distance, this
> was taken to mean that Americans were cold, aloof, withdrawn, and disinterested in
> the people of the country. USA housewives muttered about ''waste-space'' in houses
> in the Middle East. In England, Americans who were used to neighborliness were hurt
> when they discovered that their neighbors were no more accessible or friendly than
> other people, and in Latin America, exsuburbanites, accustomed to unfenced yards,
> found that the high walls there made them feel ''shut out.'' Even in Germany, where
> so many of my countrymen felt at home, radically different patterns in the use of space
> led to unexpected tensions.[9]

Cultural background can greatly alter the human use of space and the interpretation, by others, of that use of space.

Touching

Tactile communication is the use of touch in communication. Touch may be
viewed as the most extreme form of invasion of personal space. Nonetheless,
touch is essential to our growth and development. Studies have shown that an

insufficient amount of touching can result in health disorders such as allergies
and eczema, speech problems, symbolic recognition, and even death.[10] While it
may be difficult to believe, researchers have found that untouched babies and
small children grow increasingly ill and even die.

Touch is one of the most powerful ways we have of communicating with
others. The pleasure that touch causes originates in infancy. For most people,
touching is positive and enjoyable. The interpretation of the meaning of a particular touch depends, of course, on the type of touch, where a person is touched,
and the cultural background of the people involved. Still, in most cultures, touch
is associated with positive attitudes and lack of touch is associated with negative

attitudes. Touch is one of the clearest indications that we like and accept others
and that they like and accept us.

Vocal Cues

In chapter 1, we distinguished between nonverbal and nonoral communication.
While nonverbal codes include the nonoral or nonvocal codes such as bodily
movement and the human use of space, they also include pitch, duration of
sound, rate of speech, and nonwords such as *eh* and *ah*. Nonverbal codes are all
codes that do not consist of words. When we consider vocal cues, we include all
of the oral aspects of sound except the words themselves.

We can categorize vocal cues into (1) pitch—the highness or lowness of a
voice; (2) rate—how rapidly or slowly a person speaks; (3) inflection—the
change or lack of change in the pitch of a person's voice; (4) volume—the loudness or softness of a person's voice; (5) quality—the pleasant or unpleasant characteristics of a person's voice, including nasality, raspiness, and whininess; and
(6) enunciation—a person's pronunciation and articulation. In addition to these
cues, specific sounds such as *uh-huh, ah,* and *mmh,* as well as silences, com-
prise the elements taken into consideration in *paralanguage,* that which comes
with language.

Paralanguage, as we said earlier in this chapter, conveys about 38 percent of
a message. The vocal aspect of nonverbal communication frequently conveys a
speaker's personal attributes and provides information about the speaker's current emotional state. Among the personal attributes that are often communicated
are the speaker's age, height, over-all appearance, and body type.[11] A number of
studies have related various emotions to specific vocal cues. Joy and hate appear
to be the most accurately communicated emotions, and shame and love the least
accurately communicated.[12] Emotions like joy and hate appear to be conveyed
by fewer vocal cues, which makes their interpretation less difficult than the
complex sets of vocal cues that identify emotions like shame and love. Personality characteristics such as dominance, social adjustment, sociability, and tension have also been related to vocal cues.[13] For example, people who feel domi-
nant tend to speak more loudly and to enunciate very clearly. People under
tension tend to speak rapidly and in a high-pitched voice.

Clothing and Other Artifacts

Objectics, or *object language,* refers to our display of material things. Object
language is comprised of hair styles, clothing, jewelry, cosmetics, and so forth.
Our clothing and other adornments communicate our age, sex, status, role, socioeconomic class, group memberships, personality, and our relation to the opposite sex. Dresses are seldom worn by men, low-cut gowns are not the choice

of shy women, bright colors are avoided by reticent people, and the most recent Paris fashion is seldom seen in the small towns of mid-America. These cues also indicate the time in history, the time of day, and the climate. Clothing and artifacts provide physical and psychological protection, and are used for sexual attraction and to indicate self-concept.

A few years ago, the students in a female instructor's class told her that clothing was a form of communication only among older people—like herself. They argued that young people make no judgments about other people's clothing, and seldom even noticed other people's clothes, and her arguments to the contrary fell on deaf ears.

The next semester, again lecturing on object language, she told her new students about that previous discussion—but while she talked, she slipped off her jeans and sweater to reveal a leotard and tights. At the end of the hour, she gave a quiz on the material covered during the period. Not surprisingly, the students successfully answered the items on the material covered before she disrobed, but did a poor job on the questions about material she covered afterward. These students agreed—they were distracted by her unusual and provocative costume and had difficulty concentrating on the lecture. The importance of clothing as a means of nonverbal communication, to young as well as older people, was established, at least in that second class.

Clothes Communicate!

The "Tumbleweeds" cartoon derives its humor from the fact that the cowboy has a number of nonverbal cues from which to draw the conclusion that the other person is an Indian, and the fact that he calls the Indian's garb an *apron*. Our clothing does communicate who we are, what we value, how we see ourselves, and it conveys a number of other messages besides. Consider the clothing and jewelry you wear and what it might communicate about you. Keep a record for three or four days of all of the clothing, jewelry, and other adornments that you wear. Record changes in clothing within the day. After you have compiled this record, suggest why you made these choices, and what these particular clothes might communicate to others. Finally, ask two friends or acquaintances what your clothing communicates to them. Consider the similarities or differences in the perception you have of your clothing and the perceptions that your friends or acquaintances have.

T
U
M
B
L
E
W
E
E
D
S

Interpretation of Nonverbal Cues

Problems of Interpretation

Considering the importance of nonverbal codes, it is not surprising that they
provide the basis for much of the misunderstanding that occurs in communication. We have difficulty interpreting nonverbal cues for several reasons. We use
the same cue to communicate a variety of different meanings; we use a variety of
cues to communicate the same meaning; and we use conflicting verbal and nonverbal cues in our communication.

The Same Cue Communicates a Variety of Different Meanings   In this
cartoon, the young woman has reacted to a verbal instruction with an inappropriate bodily movement. True, she has responded to the request that she raise
her right hand, but she has also clenched her fist, the symbol for power in the
Sixties and early Seventies. Raising your right hand may mean that you are
taking an oath, you are demonstrating for a cause, you are indicating to an instructor that you would like to answer a question, that a physician is examining
your right side, or that you want a taxi to stop for you.

DUNAGIN'S PEOPLE

10-14

Dunagin
1975 Sentinel Star
Field Newspaper Syndicate

"THAT ISN'T WHAT
WE MEAN BY
'RAISE YOUR
RIGHT HAND'..."

We may also use the same cue to communicate different things in other nonverbal codes. We may stand close to someone else because of a feeling of affection, because the room is crowded, or because we have difficulty hearing. We may speak softly because we were taught it was the "correct" way for us to speak, because we are suffering from a sore throat, or because we are sharing a secret. We may wear blue jeans because they are the acceptable mode of dress, because they symbolize our rebellion against higher-priced clothing, or because they are the only clean clothes we have that day.

A Variety of Cues Communicate the Same Meaning   The cartoon shows an inappropriate way of communicating meaning. Yet, those of us who are parents or have younger siblings are familiar with the tendency of young children to express affection or attraction through physical aggression. As the child grows, he or she begins to experiment with more appropriate nonverbal indications of affection.

Adults have many nonverbal ways to express love or affection. We may choose to sit or stand more closely to someone we love. We might speak more softly, use a different vocal intonation, and alter how quickly we speak when we communicate with someone for whom we have affection. We often dress differently if we are going to be in the company of a person we love.

Verbal and Nonverbal Cues May Conflict   As we can see from the cartoon, we may have a positive feeling about the verbal message but a negative feeling about the nonverbal statement. The little mother approves of her doll's words, but she disapproves of the vocal cues—perhaps the intonation—that accompanies the verbal message.

We can all think of times when other people have said that they felt a certain way but told us nonverbally that they felt differently. Instructors have this experience when students tell them that they particularly enjoy their class but do not attend regularly. Students experience this form of conflict when instructors invite them into their office to talk but spend the entire time looking through memos and papers.

Bateson and others initially identified this situation as a "double bind."[14] The conflict between two contradictory messages creates a difficult situation for the person who is attempting to respond appropriately to the given cues: "He is damned if he does, and damned if he doesn't." It is particularly difficult when some of the cues are verbal and others are nonverbal.

Verbal cues can conflict with cues from any of the nonverbal codes. We may find it difficult to believe that people really care for us if they never touch us or move toward us. A person may deliver a message of anger, but in an even-toned, quiet voice. We question the credibility of people who say that money means little to them if they continually flash expensive jewelry and dress in ostentatious, costly clothing.

Solutions to Problems of Interpretation

It may appear, from our discussion, that the difficulty of interpreting nonverbal cues is insurmountable. The problems in interpretation are serious, but they can be minimized if we make use of three sets of information. First, we need to be sensitive to all of the variables in the communication situation. Second, we should attend to all of the verbal and nonverbal cues. Finally, we should use descriptive feedback to clarify unclear cues. p·5¹

Consider All of the Variables in the Communication Situation   Other
people's nonverbal communication is only a small part of a communication situation. We must also consider other aspects of other persons—ability to use
words, intentions, immediate and past history, and so forth. We also need to
consider ourselves, and how our presence might affect the behavior of others.
We should also take into account the relationship between ourselves and others.
Finally, we should consider the context—the reason for the conversation.

Consider All Available Verbal and Nonverbal Cues   Rather than focusing
on another person's clothing, or a specific facial expression, take into consideration other nonverbal cues as well. Do not forget to listen to the verbal message.
If you find contradictions between the verbal and nonverbal messages, recall the
person's past communication behavior. When contradictions in verbal and nonverbal cues occurred in the past, which was the intended message? Is it likely
that this is the intended message now?

Utilize Descriptive Feedback   One of the most accurate ways of solving the
difficulty of interpreting nonverbal cues is to use descriptive feedback. By
simply describing to the other person the conflict you find or suggesting the
meaning you understand, you can clarify things. The other person can suggest
reasons for the inconsistencies or supply the intended meaning. You can continue to request clarification until you understand and share the same message.

Summary

In this chapter we have considered the role of nonverbal codes in communication. We explained the importance of nonverbal codes and defined them as all
codes which consist of symbols which are not words. Bodily movements and
facial expression, personal space, sounds other than words, and clothing and artifacts are nonverbal codes. Kinesics is the study of people's bodily movements,
including posture, gestures, and facial expression. Proxemics is the human use
of space; included in a study of proxemics are territoriality and personal space.
Tactile communication is the use of touch in communication. Vocal cues include
pitch, rate, inflection, volume, quality, and enunciation. Objectics, or object
language, is our display of material things, including hair styles, clothing, jewelry, and cosmetics.

We have difficulty in interpreting nonverbal cues because we use the same
cue to communicate a variety of different meanings, because we use a variety of
cues to communicate the same meaning, and because we use conflicting verbal

and nonverbal cues. We can solve some of our difficulties if we consider all of the variables in the particular communication situation, if we consider all of the available verbal and nonverbal cues, and if we use descriptive feedback to minimize misunderstanding.

New Terms

Nonverbal code

Kinesics

Body position and orientation

Proxemics

Territoriality

Personal space

Tactile communication

Vocal cues

Pitch

Rate

Inflection

Volume

Quality

Enunciation

Paralanguage

Objectics

Double bind

Descriptive feedback

Additional Readings

*Ekman, Paul, and Friesen, Wallace V. *Unmasking the Face: A Guide to Recognizing Emotions from Facial Cues.* Englewood Cliffs, N.J.: Prentice-Hall, Inc., 1975.
A research-oriented look at what feelings and emotions facial expressions communicate, and how they do it. Systematic description of specific facial movements that help determine meaning. Some excellent illustrations help clarify the myriad of facial expressions that we use to convey our feelings.

Fast, Julius. *Body Language.* New York: Pocket Books, 1970.
An interesting look at nonverbal communication with numerous examples to illustrate concepts. The book tends to be a bit superficial and some of the conclusions are over-extended. Nonetheless, Fast covers many of the topics of nonverbal behavior and provides some insight into the cross-cultural aspects of nonverbal behavior.

Hall, Edward T. *The Silent Language.* Greenwich, Conn.: Fawcett Publications, 1959.
Hall compares nonverbal uses of space, time, and movement in different cultures, emphasizes the influence of culture on our behavior, and discusses the impact of cultural factors on our perception and communication. An in-depth discussion of concepts, written in an easy-to-understand style.

Knapp, Mark L. *Nonverbal Communication in Human Interaction.* New York: Holt, Rinehart, and Winston, Inc., 1972.
A summary of the research on nonverbal behavior, including appearance, use of space, movement, eye contact, and vocalics. Easy to understand, with good examples and illustrations to clarify major nonverbal principles.

*Mehrabian, Albert. "Communication without Words." *Psychology Today,* September 1968, pp. 53–55.
Mehrabian explains the relative contributions to meaning of verbal, vocal, and facial cues. He describes his research and the implications of his finding that nonverbal cues are primarily responsible for our likings, feelings, and attitudes.

Rosenfeld, Lawrence B., and Civikly, Jean M. *With Words Unspoken: The*

*Indicates more advanced readings.

Nonverbal Experience. New York: Holt, Rinehart and Winston, Inc., 1976. *A basic introduction to nonverbal behavior and the effect of nonverbal communication on our interaction with* *others. Includes a discussion of movement, touch, voice, space, and appearance, and an exploration of the relationship between culture and nonverbal behavior.*

Notes

1. Ray L. Birdwhistell, *Kinesics and Context* (Philadelphia: University of Pennsylvania Press, 1970), pp. 128–43.

2. Albert Mehrabian and Susan R. Kerris, "Inference of Attitude from Nonverbal Communication in Two Channels," *Journal of Consulting Psychology* 31 (1967): 248–52.

3. Paul Ekman and Wallace V. Friesen, "Head and Body Cues in the Judgment of Emotion: A Reformulation," *Perceptual and Motor Skills* 24 (1967): 711–24.

4. Albert Mehrabian, *Silent Messages* (Belmont, Calif.: Wadsworth Publishing Co., 1971), pp. 113–18.

5. Michael Argyle and Janet Dean, "Eye-Contact, Distance, and Affiliation," *Sociometry* 28 (1965): 289–304.

6. B. R. Addis, "The Relationship of Physical Interpersonal Distance to Sex, Race, and Age" (Master's thesis, University of Oklahoma, 1966).

7. Carol J. Guardo, "Personal Space in Children," *Child Development* 40 (1969): 143–51.

8. Robert Sommer, "The Distance for Comfortable Conversation: A Further Study," *Sociometry* 25 (1962): 111–16.

9. Edward T. Hall, "Proxemics—The Study of Man's Spatial Relations and Boundaries," *Man's Image in Medicine and Anthropology* (New York: International Universities Press, 1963), pp. 422–45.

10. Ashley Montagu, *Touching: The Human Significance of the Skin* (New York: Harper & Row, Publishers, 1971), p. 82; J. L. Desper, "Emotional Aspects of Speech and Language Development," *International Journal of Psychiatry and Neurology* 105 (1941): 193–222; John Bowlby, *Maternal Care and Mental Health* (Geneva: World Health Organization, 1951), pp. 15–29; Ronald Adler and Neil Towne, *Looking Out/Looking In* (San Francisco: Rinehart Press, 1975), pp. 225–26.

11. Ernest Kramer, "The Judgment of Personal Characteristics and Emotions from Nonverbal Properties of Speech," *Psychological Bulletin* 60 (1963): 408–20.

12. James C. McCroskey, Carl E. Larson, and Mark L. Knapp, *An Introduction to Interpersonal Communication* (Englewood Cliffs, N.J.: Prentice-Hall, Inc., 1971), pp. 116–18.

13. Kramer, 408–20.

14. Gregory Bateson, D. D. Jackson, J. Haley, and J. H. Weakland, "Toward a Theory of Schizophrenia," *Behavioral Science* 1 (1956): 251–64.

Intrapersonal and Interpersonal Communication

Intrapersonal communication is the process of understanding and sharing that occurs within a person. Interpersonal communication is the process of understanding and sharing between at least two persons. These two communication situations are highlighted in this section of the text. The roles of self and other in communication are explored.

We begin our consideration with the components of understanding and the role of self in chapter 5, "Understanding Yourself." The importance of self-awareness and self-concept are discussed, and journal writing is explained as an activity that can increase self-awareness and improve self-concept. Sharing with another is the subject of chapter 6, "Sharing Yourself." This chapter includes a definition of self-disclosure, suggests the importance of self-disclosure, identifies the attitudes that interfere with self-disclosure, and concludes with five guidelines for self-disclosure. We return to the problem of understanding, but focus our attention on the other person in chapter 7, "Understanding Another." In this chapter, the two basic skills involved in understanding another person, listening and empathy, are defined and discussed. We conclude the subject of intrapersonal and interpersonal communication with chapter 8, "The Interview and the Small Group Discussion," in which these two common types of interpersonal communication are described and analyzed.

5 Understanding Yourself

Objectives
After study of this chapter you should be able to do the following:

1. Discuss why self-awareness is important; suggest some of the barriers to self-awareness
2. Discuss ways in which we can increase self-awareness
3. Identify the factors that inhibit change of self-concept; give an example of how your self-concept has changed in the last few years
4. Discuss ways by which we can change our concepts of ourselves
5. Identify the components of self-concept and discuss how the components are related to each other
6. Define your self-image and self-esteem
7. Show that self-concept is a process by describing how your self-concept differs in different situations and at different times
8. Discuss an experience that illustrates the self-fulfilling prophecy
9. Explain the relationship between the self-fulfilling prophecy and the formation of self-concept
10. Discuss the relationship between attitudes toward others and self-concept

"I really feel great! I started jogging about a month ago and I've lost four pounds and I feel so much better."

"I can't take speech–I really freeze up when I have to speak to a large group of people."

"Who am I? Just another student trying to make it through school."

These typical statements from our everyday conversations confirm the importance of how we feel about ourselves. All of us reveal ourselves in many different ways: when we talk to ourselves; when we talk to roommates, friends, or advisors; and when we speak in public.

In chapter 1, we stated that communication begins with oneself. Communication is viewed from one's personal perspective. In this chapter, we will explore this centrality of self to communication.

Self-Awareness

The self plays a central role in communication regardless of whether the communication is in a daydream, a journal, a small group, or at a podium. The first step

in the improvement of our communication skills, consequently, is to become
aware of ourselves. Unfortunately, most of us have been taught to disregard or
minimize our feelings and emotions. As children we were told, "Be quiet,"
"Don't cry," "Don't carry on so much," or "Try to act like a man (or a lady)."

If we are sensitive to children, we recognize that the two characteristics that
are universal are their spontaneity and the completeness of their responses.
They respond immediately and completely to their world. A small child laughs
easily and with his or her whole body. A frustrated youngster responds with his
or her entire being.

Through conditioning, the child learns that many responses are inappropriate. Giggling in church is not socially approved; screaming at parents is not
condoned; loud crying in public places is not rewarded. Through training and
conditioning, the child learns to think before she or he acts.

Teaching children to think before they react may be essential in our culture,
but we pay a high price as individuals. In analyzing the situation first, and then
responding appropriately, we lose touch with our emotions. We learn to intellec-
tualize our feelings away. Many of us become so successful at this that we are
unable, as adults, to describe or even understand our own emotions.

Rediscovering ourselves is essential to our mental health and, in turn, to our
ability to communicate. Abraham H. Maslow, a well-known psychologist, was
one of the first to stress the importance of self-awareness or self-study. Maslow
felt that people must become what they could become. He constructed a hierarchy of human needs: the most basic are physical, followed by the need for

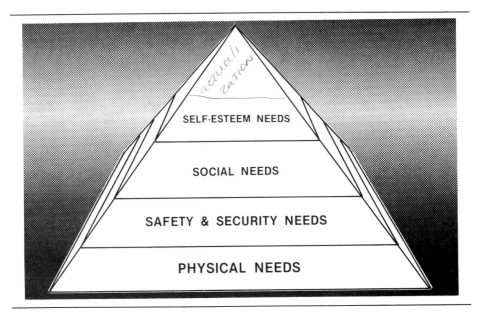

Figure 5.1   Maslow's hierarchy of needs.

safety or security, social acceptance, and self-esteem. The last is *self-actualiza-tion, living up to one's unique potentialities.*[1]

Later, other psychologists also discussed the importance of self-actualiza-tion. Carl Rogers labeled the person with this ability "the fully functioning per-son"; Sidney Jourard considered the "disclosed self"; Marie Johoda spoke of the "mentally healthy"; Charles Morris identified the "open self"; and Theo-dore Landman wrote about the "beautiful and noble person." All of these psy-chologists held an optimistic, empirically based view that recognized that in-creased self-awareness leads to self-actualization.

Will Schutz echoed this point of view and agreed about the importance of self-awareness. In *Here Comes Everybody,* Schutz considered the relationship between self-discovery and self-actualization:

> Every thought, gesture, muscle tension, feeling, stomach gurgle, nose scratch, fart, hummed tune, slip of the tongue, illness—everything is significant and meaningful and related to the now. It is possible to know and understand oneself on all these levels, and the more one knows the more he is free to determine his own life.
>
> If I know what my body tells me, I know my deepest feelings and I can choose what to do . . . Given a complete knowledge of myself, I can determine my life; lacking that mastery, I am controlled in ways that are often undesirable, unproductive, worrisome, and confusing.[2]

When we become aware of ourselves, our controlling agent becomes, not an outside force, but ourselves. Our self-awareness can be seen and heard in our communication behavior. People who are aware of themselves express emotions both verbally and nonverbally. They cry, they laugh, they speak in expressive tones. Their bodies communicate their fear, disappointment, joy, and pleasure.

Increasingly, people are becoming aware of the importance of self-awareness. Rosey Grier, the huge football star of the late 1960s, sang, "It's All Right to Cry," on *Free to Be . . . You and Me*, an album recorded in 1972. The song, reprinted here, speaks of the importance of responding honestly and spontaneously to one's emotions. It suggests that we should not allow ourselves to rationalize our problems; instead, we should work to keep in close touch with our emotions. The price of losing close touch with our emotions is too high.

It's all right to cry   (Sad and grumpy,
Crying gets the sad out of you   Down in the dumpy,
It's all right to cry   Snuggly huggly,
It might make you feel better.   Mean and ugly,
Raindrops from your eyes   Sloppy slappy,
Washing all the mad out of you   Hoppy happy)
Raindrops from your eyes   Change and change and change . . .
It might make you feel better.   It's all right to know
It's all right to feel things   Feelings come and feelings go
Though the feelings may be strange.   And it's all right to cry
Feelings are such real things   It might make you feel better.[3]
And they change and change and change

Rosey Grier is unusual. Many American men—especially men like Rosey Grier—have difficulty expressing their feelings. Sorrow, fear, anxiety, and loneliness appear to be particularly difficult for men to express. But communicating these feelings to others is psychologically healthy. Our interpersonal relationships can be enhanced by a fuller and more complete expression of our feelings.

Many adults who have learned to deny their feelings are making attempts to rediscover themselves. Warren Doyle, a Ph.D. from the University of Connecticut, approached self-discovery by backpacking alone. Doyle set two records for hiking the 2,040-mile Appalachian Trail. He reported, "There's a theory that most people have high self-concepts that crumble in situations of crisis or adversity. Many of us never have a chance to find out who we really are. . . . I was alone for 66 days. I lost my physical fat and my emotional fat as well. I saw myself as I really was."[4]

We may not be able to go hiking alone, but we can all make some moves to increase our self-awareness. We can focus on our bodies, our feelings, our emotions, and the present time. We can concentrate on how we feel about something rather than on the way we think we are expected to feel. We can look to ourselves rather than to others for solutions to problems. We can take responsibility for our own point of view as well as our own behavior. We can try to identify what we want to do and then work hard to do it well.

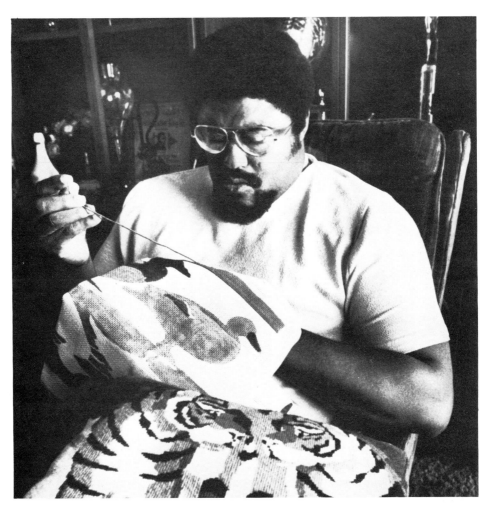

Self-awareness is essential to successful communication, even though our culture stresses self-control more than self-expression. Too much self-control can result in an avoidance of communication, on the one hand, or aggressive communication, on the other. The overly self-controlled person avoids being expressive and stating his or her own feelings, emotions, and opinions. Or, he or she may rebel and behave aggressively, trying to control and manipulate others through communication.

Consider Jim, an unassertive speaker. Jim was bright, the oldest of four children. His parents reminded him and others, "Jim always does what's right." When he was small he was praised for "not being lippy," and for "not talking back." When he became a man, people complimented him for "being such a good listener." Jim learned self-control. Now he complains, "No one knows who I am—not even me."

Marcia was taught to be "seen and not heard." She expressed herself when she was a child, but she soon learned the power of disapproval. Her parents, who tried to control her, succeeded only in making Marcia attempt to control her younger brother. Marcia monitored her brother's every expression. Now, Marcia is viewed as very domineering and unpleasant. She writes, "I know people don't like me, and I don't blame them. I don't like myself."

In order to function more fully and to communicate more effectively, we need to learn how to gain more awareness of ourselves. Self-control, like control by others, can result in a lack of self-expression. As a result, we may find that we are not sensitive to others with whom we would like to talk. We are not even aware of the topics about which we would enjoy speaking and the situations in which we would find communication pleasant. Or, we may find that we are reticent or aggressive toward others.

Kampf Um Dein Leben

Kampf um dein leben is German for "fight for your life." e. e. cummings expressed the importance of this sentiment when he wrote, "To be nobody—but—yourself in a world which is doing its best, night and day, to make you everybody-else means to fight, and never stop fighting."

Explain the significance of cummings' statement. From your own life, describe situations that illustrate the difficulty of self-awareness and self-actualization. How is the fight to be yourself evidenced in your communication with yourself and with others?

Self-Concept

Self-concept is each person's consciousness of his or her total, essential, and particular being. Included in self-concept are all of our physical, social, and psychological perceptions about ourselves. These perceptions are a result of our past, present, and projected experiences and interactions with our environment —including the people in our environment.

Two Components of Self-Concept

Researchers tell us that self-concept is composed of two parts. Your *self-image* is the picture you have of yourself, the sort of person you believe you are. Included in your self-image are the categories in which you place yourself, the roles you play, and other similar descriptors that all of us use to identify ourselves. If you tell an instructor that you are a married woman with three children and "only" a part-time student, you are calling attention to several aspects of your self-image—the roles of wife, mother, and part-time student.

Consider what you say about your academic status. Do you tell people that you are a "part-time student," a "commuter student," a "community college student," a "dormie," a "college student," a "university student," or simply "a student"? The label that you use to identify yourself indicates your self-image and, to some extent, affects your communication.

Our self-image is originally based on categorization by others. Other people categorize us by role: husband, father, boss, woman, wife, student. Others categorize us by personality traits: intelligent, happy, enthusiastic, shy, neurotic, superstitious. Or by physical characteristics: fat, tall, beautiful, heavy, wiry. A study a few years ago showed that family roles are used most often in the categorization of other people, followed by occupation, marital status, and religious affiliation.[5]

The roles we play directly influence the way we communicate. The role of parent calls for a kind of communication that is different from a student's or wife's. The young woman who plays the role of flirt has a different script than the working woman has. What you say, how you say it, to whom you speak, and how frequently you speak are largely determined by the roles you play.

Self-esteem is the other component of self-concept. *Self-esteem* is how we feel about ourselves, how well we like ourselves. A professional woman shares her self-esteem when she explains that she really enjoys being both a mother and a college professor and seldom feels any conflict between the two roles. You share your self-esteem when you say how excited you are by the prospect of a career in retail sales or industrial management, and how eager you are to begin your work.

Our self-esteem is usually based on our success or failure. If you have a favorable attitude toward yourself, you are said to have "high self-esteem"; if you have unfavorable or negative attitudes toward yourself you have "low self-esteem." Our self-esteem—whether high or low—is easily observed when we communicate with other people. The way they communicate to us, in turn, affects our own degree of self-esteem.

Excessive concern over self-esteem, however, is often associated with *self-consciousness*. People who are self-conscious are usually shy, easily embarrassed, and anxious in the presence of other people. Most of us are sometimes shy, embarrassed, or anxious. Nearly all public speakers experience stage fright from time to time. A self-conscious person, to make it clearer, suffers stage fright in all situations, to the point of being unwilling to even try to speak before any group. Self-conscious people experience shyness, embarrassment, and anxiety regularly.

Self-Concept in Process

If someone asks you who you are, you might respond in a variety of ways—depending upon the situation, the other person, and the way you feel at the moment. If you are applying for a job and the person requesting information is the prospective employer, you might identify yourself in terms of specific work experience or educational background. If the situation involves an intimate friend or spouse, you would probably respond with far different information—perhaps with more emphasis on your feelings than on your specific experiences.

When we say that one's *self-concept is in process*, we mean that it is not the same in all situations, with all people, and at all times. The view of yourself that you share in class is different from the view of yourself that you share at a party. The self that your employer knows is not the same person your family knows. The stumbling adolescent you once were has become a young adult.

In considering the notion that self-concept changes, we should also consider how it was originally formed. In essence, our self-concepts are determined by the treatment we receive from others and the relationships we have with them. Our self-image, as we have stated, occurs as a result of our being categorized by others. Our self-esteem depends on whether we have been rewarded or punished by others, and for what.

From the moment we were born, and some scholars believe even earlier, the treatment we received from others has influenced who we believe we are. As babies, we responded to the nonverbal messages of hugging, kissing, cuddling, and touching. As we began to understand language, we responded to verbal messages as well. Early verbal messages—"Big boys don't cry," "Little ladies don't make messes," and "Daddy thinks you're the best baby in the whole world,"—influenced our self-concept.

Small children are trusting, and they have little experience on which to draw; consequently, they believe what other people tell them. Parental evaluation—verbal and nonverbal—has a particularly strong effect on the development of the child's self-concept. And what the parents believe about the child has a tendency to become a self-fulfilling prophecy.

IMP IN DAILY LIFE

Dorothy Law Nolte's poem, "Children Learn What they Live," frequently seen in elementary schools and day-care centers, suggests the importance of other people in the perception we hold of our self:

If a child lives with criticism
  he learns to condemn.
If a child lives with hostility
  he learns to fight.
If a child lives with ridicule
  he learns to be shy
If a child lives with shame
  he learns to feel guilty
If a child lives with tolerance
  he learns to be patient.
If a child lives with encouragement
  he learns confidence.
If a child lives with praise
  he learns to appreciate.

If a child lives with fairness
  he learns justice.
If a child lives with security
  he learns to have faith.
If a child lives with approval
  he learns to like himself.
If a child lives with acceptance
  and friendship
  he learns to find love in the world.[6]

Select two of the predictions Nolte makes and illustrate their truth or falsity by your own way of communicating. If, for example, your parents were very critical of you, have you, in turn, learned to condemn others? If you are self-confident, does it have anything to do with the encouragement you have received from others?

The *self-fulfilling prophecy* is the tendency to become what people expect you to become. In the book *Pygmalion in the Classroom: Teacher Expectation and Pupils' Intellectual Development,* Rosenthal and Jacobson spoke of the importance of the self-fulfilling prophecy. These two researchers summarized a number of studies of academic performance that show that students who are expected to do well actually do perform better. Rosenthal and Jacobson conclude:

> To a great extent, our expectations for another person's behavior are accurate because we know his past behavior. But there is now good reason to believe that another factor increased our accuracy of interpersonal predictions or prophecies. Our prediction or prophecy may in itself be a factor in determining the behavior of other people.[7]

The self-fulfilling prophecy is relevant to self-concept. Our concepts of ourselves originated in the responses we received when we were young, but it is the self-fulfilling prophecies that maintain them. Apparently, we attempt to behave in a way that is consistent with other people's expectations, regardless of whether those expectations are positive or negative. Suppose a small girl is complimented by her family for being quiet, praised by her elementary school teachers for her lack of assertiveness, and encouraged by cultural constraints not to speak up. The result can be a reticent young woman who is afraid to make a speech. On the other hand, suppose a child is praised for talking, is encouraged to put his ideas into words, and is congratulated for winning debates. The result might be a young man who truly enjoys talking. The self-fulfilling prophecy affects our self-concept, which, in turn, affects our communication with others.

Improving Self-Concept

There are numerous recent examples of people who have made dramatic changes in their life style, behavior and, in turn, their self-concept. Patricia Hearst confused everyone in 1975 and 1976, when she behaved, first, like a wealthy socialite who was also a college student, then like the victim of a political kidnapping and, later, like a member of the political underground.

Abbie Hoffman, one of the Chicago Seven, underwent a similar alteration when he went underground in 1975. Hoffman made numerous changes in his outward appearance and explained, to a *Playboy* interviewer, that he had altered the way he thought about himself. Hoffman said, "Your face changes, you have to be different all the way through."[8]

Charles W. Colson, former special counsel to President Richard M. Nixon, also underwent a profound change. Colson, a "hatchet man" in the Watergate scandal, was tried, found guilty, and sent to prison. When he came out of prison, he professed a deep faith in Jesus Christ and was labeled a "born-again Christian."

Dramatic changes do occur in people. Although none of us might choose to follow the paths of Hearst, Hoffman, or Colson, we can see, in these three people, the possibility of change. If others can change so much, we can at least hope to make small alterations in our own perception of ourselves.

Altering one's self-concept is not a simple matter, however. The "Animal Crackers" cartoon exemplifies the difficulty of change and suggests one of the factors that make change difficult. The people who know us expect us to behave in a certain way. In point of fact, they helped to create and maintain the self-concept that we have. These people will continue to insist that we maintain a particular self-concept, even when we are attempting to change.

This point can be clarified with an example that may be familiar to you. If your family believes that you are hard to get along with in the morning, you may establish a self-concept that includes being temperamental before 9 A.M. You may wish to be as even tempered in the morning as you are the rest of the day, and you may have attempted to alter your behavior. Nonetheless, your family tells you that you remain difficult to deal with at breakfast. You may find it almost impossible to convince yourself that you are the even-tempered person you wish to be, when your family continues to tell you otherwise.

Sometimes we find ourselves working against ourselves when we try to change our self-concept. For instance, you may see yourself as a procrastinator. Even when you set out to do things on time, you may find that you never quite finish them until it is almost too late. You may be behaving this way because it fits in with another element of your self-concept: "responds to pressure," "does magic overnight," or "never lets his friends or family down." We can alter one aspect of our self-concept only to the extent that it is out of line with the others.

Another problem occurs even when we have changed and others recognize that we have changed. Sometimes we hamper the development of our concepts of ourselves. For example, if you were overweight as a youngster but have now lost the extra poundage, you may properly think you are average weight. Others agree. And still, you may continue to worry about being fat. We must learn how to change our self-concepts and then to allow the process to occur.

ANIMAL CRACKERS

If we wish to change our self-concept in order to improve our ability to communicate with others, at least two steps are essential. First, we need to become aware of ourselves; then we need to establish a positive attitude toward ourselves and, thus, toward others. The first step is not an automatic, natural process, as we said at the beginning of this chapter. We are conditioned to be out of touch with ourselves. We need to develop sensitivity to our own feelings and our own thoughts.

It is essential that we acknowledge *all* our feelings. We are all more familiar with certain aspects of ourselves than others. If we have low self-esteem, we probably focus on those aspects of ourselves that we see as problems or deficiencies. If we have a high self-esteem, we probably ignore our liabilities and focus on our assets. All of us have negative as well as positive characteristics, and it is important that we recognize both of these aspects of ourselves.

Let's take the study of communication as an example. Some people feel that studying communication is a waste of time because they are experienced public speakers. Others feel that they have been successful in small group discussions. Still other people feel that they have successfully communicated—with one other person at a time—and that is all they need.

On the other hand, another group of people feels that the study of communication is useless to them because they simply cannot give a speech. Or they feel that they never have been able to talk to a member of the opposite sex, and never will. Or, they find that communication is just plain frustrating to them in any situation.

The second group, people who suffer from low self-esteem, generalize from one type of communication situation, in which they feel they fail, to all other communication situations. The first group, people who enjoy high self-esteem, generalize from their successes to all other communication situations. It is essential to our understanding of ourselves that we acknowledge all of our abilities and failings and do not make the error of generalizing from one or two specific cases. Few people are competent in every communication situation; fewer still are incompetent in all communication situations.

It is also necessary that we focus on ourselves rather than on others. Instead of using your parents' perception of you, try to establish your own view. Rather than deciding "who you are" on the basis of cultural standards and norms, attempt to make your assessment on the basis of your own standards and norms. No one else knows us as well as we do—it is important that we use the best source available to us.

One woman, Alice, can illustrate the importance of focusing on ourselves instead of on others. She attended an assertiveness training workshop because she was unable to talk to her husband about family finances. She was sure that her husband felt that he should be the family financial expert; yet during the ten years of marriage, Alice witnessed countless near-crises of a financial nature. Every time she tried to talk to her husband, he acted sullen and withdrawn. His responses encouraged her to keep her ideas about finances to herself. Alice found herself in a vicious circle: She believed that she was not competent to handle money and she was unassertive in talking about it.

As Alice worked through her communication problem, she made a number of discoveries. Confronting her husband with the situation, Alice found that he did not really want to handle the money and would prefer her to do it. He had only seemed sullen and withdrawn, because he was embarrassed by his ineptitude in economics and simple math. Alice also found that she was more capable than he of balancing the checkbook, budgeting the family resources, and making investigations into investments. She finally realized that she had been taking her cues from her husband rather than herself. Focusing on ourselves, rather than on others, is essential in becoming aware of who we are.

The second step, establishing a positive attitude toward yourself and others, is more difficult. A popular book, a few years ago, entitled *I'm OK–You're OK,*

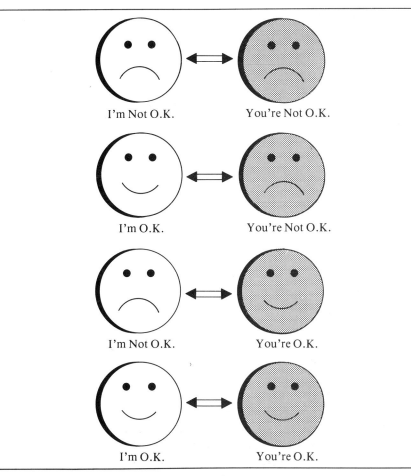

Figure 5.2

suggested four possible positions in which people could find themselves. The first occurs when they believe that neither they nor other people are worthy of being liked or accepted: I'm not OK and you're not OK. The second occurs when they believe that they are worthy of liking and acceptance, but others are not: I'm OK, but you're not OK. The third position is when they believe that others are worthy of liking and acceptance, but they are not: I'm not OK, but you're OK. The final position, the best situation, is one in which people feel that they and others are worthy of being liked and accepted: I'm OK and you're OK.[9]

If we are to alter our self-concept, we must strive for the situation in which we believe that we, and other people also, are worthy of liking and acceptance. We need to reject highly critical attitudes both of ourselves and of others. We need to develop the belief that we, and others, have potentialities which are worthy of respect. We need to free ourselves of anxiety, insecurity, cynicism, defensiveness, and the tendency to be highly evaluative. Our goal should be to free ourselves so we can establish meaningful relationships with ourselves and with others.

It was very important that Alice, whom we mentioned a moment ago, did not verbally attack her husband for his nonverbal behavior. When she approached him about the problem, she did so in a clear and straightforward way. She did not criticize his inability to handle the finances or his inability to talk to her about his problem. Instead, she tried to communicate her respect for him, while, at the same time, she discussed a problem. She showed her concern about their family's problem while maintaining her love for her husband.

Alice exemplifies the kind of respect that we should feel for everyone. We may not accept another person's behavior, but we need to maintain an appreciation for his or her potentialities which goes beyond the immediate situation. This kind of respect or appreciation of other people allows us to become the kind of person we truly wish to become.

In the album notes for *Sharepickers,*
Mason Williams wrote the following:

Here I Am Again

One night after a concert with a symphony orchestra, I was sitting by myself in my room, wondering what a super-duper love star like me is doing all alone, and I began to feel sorry for myself. I started thinking about where I was and how I had got here. I felt like I was going to cry, so naturally I grabbed my guitar to catch the tears and wrote this song, which is about living a way of life and writing songs off to it beyond the need to.

I realized I was just another blues singer with nothing to be blue about except being stuck having to sing the blues, trapped by the truth—it's not what you don't do that holds you back, it's what you do well that gets you. It seems like if you're successful at something and it comes easy, you always try to free ride it past the right point. I've met a lot of people who are stuck in spiritual ruts because they'd latched onto a magic and tried to ride it too far. Good luck turns bad on you after awhile; you have to learn where to get off. I realized I'd missed my stop. Here I was alone again writing another lonely song about being alone again, instead of really being with a friend. I had used music, God bless it, just to get to the top. It was only a ticket, and here I was fondling my ticket in a hotel room in Hartford, Connecticut, way off the track.

I realized that all my life I'd been afraid—afraid to ask for what I wanted—because of what I wanted. I realized that I had become rich and famous, a star, just so everything would come to me—even more than I could use—and I could take my pick from it without risking rejection. Suddenly it struck me that that's probably why most successful people are unhappy. They get themselves into a position where they don't have to ask for things, without realizing that if they don't practice asking for what they want from others, they're not good at asking for what they want from themselves—which means they don't know what they want. And you know, you never can satisfy somebody who doesn't know what he wants.

You have to practice asking to be a good asker. What's more, you have to practice *true* asking. You've got to ask for what you really want and not what somebody else wants you to ask for or what you think is right to want. Practice doesn't make perfect unless you practice perfectly.

That's what praying is all about, my friends. To pray is to practice asking, and if you're not really asking, you're not really practicing. A person could spend the rest of his life afraid to ask for what he wants, because of what he wants, whether he really wants it or not.[10]

Williams lends support to the idea that it is essential to know ourselves and our needs in order to be satisfied. Suggest needs of your own that must be fulfilled in order for you to be satisfied. Is it necessary for you to alter your self-concept in order to meet these needs? For instance, if you feel that you need a full-time career in teaching in order to satisfy your desire to serve others, you might have to change your view of yourself as someone who is too busy with a family to pursue a career. If you need a certain amount of time alone each day, you may have to alter your view of yourself as a person who always has time for everybody.

Journal Writing

Journal writing has a long and varied history. The journal has been known as a diary, a memoir, a personal journal, an autobiography, a personal notebook, and a private chronicle. Recently, the journal was discussed in the novel by Erica Jong entitled *How to Save Your Own Life*. Jong suggests that the journal is a way for a person to understand his or her own life. Essentially, the *journal* can be defined as a daily or periodic record of personal experiences and impressions.

In the past, journals have served a variety of functions, including the recording of the events of the day when other means were unavailable, the preservation of the truth as someone perceived it, or the satisfaction of egotistical needs. Journals serve all of these needs today.

The journal is introduced in this chapter because it can serve two basic functions: allowing a person to increase his or her self-awareness, and allowing a person to improve his or her self-concept. The journal can increase self-awareness by encouraging self-assessment and self-understanding. The journal can improve self-concept by assisting in self-improvement, by providing an outlet for emotional expression, and by offering the possibility of celebrating a person's

selfhood. The journal allows us to communicate with ourselves while helping us
to improve a basic skill, the ability to communicate.

Increasing Self-Awareness

The journal allows people to become increasingly aware of themselves as they
assess their characteristics and behavior, and as they attempt to understand
themselves. One student recognized this function of journal writing after she had
written a journal. She commented, ''A lot of the factors that have shaped my life
seem more clear to me now and I feel more aware of my strengths and weaknesses than before.''

Another student was able to relate some of her feelings and thoughts to
those she perceived in others. She wrote,

> The most surprising thing that I realized while writing this journal is that I'm not alone
> in my feelings and thoughts. I'm like everyone else in some aspects and unique in
> others. But, basically, I realized that my problems aren't so different from other
> people's problems. Right now, I'm really relieved about that. That's not to say that I
> didn't know it before. I just never sat down and talked about it before and really
> thought about it.

The principal function of the notebook in Erica Jong's book was to increase her self-awareness and to find patterns in her life. Other authors also emphasize this function of the journal. John Powell, author of *Why Am I Afraid to Tell You Who I Am?* and *The Secret of Staying in Love,* discussed the importance of journal writing in *Fully Human, Fully Alive:*

> If people were regularly to practice this kind of gentle but persistent self-examination of their vision, I am sure they would find, as I have, many new insights and an immediate change in the emotional patterns of their lives. Obviously, the more precise and vivid the verbalization in writing of this kind, the greater the likelihood that misconceptions will surface for recognition.[11]

Improving Self-Concept

Journal writing can result in an improvement of a person's self-concept as well as in increased self-awareness. Writing a journal can help you to identify problems in your life and alter your behavior so that you have better relationships with others. You can also rid yourself of strong, negative emotions by putting them on paper. And, in a journal, you can celebrate your joys and successes. An improved self-concept can easily result.

Self-improvement, a worthy function of the journal, can occur in a number of ways. You can review your journal entries to determine if the difficulties you encounter form some kind of pattern. You can confront your problems more directly when you write about them than when you are just thinking about them. This direct confrontation can cause you to consider alternative behavior. Moreover, recording negative experiences is uncomfortable. You may choose, rather than deceive yourself by ignoring them, to change your behavior to minimize such experiences.

The second way that a journal can help you to improve your self-concept is by providing an outlet for your strong emotions. All of us feel anger, bitterness, resentment, impatience, and other emotions which often result in unhappiness if we express them to others. The journal is a ready listener for such emotions, and it will not judge you. One student noted that her journal served as an outlet for her emotional expressions. She discussed her "emotional traumas," and stated that "it is nice to get them on paper. I need to tell someone to relieve my distress and the paper is a patient listener—[I have found] an outlet for my emotions."

A number of writers talk about this function of the journal. In her book, *Widow,* Lynn Caine entitles one chapter, "Dear Paper Psychiatrist," and in it discusses the journal she kept after the death of her husband. She considers the various ways that the journal helped her to record the events of her life and her emotional reactions to them. John Powell, in *Fully Human, Fully Alive,* shares an excerpt from his journal and then advises, "I would strongly recommend the use of such a journal every day but especially on those days when emotions have been vibrating uncomfortably."[12]

Your self-concept can be improved in yet another way because journal writing offers you the opportunity to celebrate yourself. One student who appreciated the journal assignment said that she had never before been given credit in college for focusing on herself. Another wrote, "The fact that I was writing about my favorite subject—myself—I found that writing this journal was interesting and enjoyable; I found myself to be deep and interesting."

Throughout history, journal writers have found that the journal allows a celebration of self. Fothergill discusses this motive for writing a journal. He considers the journal of the eighteenth-century English figure, James Boswell, and concludes,

> Boswell discusses with himself his purposes in keeping so energetic a journal. . . . Two themes run through his formulations on the subject. One is the conventional rationale in terms of self-knowledge and self-improvement, the other a sheer and unabashed celebration of his own personality. . . . It is a book of the self in the fullest sense, the book of Boswell, intended for readers who love a parade.[13]

Summary

In this chapter we continued our discussion of the importance of self in communication. We discussed self-awareness and considered the parental and social conditioning that reinforces our lack of self-awareness. We stated that self-awareness is essential to our mental health and to our ability to communicate competently.

Self-concept was defined as each person's consciousness of his or her total, essential, and particular being. Self-concept consists of self-image and self-esteem. Self-images are the pictures we have of ourselves or the sort of persons that we believe we are. Included in our self-images are the categories in which we place ourselves, the roles we play, and the other ways in which we identify ourselves.

Self-esteem is how we feel about ourselves, or how well we like ourselves. To have a high self-esteem is to have a favorable attitude toward yourself; to have a low self-esteem is to have an unfavorable attitude toward yourself. Self-consciousness is excessive concern about self-esteem; it is characterized by shyness, embarrassment, and anxiety in the presence of others.

Self-concept is in process. Our self-concepts change with the situation, the other person or people involved, and our own moods. One's self-concept is originally formed by the treatment received from others and one's relationships with them. It is maintained largely as a self-fulfilling prophecy. The self-fulfilling prophecy is the tendency to become whatever people expect you to become.

how we
like ourselves

Self-concept can be improved. We considered the difficulty, but possibility, of altering our concepts of ourselves. The two essential steps in changing self-concept are: (1) becoming aware of ourselves; and (2) establishing a positive attitude toward ourselves and others.

In the final section of this chapter, we considered journal writing. The journal was defined as a daily or periodic record of personal experiences and impressions. Although the journal can serve a variety of functions, it is introduced in this text in order to help you increase your self-awareness and improve your self-concept. The journal allows us to increase self-awareness through self-assessment and self-understanding. It allows us to improve our self-concepts through self-improvement, by providing an outlet for emotional expression, and by affording us the possibility of celebrating ourselves.

New Terms

Self-awareness	Self-image	Self-focus
Maslow's "Hierarchy of Needs"	Self-esteem	*I'm OK—You're OK*
	Roles	Needs
Self-control	Self-consciousness	Journal
Self-expression	Self-fulfilling prophecy	Self-improvement
Self-concept		

Additional Readings

*Gergen, Kenneth J. *The Concept of Self.* New York: Holt, Rinehart and Winston, Inc., 1971.
A research approach to the definition and development of self-concept. Describes the influence of self-concept on our behavior and summarizes research findings about factors which affect our self-concept.

Goffman, Erving. *The Presentation of Self in Everyday Life.* Garden City, N.Y.: Doubleday & Co., Inc., 1959.
Goffman discusses the intentional and unintentional, the honest and the deceitful ways in which we tell others and ourselves who we are. By using the analogy of the theatre, the author explains how we present and maintain masks in our interactions with others.

*Horrocks, John E., and Jackson, Dorothy W. *Self and Role: A Theory of*

Self-Process and Role Behavior. Boston: Houghton Mifflin Company, 1972.
A scholarly discussion of the definition, development, and presentation of self, including the factors which influence the self and ways in which the self influences our thinking, perception, and communication.

Jourard, Sidney M. *The Transparent Self: Self-Disclosure and Well-Being.* New York: Van Nostrand Reinhold Company, 1964.
The skill of self-disclosure: how to develop an honest and open self, barriers to effective self-disclosure, and the role of self-disclosure in improving interpersonal relationships.

*Indicates more advanced readings.

Laird, Jess. *I Ain't Much Baby, but I'm
All I've Got.* New York: Doubleday &
Co., Inc., 1972.
*Advice on how to become a genuine, real
person by understanding and controlling
your behavior. Laird believes that trust
and love stem from an honest knowledge
and acceptance of yourself. Written from
personal experience in an interesting and
stimulating manner.*

Powell, John. *The Secret of Staying in
Love.* Niles, Ill.: Argus
Communications, 1974.
*Powell focuses on the fundamental
human need for a "true and deep love of
self," explores the problems of loving,
the nature of love, and ways to find and
maintain a high self-esteem. Written in a
direct and personal style that holds one's
attention.*

Prather, Hugh. *Notes to Myself.* Moab,
Utah: Real People Press, 1970.
*An easily read, highly thought-provoking
collection of thoughts tracing one man's
struggle for self-awareness. Insightful,
nontheoretical treatment of self-concept,
self-awareness, and self-expression.*

*Wiley, Ruth C. *The Self Concept: A
Critical Survey of Pertinent Research
Literature.* Lincoln, Nebr.: University
of Nebraska Press, 1961.
*A definitive exploration of self-concept.
In-depth discussion of methodologies of
research on the self and their
implications. Good source for research
papers or for a more complete look at the
research behind the conclusions drawn
in this text.*

Notes

1. Abraham H. Maslow, "Hierarchy of
Needs," in *Motivation and Personality*, 2d
ed. (New York: Harper & Row,
Publishers, 1970), pp. 35-72. Copyright ©
1970 by Abraham H. Maslow.

2. Will Schutz, *Here Comes Everybody* (New
York: Harper & Row, Publishers, 1971), p.
1. Reprinted by permission.

3. "It's All Right to Cry" by Carol Hall,
from *Free To Be . . . You and Me*
published by McGraw-Hill. Copyright ©
1972 Free To Be Foundation, Inc. Used
by permission.

4. Jane Anderson, "Discover Yourself: Go
Hiking Alone," Fort Wayne *Journal-
Gazette*, March 21, 1976.

5. Michael Argyle, *Social Interaction* (New
York: Atherton Press, 1969), p. 133.

6. Dorothy Law Nolte, "Children Learn
What They Live," 1954.

7. Robert Rosenthal and Lenore Jacobson,
*Pygmalion in the Classroom: Teacher
Expectation and Pupils' Intellectual
Development* (New York: Holt, Rinehart
and Winston, Inc., 1968), p. vii.

8. "Playboy Interview: Abbie Hoffman,"
Playboy, May 1976, p. 64.

9. Thomas A. Harris, *I'm OK—You're OK*,
(New York: Harper & Row, Publishers,
1967).

10. Mason Williams, "Here I Am Again,"
liner notes from *Sharepickers*. Copyright
by Mason Williams. Used by permission.
All rights reserved.

11. Reprinted from John Powell, *Fully
Human, Fully Alive*, p. 152. Copyright ©
1976 by Argus Communications. Used
with permission from Argus
Communications, Niles, Ill.

12. Reprinted from John Powell, *Fully
Human, Fully Alive*, p. 154. Copyright ©
1976 by Argus Communications. Used
with permission from Argus
Communications, Niles, Ill.

13. Robert A. Fothergill, *Private Chronicles:
A Study of English Diaries* (London:
Oxford University Press, 1974), p. 77.

6

Sharing Yourself

Objectives
After study of this chapter you should be able to do the following:

1. Define self-disclosure and explain its importance
2. Discuss the relationship among trust, respect, and self-disclosure
3. Identify what you risk when you engage in negative self-disclosure and positive self-disclosure
4. Describe an experience that illustrates the reciprocal nature of self-disclosure
5. List the factors that affect your willingness to self-disclose
6. Discuss the relationship between self-disclosure and the growth of a relationship
7. Name five guidelines to appropriate self-disclosure

conchy

"In order to see I have to be willing to be seen." [1]

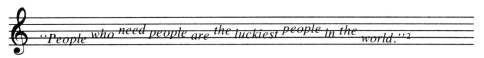

"People who need people are the luckiest people in the world." [2]

The cartoon, the portion of the poem, and the excerpt from the song all serve to introduce us to the specific topic of this chapter. Understanding and sharing form the basis of communication. In the last chapter we talked about understanding ourselves. In this chapter we will focus on sharing ourselves with others. Self-disclosure is considered essential to interpersonal communication.

Definition of Self-Disclosure

The term that is most frequently associated with a person's ability to share himself or herself with others is *self-disclosure*. The current definition of self-disclosure is broad: it includes any statement a person makes about himself or herself. A few researchers have narrowed this definition to include only statements that are intentional, conscious, or voluntary. Other writers have suggested that the term *self-disclosure* should be reserved for statements about oneself that another person would be unlikely to know or discover. Because we are more interested in intentional communication, rather than in random and unplanned statements, and because we are more interested in those statements about ourselves that others are unlikely to discover through observation, we will focus on the most limited definition of self-disclosure. For our purposes, *self-disclosure* consists of those statements about oneself that are intentional and that the other person is unlikely to know. Self-disclosure can be as unthreatening as saying how you feel about a particular movie or how much studying you have been doing, or it can be as difficult as telling someone that her use of obscenity makes you feel uncomfortable or that you have allowed your baby to be adopted.

Importance of Self-Disclosure

Self-disclosure is important for a variety of reasons. When we talk about ourselves, about our feelings and perceptions, we develop a greater understanding and awareness of ourselves. Self-disclosure can also result in self-improvement. As other people provide feedback to us, we can identify some of the problems we face and some mistakes we are making. However, others cannot provide accurate or helpful feedback unless we self-disclose.

Self-Disclosure Allows Us to Develop a Greater Understanding of Ourselves

In order to understand the degree of self-understanding and self-improvement that is possible through self-disclosure, consider the Johari Window depicted in

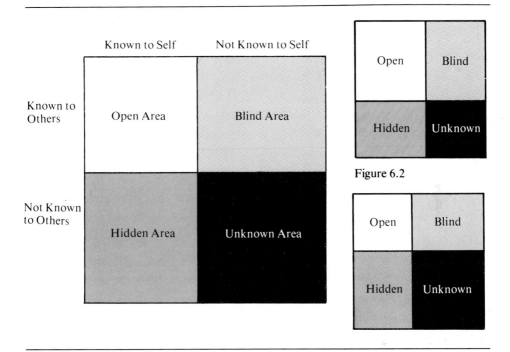

Figure 6.1   The Johari Window.   Figure 6.3

figure 6.1. This diagram, created by Joseph Luft and Harrington Ingham, depicts four kinds of information about a person. The *open area* consists of information that is known to you and known to other people. It includes such information as your height, your approximate weight, and your sex—obvious to an observer—as well as information you freely disclose, such as the courses in which you are enrolled, your major, and your home town. The *blind area* consists of information that is known to others, but unknown to you. Included in this area are personality characteristics—you are temperamental in the morning, you are assertive, or you are cynical—which others perceive but which you do not recognize or acknowledge. The *hidden area* includes information that is not known to other people, but that is known to you. It includes any information that you choose not to disclose to others. The *unknown area* includes information that is unknown to you and to others. Any characteristics or potentialities that you may have that have not been considered by yourself or by others is included in this area.

The Johari Window does not consist of four areas that are unchanging in size, nor of four necessarily equal areas. The four areas differ dramatically from person to person and vary within the same person and in the same relationship. Figure 6.2 might represent your Johari Window now, and figure 6.3 might better

depict your Johari Window when you were in high school. As the size of one of
the areas changes, the size of the other areas also changes.

Self-Disclosure Can Result in Self-Improvement

Self-disclosure allows you to increase the size of the open area and to decrease
the size of the other three areas. In talking about a number of happy experiences
you have had, you may suddenly realize why they were all happy. In learning
more about yourself, you decrease the unknown area and increase the open
area. In discussing clothes with a friend, you may discover that others view you
as a style setter: since others share this perception of you, and you have been
unaware of it, you reduce the blind area on the Johari Window and increase the
open area. The Johari Window illustrates that increased self-disclosure can result in greater understanding and awareness of ourselves and can result in self-
improvement.

Self-Disclosure Allows Us to Establish More Meaningful Relationships with Others

Self-disclosure, which makes us more open, often generates self-disclosure from
others. In this way, we can all become more open to ourselves and to others.
Both self-knowledge and knowledge of others increases.

Consider your communication with the person to whom you feel closest.
Have you engaged in a great deal of self-disclosure? Now consider what you say
or write to someone with whom you have only an acquaintanceship. How does
your self-disclosure differ? Most self-disclosure is offered most frequently and
regularly to close friends. Self-disclosure allows relationships to grow in depth
and meaning.

An inability to self-disclose, on the other hand, can result in the death of a

relationship. One of the common explanations for divorce given by women is their need to self-disclose. Divorced women are increasingly identifying their own lack of opportunity to express who they are as the cause of the breakup of their marriages. Without opportunities for self-disclosure, relationships appear to be doomed to shallowness, superficiality, or death.

Self-Disclosure Allows Us to Establish More Positive Attitudes Toward Ourselves and Others

In an article entitled "Shy Murderers," Lee, Zimbardo, and Bertholf discuss the person who is overcontrolled and shy, and, because of his frustration, attacks others. They suggest that this kind of person needs to learn how to express feelings directly to others. They continue:

> The social skills we've outlined should be learned by every child as a normal part of socialization. Children should be encouraged to express their feelings and to like themselves. They should come to see other people as sources of positive regard and interest, not as critical, negative evaluators who might reject them. They, and we, must be seen *and* heard.[3]

Both positive and negative self-disclosure can result in more positive attitudes about ourselves and others. If we disclose positive information about ourselves, we share the joy that we feel about ourselves. When we tell others about our hopes and dreams, when we share happy moments, and when we recall exciting experiences, we feel encouraged. Others reinforce our feeling by offering their support, enthusiasm, and encouragement.

Although it may seem paradoxical, negative self-disclosure can also result in more positive attitudes about ourselves and others. When we are able to expose our negative qualities, our mistakes, our failings, and our shortcomings, and when others are able to do the same, we can recognize that we are all fallible, that no one is perfect. We become more understanding and forgiving and we develop more positive attitudes about all humankind by sharing negative disclosures.

One student wrote that she originally had not seen the importance of self-disclosure in interpersonal communication, but during the course of the quarter, she learned its significance. She wrote:

> I always thought that interpersonal communication would be like the required English courses that I took. It might be interesting, but it would not be applicable in the real world. As I sat listening to the professor's lecture on self-disclosure, I recall thinking, "How nice, but does it really matter? Does your interpersonal communication really improve when you are aware of your own feelings and are able to communicate them to others?"

Like many times in my life before, I found I was wrong. The amazing thing was, I proved myself wrong, not in class, but in a real life situation, in the bar where I work as a waitress. One night, two girls were holding hands and another waitress told me about it. As I always had, I just said, "If that's their bag, it doesn't bother me."

Many of my customers commented on the girls, especially after they got up and slow-danced together. The remarks ranged from "Isn't that sickening?" to "I think I need a double." I just repeated to each of them what I had told the waitress who first pointed them out to me, "If that's their thing, then I don't mind."

After about twenty minutes, the girls got up to leave. I had my back to them as they were walking out, but I saw them out of the corner of my eye. As they passed, one of the girls slapped my bottom. In a rage of anger, humiliation, and indignation, I whirled with clenched fists to strike her. Fortunately, as it later turned out, they were out the door before I could get to her. I ran to the bar manager, practically in tears and shaking like a leaf, and yelled at him that if they came back in again and one of them touched me, he'd better call an ambulance because I would kill her.

They did return a few minutes later. To my embarrassment, the band playing stopped. One of the girls announced that she and her friend were anthropology majors at the university and were completing a term project. She asked for any feedback and reactions that the crowd had.

I did not talk to them, mainly because I was too confused, and too surprised by my own reaction. That night, in bed, I ran the incident over and over in my mind and tried to examine my true feelings. By examining my reaction, I came to many conclusions about myself that I had never realized before.

First, my statement, "Let them do their own thing," was far from my true feeling —so far off that it surprised even me when I admitted it. I really felt hatred for these people because they dared to break a norm. I felt threatened by them.

Second, my reaction to the two women was similar to other statements I had made, but didn't really feel. I guess that a lot of the statements I make are because I want to seem better than everyone else. I want to appear as though I can accept things that others can't.

If the anthropology majors learned nothing from their experiment, I learned a great deal. Since then I have tried to think about how I really feel before I say anything. I still catch myself saying things that I don't really mean, but at least now I realize it afterwards. I'm glad I enrolled in interpersonal communication—if nothing else, I learned the importance of genuine self-disclosure.

Interference with Self-Disclosure

If self-disclosure is an aspect of interpersonal communication that is important to the way we view ourselves and others, we should consider why we are often unwilling to self-disclose to others. In general, we can say that people are reluctant to self-disclose because of their negative feelings about themselves or their negative feelings about others. In other words, they do not respect themselves, they do not trust others, or both. Lana, in the cartoon, does not appear to trust Lyle's motives.

The Risk of Self-Disclosure

Franz Kafka wrote the following short story, entitled "Give it Up!"

> It was early in the morning, the streets clean and empty, I was going to the train station. When I compared a tower clock with my watch, I saw that it was already much later than I had thought. I had to hurry, the terror over this discovery made me uncertain as to the way. I did not know this city very well yet. Fortunately, a police officer was nearby. I ran to him and asked him breathlessly for the way. He smiled and said: "You want to know the way from me?" "Yes," I said, "since I can't find it myself." "Give it up, give it up," he said and turned away with a wide sweep, just like people who want to be alone with their laughter.[4]

It is unclear why the police officer answered as he did and it is unclear what he meant by his answer. It is clear that he failed to respond to the first person's negative self-disclosure—that he was unable to find his way. Suggest explanations for his answer. What response would have been appropriate to such an answer? Could the first person have asked his first question in a different way in order to elicit a different answer?

Two contemporary writers have discussed the risk involved in self-disclosure. In *The Shoes of the Fisherman,* Morris L. West wrote:

> It costs so much to be a full human being that there are very few who have the enlightenment or the courage to pay the price. . . . One has to abandon altogether the search for security, and reach out to the risk of living with both arms. One has to embrace the world like a lover. One has to accept pain as a condition of existence. One has to court doubt and darkness as the cost of knowing. One needs a will stubborn in conflict, but apt always to total acceptance of every consequence of living and dying.[5]

In *Why Am I Afraid to Tell You Who I Am?* John Powell writes that he asked a number of people the question which forms the title of his book. The response of one of his friends to the question, "Why are you afraid to tell me who you are?" was to the point. He answered, "Because if I tell you who I am, you may not like who I am, and that's all that I have."[6] In essence, his friend was stating that he did not respect himself enough to trust others with the information. Frequently, our lack of positive feelings about ourselves or about others contributes to our inability to self-disclose.

A Fuzzy Tale

O nce upon a time, a long time ago, there lived
two very happy people called Tim and
Maggie with two children called John and
Lucy. To understand how happy they were, you
have to understand how things were in those days.
You see, in those days everyone was given at birth
a small, soft, Fuzzy Bag. Anytime a person reached
into this bag he was able to pull out a Warm Fuzzy.
Warm Fuzzies were very much in demand because
whenever somebody was given a Warm Fuzzy it
made him feel warm and fuzzy all over. People who
didn't get Warm Fuzzies regularly were in danger of
developing a sickness in their back which caused
them to shrivel up and die.

In those days it was very easy to get Warm
Fuzzies. Anytime that somebody felt like it, he
might walk up to you and say, "I'd like to have a
Warm Fuzzy." You would then reach into your bag
and pull out a Fuzzy the size of a little girl's hand.
As soon as the Fuzzy saw the light of day it would
smile and blossom into a large, shaggy, Warm
Fuzzy. You then would lay it on the person's
shoulder or head or lap and it would snuggle up and
melt right against their skin and make them feel
good all over. People were always asking each other
for Warm Fuzzies, and since they were always
given freely, getting enough of them was never a
problem. There were always plenty to go around,
and as a consequence everyone was happy and felt
warm and fuzzy most of the time.

One day a bad witch became angry because
everyone was so happy and no one was buying
potions and salves. The witch was very clever and
devised a very wicked plan. One beautiful morning
the witch crept up to Tim while Maggie was playing
with their daughter and whispered in his ear, "See
here, Tim, look at all the Fuzzies that Maggie is
giving to Lucy. You know, if she keeps it up,
eventually she is going to run out and then there
won't be any left for you!"

Claude M. Steiner

Reprinted from Scripts People Play: Transactional Analysis of Life Scripts *(New York: Bantam Books, 1974), pp. 127-31. Copyright by Claude M. Steiner. Used with permission.*

Tim was astonished. He turned to the witch and said, "Do you mean to tell me that there isn't a Warm Fuzzy in our bag every time we reach into it?"

And the witch said, "No, absolutely not, and once you run out, that's it. You don't have any more." With this the witch flew away on a broom, laughing and cackling all the way.

Tim took this to heart and began to notice every time Maggie gave up a Warm Fuzzy to somebody else. Eventually he got very worried and upset because he liked Maggie's Warm Fuzzies very much and did not want to give them up. He certainly did not think it was right for Maggie to be spending all her Warm Fuzzies on the children and on other people. He began to complain every time he saw Maggie giving a Warm Fuzzy to somebody else, and because Maggie liked him very much, she stopped giving Warm Fuzzies to other people as often, and reserved them for him.

The children watched this and soon began to get the idea that it was wrong to give up Warm Fuzzies any time you were asked or felt like it. They too became very careful. They would watch their parents closely and whenever they felt that one of their parents was giving too many Fuzzies to others, they also began to object. They began to feel worried whenever they gave away too many Warm Fuzzies. Even though they found a Warm Fuzzy every time they reached into their bag, they reached in less and less and became more and more stingy. Soon people began to notice the lack of Warm Fuzzies, and they began to feel less warm and less fuzzy. They began to shrivel up and, occasionally, people would die from lack of Warm Fuzzies. More and more people went to the witch to buy potions and salves even though they didn't seem to work.

(Continued)

Well, the situation was getting very serious indeed. The bad witch who had been watching all of this didn't really want the people to die (since dead people couldn't buy his salves and potions), so a new plan was devised. Everyone was given a bag that was very similar to the Fuzzy Bag except that this one was cold while the Fuzzy Bag was warm. Inside of the witch's bag were Cold Pricklies. These Cold Pricklies did not make people feel warm and fuzzy, but made them feel cold and prickly instead. But, they did prevent peoples' backs from shriveling up. So, from then on, every time somebody said, "I want a Warm Fuzzy," people who were worried about depleting their supply would say, "I can't give you a Warm Fuzzy, but would you like a Cold Prickly?" Sometimes, two people would walk up to each other, thinking they could get a Warm Fuzzy, but one or the other of them would change his mind and they would wind up giving each other Cold Pricklies. So, the end result was that while very few people were dying, a lot of people were still unhappy and feeling very cold and prickly.

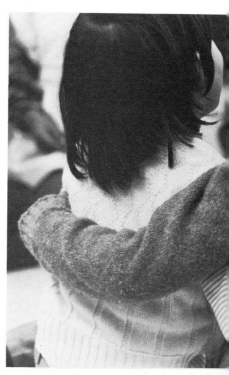

The situation got very complicated because, since the coming of the witch, there were less and less Warm Fuzzies around; so Warm Fuzzies, which used to be thought of as free as air, became extremely valuable. This caused people to do all sorts of things in order to obtain them. Before the witch had appeared, people used to gather in groups of three or four or five, never caring too much who was giving Warm Fuzzies to whom. After the coming of the witch, people began to pair off and to reserve all their Warm Fuzzies for each other exclusively. People who forgot themselves and gave a Warm Fuzzy to someone else would immediately feel guilty about it because they knew that their partner would probably resent the loss of a Warm Fuzzy. People who could not find a generous partner had to buy their Warm Fuzzies and had to work long hours to earn the money.

Some people somehow became "popular" and got a lot of Warm Fuzzies without having to return them. These people would then sell these Warm Fuzzies to people who were "unpopular" and needed them to survive.

Another thing which happened was that some people would take Cold Pricklies—which were limitless and freely available—coat them white and fluffy and pass them on as Warm Fuzzies. These counterfeit Warm Fuzzies were really Plastic Fuzzies, and they caused additional difficulties. For instance, two people would get together and freely exchange Plastic Fuzzies, which presumably should have made them feel good, but they came away feeling bad instead. Since they thought they had been exchanging Warm Fuzzies, people grew very confused about this, never realizing that their cold prickly feelings were really the result of the fact they had been given a lot of Plastic Fuzzies.

So the situation was very, very dismal and it all started because of the coming of the witch who made people believe that some day, when least expected, they might reach into their Warm Fuzzy Bag and find no more.

Not long ago, a young woman with big hips born under the sign of Aquarius came to this unhappy land. She seemed not to have heard about the bad witch and was not worried about running out of Warm Fuzzies. She gave them out freely, even when not asked. They called her the Hip Woman and disapproved of her because she was giving the children the idea that they should not worry about running out of Warm Fuzzies. The children liked her very much because they felt good around her and they began to give out Warm Fuzzies whenever they felt like it.

(Continued)

The grownups became concerned and decided to pass a law to protect the children from depleting their supplies of Warm Fuzzies. The law made it a criminal offense to give out Warm Fuzzies in a reckless manner, without a license. Many children, however, seemed not to care; and in spite of the law they continued to give each other Warm Fuzzies whenever they felt like it and always when asked. Because there were many, many children, almost as many as grownups, it began to look as if maybe they would have their way.

As of now it is hard to say what will happen. Will the grownup forces of law and order stop the recklessness of the children? Are the grownups going to join with the Hip Woman and the children in taking a chance that there will always be as many Warm Fuzzies as needed? Will they remember the days their children are trying to bring back when Warm Fuzzies were abundant because people gave them away freely?

Fear of situations that are not under our control and our lack of trust of other people can result in our refusal to self-disclose to others. In time, this fear and lack of trust becomes permanent and our refusal to self-disclose becomes habitual.

We are probably taught very early in our lives to avoid self-disclosure. The same kinds of responses that interfere with our self-awareness contribute also to our difficulty in self-disclosing. Our parents taught us that positive self-disclosure was bragging. Significant others responded negatively to us when we made negative self-disclosures. The message we seemed to hear was that self-disclosures should be avoided.

Claude Steiner's fable "A Fuzzy Tale," which you just read, illustrates sensitively the natural desire to share ourselves that we have as children and the way in which we lose this natural ability and learn to avoid self-disclosure.

Guidelines for Self-Disclosure

Self-disclosure, as we have defined it, occurs when we voluntarily tell someone else about ourselves. It should reflect our present reactions to people and situations. In other words, self-disclosure should be spontaneous, rather than manipulative or planned. In the student paper at the beginning of this chapter, the student wrote that she had often said things in order to appear superior to others. Those statements were not only untrue, but they lacked spontaneity and tended to be manipulative.

Self-disclosure is also probably better when it is specific rather than general, tentative rather than unchanging, and informing rather than threatening. We should not self-disclose in a general, arrogant, or threatening way. Self-disclosure should help us to build relationships, rather than destroying those that already exist.

The research into self-disclosure is fairly recent, and there are few consistent conclusions. Nonetheless, the studies suggest that there are norms governing self-disclosure. These norms strongly influence the appropriateness and inappropriateness of self-disclosure in particular situations, at particular points in a relationship, for particular persons, and for specific topics. Let us consider some generalizations from the research that should guide our self-disclosure.

Self-Disclosure Should Be Reciprocal or Shared

Self-disclosure cannot be one-sided in a successful interpersonal relationship. No characteristic of self-disclosing communication is documented as well as the finding that as the disclosure of one person increases, so does the self-disclosure of the other person.[7]

Two interpretations of this phenomenon have been offered. Jourard suggested that people disclose only when they feel safe and that being able to disclose is positively valued by others. As a consequence, persons self-disclose after another person has self-disclosed because they feel safe and able to do so.[8] Worthy, Gary and Kahn used a social exchange theory—a theory which holds that we exchange communication of an equal or comparable value—to explain reciprocal self-disclosure. They suggest that people only reveal themselves to friends. And when they are the recipients of self-disclosure, they feel that they are liked or trusted. Being trusted or liked is rewarding. It also obligates the receivers of self-disclosure to reciprocate by disclosing themselves to the other person.[9]

The implication of these findings is that appropriate self-disclosure is reciprocal. If the person to whom you are self-disclosing refuses to self-disclose, you should stop. If a person with whom you are communicating is freely self-dis-

closing, you, too, should feel free to self-disclose. If you wish to self-disclose in the course of a conversation, you might try some low-risk self-disclosure to determine if the other person can, and will, make a similar disclosure.

Self-Disclosure Is Related to the Duration of a Relationship

Self-disclosure usually develops slowly, increasing as the relationship endures and becomes more stable and permanent. The only exception occurs when strangers, who expect no future interaction, meet. In such situations, self-disclosure may occur quickly.[10] In one study which dealt with male freshman roommates, the pattern of self-disclosure that emerged seemed fairly generalizable. First, a relatively high level of ordinary information was disclosed, then intimate information was disclosed at a gradually increasing rate.[11]

Most of us have had the experience of sitting next to a stranger whom we expect never to see again, on a bus, an airplane, or in some other public place. The other person may have disclosed a great deal, or we may have disclosed a great deal about ourselves to the other person. This tendency to talk about ourselves to strangers has been demonstrated in studies. On the other hand, people do not prefer this setting for self-disclosure. In one study, it was found that people who were strangers preferred the company of those who disclosed very little rather than of those who disclosed a great deal.[12] Three other researchers have concluded that if intimate disclosures are inappropriately timed, others may perceive the person who is disclosing as suffering from maladjustment or inappropriate socialization.[13] This conclusion was verified by two other psychologists who stated, ''Intimate disclosure to a stranger or an acquaintance was seen by observers as less appropriate and more maladjusted than nondisclosure.''[14]

In a more recent study, two communication scholars were able to secure more specific information about the effect of the length of a relationship on self-disclosure. Gilbert and Whiteneck found that if a person were going to disclose ordinary facts, he or she would first disclose positive statements, then neutral statements, and, finally, negative statements. If the person were disclosing intimate information, the likelihood of disclosure would be negative statements, followed by positive, and ending with neutral. They concluded that the duration of a relationship affected the kind of self-disclosure that seemed appropriate.[15]

Gilbert and Whiteneck's conclusion can be explained by Blau's earlier hypothesis. Blau suggested that one person's attraction to another was dependent on the anticipation and belief that the association would be rewarding.[16] In other words, we are attracted to people who seem impressive, who have attractive qualities, and who create the impression that associating with them will be rewarding. To be attractive, therefore, people should present themselves positively in the initial stages of a relationship. Disclosure of one's negative aspects should be reserved for relationships that have persisted longer.

Self-disclosure should be appropriate to the length of a relationship. You
can apply this principle to your own life. You should not disclose yourself to
strangers; you should reserve intimate self-disclosures for persons whom you
have known for some time; and you should disclose positive information about
yourself before you disclose negative information.

Self-Disclosure Should Be Appropriate for the Person to Whom You Are Self-Disclosing

In general, except for strangers whom we do not expect to see again, the research shows that we disclose ourselves most to persons to whom we feel close
or toward whom we feel affectionate.[17] Jourard and Lasakow showed that the
willingness of people to disclose is dependent on their relationship with the other
person. Young unmarried people disclosed most to their mothers, their fathers,
their male friends, and their female friends, in that order. Married people disclosed more to their spouses than to any other people.[18]

It has also been shown that the verbal and nonverbal behavior of the other
person affects people's willingness to self-disclose. Researchers found that
people will disclose more to persons who are perceived as warm, genuine, and
understanding than to others.[19]

The Gilbert and Whiteneck study we have already cited concluded that
highly negative disclosures are reserved for intimate relationships. The relationship should be intimate before you disclose highly negative information about
yourself.[20]

The implications of this research are clear. You should disclose most to
people for whom you have affection and to whom you feel close. You should be
sensitive to the verbal and nonverbal cues that the other person transmits, particularly as they relate to that person's warmth, genuineness, and understanding.
And you should reserve disclosures of highly negative information for your intimate friends or members of your family.

Self-Disclosure Is Related to the Topic Under Discussion

The topic under consideration also affects self-disclosure. Taylor and Altman
determined that the type of information to be disclosed influenced the level of
self-disclosure.[21] Marital satisfaction was found to be affected more by the couple's satisfaction with the topics being considered and the information disclosed
rather than by the amount of disclosure.[22] One researcher found that "shared
activities" and "children and careers" were the only two of seventeen different
topics in which disclosure was related to marital satisfaction.[23]

Because the research is limited, the implications are ambiguous. You should
keep in mind, however, that the topic under discussion may affect the amount of
self-disclosure that is appropriate and satisfying.

Self-Disclosure Depends on the Person Who Is Disclosing

We must consider ourselves in the process called "self-disclosure." Who we are affects our willingness and our ability to self-disclose and our willingness to engage in self-disclosive communication. But we know relatively little about what kinds of people self-disclose and what distinguishes them from people who do not. In a recent study of the role of sex in self-disclosure, Gilbert and Whiteneck found that men are more likely to disclose earlier in the development of a relationship than women; that men are less likely to make positive statements about themselves than women; but that both sexes are equally likely to make negative statements about themselves.[24] Positive statements included statements such as "I really did well on the English exam," "My wife is really helpful in my career," "I scored sixteen points in the last basketball game." Negative statements included "I think I have to drop out of school," "My girlfriend wants to break up," and "I don't seem to be able to make any friends."

We must keep in mind, then, that in self-disclosure, we have to suit ourselves. Many factors affect our ability and our willingness to self-disclose. Our own comfort, satisfaction, and needs must be taken into account when we share ourselves with others.

Applying the Principles

The guidelines for self-disclosure are somewhat abstract. In order to test your understanding and ability to apply these guidelines to specific situations, complete the following exercise.

For each situation, determine whether the information that is disclosed is appropriate or inappropriate. Write "Appropriate" in the blank if the self-disclosure is appropriate for the people involved, their relationship to each other, and other relevant variables. Write "Inappropriate" if one of the guidelines has been disregarded and try to identify the specific one.

Appropriate or Inappropriate

1. You are with a friend who seems distracted and you begin to talk about your marital problems. _____
2. You are being interviewed for a job and you tell your prospective employer that you must have the job so that you won't have to move back home with your parents. _____
3. You are on a bus and the woman next to you begins to tell you about her abortion. _____
4. You are a woman, and you walk up to a stranger in a bar and begin to tell him about yourself. _____
5. You tell your wife or husband that you suspect that you have lung cancer and that your fear of the disease is unbearable. _____

Summary

In this chapter we considered self-disclosure. We defined self-disclosure as the ability to voluntarily tell other people things about ourselves that they are unlikely to know or to learn from others.

Self-disclosure is important because it allows us to develop a greater understanding and awareness of ourselves, because it can result in self-improvement, because it allows us to establish more meaningful relationships with others, and because it allows us to establish more positive attitudes about ourselves and others. We show reluctance to disclose ourselves because we do not respect ourselves and because we do not trust others.

We can find five guidelines for self-disclosure in the research on the subject: (1) self-disclosure should be reciprocal, or shared; (2) it is related to the duration of a relationship; (3) self-disclosure should be appropriate for the person to whom you are self-disclosing; (4) it should be appropriate to the topic under discussion; (5) self-disclosure depends on the person who is making the disclosure.

We turn from this focus on the self to a consideration of the other person. Interpersonal communication involves at least two people. Self-disclosure is important, but equally important is our ability to understand others through listening and empathy, the topic of chapter 7.

New Terms

Self-disclosure	Unknown area	Reciprocity
Johari Window	Positive self-disclosure	Appropriate self-disclosure
Open area	Negative self-disclosure	
Blind area	Spontaneity	Intimate self-disclosure
Hidden area	Manipulation	

Additional Readings

Egan, Gerard. *Interpersonal Living: A Skills/Contract Approach to Human Relations Training in Groups*. Belmont, Calif.: Wadsworth Publishing Co., Inc., 1976.
Self-disclosure is discussed as a prerequisite for the development of a meaningful relationship. A brief theoretical explanation of self-disclosure is offered, and a detailed list of behavioral guidelines to appropriate self-disclosure.

Gordon, Chad, and Gergen, Kenneth J. *The Self in Social Interaction*. New York: John Wiley & Sons, Inc., 1968. Pages 299–308.
The authors relate the need for consistency to the factors of motivation, environment, and other people that determine the way we present ourselves to others. Contains some interesting insights into why we tend to disclose certain kinds of information to others, and into some of the problems associated with full self-disclosure.

*Goffman, Erving. *The Presentation of Self in Everyday Life*. Garden City, N.Y.: Doubleday & Co., Inc., 1959. *Goffman discusses self-disclosure as a method of presenting our characters to others and advises that we manage the impression of ourselves to others by wearing masks which may hinder communication.*

*Jourard, Sidney. "Healthy Personality and Self-Disclosure." In *The Self in Social Interaction*, edited by Chad Gordon and Kenneth J. Gergen, pp. 423–34. New York: John Wiley & Sons, Inc., 1968. *A synthesis of several works by Jourard, this selection is a discussion of the relationship between the ability to disclose the self and the development of a healthy self-concept. Self-disclosure is related to age, sex, interpersonal competence, personality, and interpersonal contexts.*

McCroskey, James C., and Wheeless, Lawrence R. *Introduction to Human Communication*. Boston: Allyn & Bacon, Inc., 1976. Pages 205–29. *A fundamental discussion of the nature, effect, and patterns of self-disclosure. A good summary of the important research findings relating sex, age, family, marriage, and race to our willingness to disclose ourselves and the depth and accuracy of our self-disclosure.*

Phelps, Lynn A., and DeWine, Sue. *Interpersonal Communication Journal*. New York: West Publishing Company, 1976. *A workbook approach to developing self-awareness and self-confidence as a communicator. Provides numerous opportunities for practice of self-disclosive messages. A helpful introduction to the value of journals to help you practice expression of your ideas, feelings, and needs.*

Rogers, Carl R. *On Becoming A Person*. Boston: Houghton Mifflin Company, 1961. *A thorough discussion of trust, self-awareness, and self-disclosure as they relate to the growth of a fully functioning self. Rogers discloses the decisions and guidelines which have helped him become more effective in presenting his self-image to others. Insightful reading.*

*Indicates more advanced readings.

Notes

1. Hugh Prather, *Notes to Myself* (Moab, Utah: Real People Press, 1970). Used with permission.
2. From the song "People" by Bob Merrill and Jule Styne. Copyright © 1963 and 1964 by Bob Merrill and Jule Styne, Chappell-Styne, Inc., and Wonderful Music Corp., owners of publication and allied rights throughout the world. Chappell & Co., Inc., sole and exclusive agent. International Copyright Secured. All Rights Reserved. Used by permission.
3. Melvin Lee, Philip G. Zimbardo, and Minerva Bertholf, "Shy Murderers," *Psychology Today* 11 (November 1977): 148.
4. Franz Kafka, "Give It Up!" in *The Complete Stories*, ed. Nathum N. Glatzer (New York: Schocken Books, Inc., 1972), p. 456.
5. Reprinted by permission of William Morrow & Company, Inc. from *The Shoes of the Fisherman* by Morris L. West. Copyright © 1963 by Morris L. West.
6. Powell, p. 12.
7. P. C. Cozby, "Self-Disclosure: A Literature Review," *Psychological Bulletin* 79 (1973): 73–91; S. Jourard and M. J. Landsman, "Cognition, Cathexis, and the 'Dyadic Effect' in Men's Self-Disclosing Behavior," *Merrill-Palmer Quarterly of Behavior and Development* 9 (1960): 141–48; S. Jourard and J. L. Resnick, "Some Effects on Self-Disclosure Among College Women," *Journal of Humanistic Psychology* 10 (1970): 84–93; S. Jourard and P. Jaffe, "Influence of an Interviewer's Disclosure on the Self-Disclosing Behavior of Interviewees," *Journal of Counseling Psychology* 17 (1970): 252–97; H. Erlich and

D. Graeven, "Reciprocal Self-Disclosure in a Dyad," *Journal of Experimental Social Psychology* 7 (1971): 389–400; G. Levinger and D. Senn, "Disclosure of Feelings in Marriage," *Merrill-Palmer Quarterly of Behavior and Development* 13 (1967): 237–49; P. Cozby, "Self-Disclosure, Reciprocity, and Liking," *Sociometry* 35 (1972): 151–60; and F. M. Levin and K. Gergen, "Revealingness, Ingratiation, and the Disclosure of Self," *Proceedings of the 77th Annual Convention,* American Psychological Association, 1969, pp. 447–48.

8. S. Jourard, *The Transparent Self,* 2d ed. (New York: Van Nostrand Reinhold Company, 1971).

9. W. Worthy, A. Gary, and G. M. Kahn, "Self-Disclosure as an Exchange Process," *Journal of Personality and Social Psychology* 13 (1969): 59–63.

10. P. T. Quinn, "Self-Disclosure as a Function of Degree of Acquaintance and Potential Power," (Master's thesis, Ohio State University, 1965).

11. D. A. Taylor, "Some Aspects of the Development of Interpersonal Relationships: Social Penetration Process," *Technical Report No. 1* (Center for Research on Social Behavior, University of Delaware, 1965).

12. S. A. Culbert, "Trainer Self-Disclosure and Member Growth in Two T-Groups," *Journal of Applied Behavioral Science* 4 (1968): 47–73.

13. C. A. Kiesler, S. Kiesler, and M. Pallack, "The Effects of Commitment on Future Interaction on Reactions to Norm Violations," *Journal of Personality* 35 (1967): 585–99.

14. A. L. Chaikin and V. J. Derlega, "Variables Affecting the Appropriateness of Self-Disclosure," *Journal of Consulting and Clinical Psychology* 42 (1974): 588–93.

15. Shirley J. Gilbert and Gale G. Whiteneck, "Toward A Multidimensional Approach to the Study of Self-Disclosure," *Human Communication Research* 4 (1976): 347–55.

16. P. M. Blau, *Exchange and Power in Social Life* (New York: John Wiley and Sons, Inc., 1964), p. 21.

17. S. Jourard, "Self-Disclosure and Other-Cathexis," *Journal of Abnormal and Social Psychology* 59 (1959): 428–31; Jourard and Lasakow, 1958; Worthy, Gary and Kahn, 1969; and Cozby, 1972.

18. Sidney Jourard and Paul Lasakow, "Some Factors in Self-Disclosure," *Journal of Abnormal and Social Psychology* 51 (1958): 91–98.

19. Jeffrey G. Shapiro, Herbert H. Krauss, and Charles B. Truax, "Therapeutic Conditions of Disclosure beyond the Therapeutic Encounter," *Journal of Counseling Psychology* 16 (1969): 290–94.

20. Gilbert and Whiteneck, 347–55.

21. D. Taylor and I. Altman, "Intimacy Scaled Stimuli to Use in Studies of Interpersonal Relations," *Psychological Reports* 19 (1966): 729–30.

22. Levinger and Senn, 1967.

23. F. Voss, "The Relationships of Disclosure to Marital Satisfaction: An Exploratory Study" (Master's thesis, University of Wisconsin, 1969).

24. Gilbert and Whiteneck, 347–55.

7 Understanding Another

Objectives

After study of this chapter you should be able to do the following:

1. Differentiate between hearing and listening
2. Name three common misconceptions about listening
3. Discuss the importance of listening in communication
4. Define empathy and differentiate it from sympathy and neutrality
5. Give examples of four kinds of external distractions that interfere with listening and empathy
6. Give examples of the internal factors that interfere with empathy and listening
7. Explain how status and stereotypes interfere with our ability to listen and empathize
8. Discuss one of your stereotypes and explain how it influences your communication with people who fit that stereotype
9. Discuss the ways in which we can overcome the barriers to effective listening and improve our ability to empathize with other people
10. Discuss a personal experience in which you wanted to empathize but could not and relate it to the concepts explained in this chapter. Explain the factors that prevented effective listening and the ways in which you might have overcome those barriers

"My younger sister goes to college in Illinois. She said that her speech department runs a contest on listening. The guy who won this year said he had an advantage over the other contestants–he's been married for twelve years!"

"My husband says I don't understand him. How can I understand *him? With two kids, a baby, and a dog all making noise at the same time, I can't even* hear *him!"*

"The Indians who live in the part of the country I come from had a belief that really made a difference in their behavior. They said that if someone wanted to understand someone else, they had to walk in the other person's moccasins for a fortnight."

In the last chapter, we discussed the importance of sharing ourselves in interpersonal communication. In this one we turn our consideration to the other person. We suggest that two basic skills must be practiced if our goal is to understand another person. Listening and empathy—as suggested in the introductory statements—are the focus of this chapter.

Two Basic Skills in Understanding Another

Listening

When we think about communication, we usually focus on the speaking, or sending, aspect. If someone says he is enrolled in a speech class, we ask how many speeches he has to make. If he says he had a talk with his family, we ask him what he said. The other activity involved in communication—listening— should be given equal consideration. *Listening* is the process of receiving and interpreting aural stimuli.

There are a number of popular misconceptions about listening. Most people assume that (1) they are already good listeners; (2) they cannot be taught how to become better listeners; and (3) listening and hearing are the same thing.

Ask people you know if they listen well. Most likely, they will say that they do. Most of us believe that we listen well. Unfortunately, a number of studies demonstrate that our perceptions of our own ability to listen are inaccurate.[1]

Ralph Nichols and his associates at the University of Minnesota tested the ability of thousands of students and hundreds of business and professional people to understand and remember what they heard. His research led to two conclusions: On the average, people remember only about half of what they have heard, even when they are tested immediately, and no matter how intently they believed they were listening. Then, two months later, they only remember 25 percent of what they heard.[2] These test results demonstrate our inability to hear and retain a message. *Listen*

A misconception most of us have is that people cannot be taught to become better listeners. P. T. Rankin determined that people spend about 70 percent of their waking time in communication. Listening, talking, reading, and writing occurred in the percentages listed:

Listening	42%
Talking	32%
Reading	15%
Writing	11%

In other words, more of the time devoted to communication is spent listening than in any other single activity.[3] Television has probably increased our listening time even further. And Rankin did not include intrapersonal communication, the communication that occurs within a person, in his study. If he had included intrapersonal communication, he might have found that we spend 100 percent of our waking time engaged in communication.

Another study, completed by D. Bird, confirmed Rankin's findings. Bird asked college women to record the amount of time they were involved in different aspects of communication. Again, 42 percent of the time spent in communication was spent in listening. These women also indicated that listening was as or more important than reading to their success in college.[4] Many other studies have documented the great amount of time we spend listening.[5]

Even though we have evidence of the central role of listening in communication and have had such evidence for over fifty years, we rarely study the subject. You have probably attended classes in reading and writing since the time you first started school. Most colleges require one or two courses in English composition and literature. You may have had one or more formal courses in speech before this one. You probably had Show-and-Tell or Sharing Time in elementary school. And yet, you probably have never studied listening or enrolled in any course that emphasized listening to any large extent. The conclusion is obvious: we assume that listening cannot be learned. If we thought it could be, our educational institutions would offer courses in listening at all levels.

Perhaps this is because we assume that listening and hearing are one and the same. That is untrue. Once in a while, we might have difficulty distinguishing between listening and hearing, but the two processes are generally distinct. Hearing is a natural process, and unless we suffer from physiological damage or some form of cerebral dysfunction, we cannot help hearing loud sounds. Listening, on the other hand, is a selective activity; it involves the reception *and* the interpretation of aural stimuli.

Most of us have been in situations in which another person assumed that listening and hearing were the same. We can all recall reprimands from our parents, like, "What do you mean you didn't clean your room? I came into the living room, where you were watching TV, and told you to do it. I know you heard me." An instructor might have said to you, "I just asked you a question.

Everyone else in the room heard it. Why didn't you?'' Many people incorrectly assume that listening and hearing are the same.

Listening, the process of receiving and interpreting aural stimuli, is an integral part of communication. Simply hearing, receiving aural stimuli, is not sufficient. As we said in chapter 1, both encoding, or putting messages or thoughts into codes, and decoding, or assigning meaning to codes, are essential to communication.

Empathy

Empathy is a second skill that helps us to understand another person. We define *empathy* as the ability to perceive the other person's view of the world as though that view were our own. When we talk about "putting ourselves in someone else's shoes," as Wellington literally does in the cartoon, we are talking about empathy.

Most of us assume that other people perceive things the way we do. But, as we said in chapter 2, great variations in perceptions exist. If we wish to be more understanding of others, we need to recognize that such differences occur and that we should attempt to determine what other people's experiences are. Bochner and Kelly, two communication scholars, wrote that empathy is "the essence of all communicative process."[6]

Empathy is distinct from neutrality and sympathy. We exhibit neutrality when we show indifference to another person. We show sympathy when we share the feelings of others—their pain or sorrow, their joy or happiness. When we sympathize with others, we may show that we care by expressing the same emotional response to a situation that they have made. It is possible that sympathy will not be helpful since we may find ourselves limited by the strong emotions of the moment. It can be difficult to be supportive of others when we are laughing or crying or shouting with them.

Neutrality is harmful because it indicates that we do not have respect or positive regard for the other person. Sympathy may also be destructive when it connotes or suggests superiority. In feeling sorry for another person, we may be

WEE PALS

communicating that we are somehow better off, more advanced, or without need for sympathy ourselves. It is possible that our sympathetic responses may be regarded as patronizing and may not be appreciated by others.

When we empathize with others, we do not need to feel the same fear or anxiety that they are experiencing. What we communicate to them is an awareness and appreciation of their emotions. Empathy requires sensitivity to others and an ability to demonstrate this sensitivity. We should strive to communicate that we are with them, not because we are sharing their emotions, but because we understand their feelings.

If we fail to empathize with others, we fail to understand them. In a very real sense, we are hurting ourselves. To the extent that we do not empathize with others, we restrict ourselves to our personal experiences and feelings.

Nonetheless, empathy is not easy to achieve. We need to empathize with others precisely when it is most difficult for us to do it. When we disagree most with someone else, it is then that we most need to show that we understand them and their point of view. Seeing the other side is the most difficult when we do not agree with it. Our tendency in such situations is to spend a great deal of energy and time defending our own position and finding fault with the other person's point of view. We feel a need to prove that we are right, and the other person wrong.

And yet empathy can be a most important emotion. Empathy allows us to enter another person's world as though it were our own. It implies understanding, rather than judgment. Carl Rogers has expressed the importance of empathy:

> A person who is loved appreciatively, not possessively, blooms, and develops his own unique self. The person who loves non-possessively is himself enriched.[7]

Empathy is satisfying and enriching to both parties in an interpersonal relationship.

Who's Right?

The goal of empathic understanding is acceptance of ourselves and acceptance of others. We should strive to appreciate our own points of view as well as the positions of other people. We have empathized when we can honestly say, "You're right and I'm right." But usually, when we are engaged in an argument, we say, "You're wrong and I'm right." Other positions we could take are, "You're wrong and I'm wrong," which demonstrates negative feelings about both positions and both people; or, "I'm wrong and you're right," which demonstrates a lack of confidence and perhaps a poor self-concept. In order to gain experience in empathizing, try to explain how both of the contradictory statements made by two different people might be seen as "right."

1. "Abortion is the best form of birth control."

Right, because _____

_____

"Abortions should be illegal—regardless of the reason for them."

Right, because _____

_____

2. "Marijuana should be sold in all the same places that sell tobacco."

Right, because _____

_____

"Smoking marijuana should be considered a felony."

Right, because _____

_____

3. "The drinking age should be raised to 25."

Right, because _____

_____

"The drinking age should be lowered to 15."

Right, because _____

_____

4. "People should pass a test before they can marry."

Right, because _____

_____

"Marriage laws should be liberalized so people can
marry more easily."

Right, because _____

_____

5. "Women belong in the home."

Right, because _____

_____

"Women should be responsible for their own support."

Right, because _____

_____

6. "President Carter did an excellent job."

Right, because _____

_____

"President Carter is the poorest American president to
date."

Right, because _____

_____

You probably found it relatively easy to support both sides of some of these issues. Others were no doubt more challenging. The conflicting statements that were easy for you to support probably concern issues that affect you very little; those that were difficult possibly deal with matters about which you have a great deal of concern and a specific position. We all need to develop empathic understanding for the points of view with which we disagree.

Interference with Our Ability to Listen and to Empathize

The studies cited earlier show that we do not listen well. Similar studies of empathy have not been done, but the results would probably be the same. Empathizing with someone else is even more difficult than listening. Understanding another by listening and empathizing requires that we hear both their verbal and nonverbal messages; that we understand the content, the intent, and the accompanying emotions; and that we communicate our understanding to them. A number of difficulties and breakdowns in communication can occur on the way. Let us consider some of the factors that may interfere with our ability to listen and to empathize.

The Message and the Occasion

A number of distractions occur both in the message itself and in the situation in which it is received: (1) factual distractions; (2) semantic distractions; (3) mental distractions; and (4) physical distractions. Factual distractions occur because we *EMOTION* tend to listen for facts instead of ideas. Perhaps our educational institutions encourage this tendency. Instead of looking at the whole, we focus on the parts. We can lose the main idea or the purpose behind a message if we jump from fact to fact instead of attempting to weave them together into a total pattern. For example, a friend might relate an experience from her past in which she felt devastated by circumstances beyond her control. Friends may tell us stories about their childhood, stories of fear, frustration, or anger. We listen to the facts—he comes from a small town, she had a pet hamster—and we do not grasp the emotion.

Semantic distractions are similar, in that they are also caused by elements of the message. Semantic distractions occur when someone uses a word or phrase differently or uses one to which we react emotionally. Regionalisms, different names for similar things used in different parts of the country, can be semantic distractions. In different parts of the country, people may ask for a "pop," a "soda," a "coke," or a "tonic"—merely different names for a soft drink. Emotional reactions to words often occur when people are classified in a denigrating way: "girl" for women over twenty-one, "Polacks" for Polish people, "Jew" for anyone who tends to be thrifty.

Mental distractions occur when we engage in intrapersonal communication, in communicating with ourselves, when we are talking with others. The mental side trips, daydreams, counter-arguments, and recollections that we engage in when someone is talking to us distract us from receiving the other person's message. These side trips can be suggested by something the other person says or by our own preoccupation. Mental distractions may occur because of the great difference between the speed at which we hear and the speed at which we speak. Most Americans talk at a rate of about 125 words per minute, but we are able to receive about 800 words per minute. This discrepancy allows us great freedom to consider other matters that may be more important to us. A cook can easily plan dinner while listening to a psychology lecture. Someone else can review the exciting events of the previous evening while listening to the news. We can decide whether to accept an invitation while listening to a friend's account of an argument with another friend.

Physical distractions include all the stimuli in the environment that might interfere with our focusing on the other person and his or her message. We can be distracted by sound—a buzzing neon light, loud music, or the speaker's lisp;

by visual stimuli—a poster of a nude on the wall, bright sunlight, or the speaker's beauty; or by any other stimuli—an unusual odor, an uncomfortable article of clothing, or an unpleasant aftertaste in our mouth.

Ourselves

Another set of factors that interferes with our ability to listen and to empathize is related to ourselves. If we constantly focus on ourselves, we cannot be sensitive to others. In order to understand another person, we need to be open to them. Self-focus, or a preoccupation with thoughts about ourselves, hampers listening and empathy. As we suggested in the exercise entitled, "Who's Right?" we need to develop positive feelings about ourselves and about other people. Self-focus suggests that we have developed regard for ourselves, but that we have failed to develop the same feeling toward others. In the conversation that follows, Tom is unable to listen or empathize with Karen because he allows his personal concerns to dominate his thinking and his communication.

Karen has just received word that her grandmother has died. Tom is the counselor at the agency where she works. Karen is extremely upset and goes to Tom because she needs to talk to someone. She has talked with him only casually in the past, but she feels he will understand because he is a trained counselor.

Karen: "Tom, do you have a minute?"

Tom: "Sure Karen, come on in."

Karen: "I wanted to talk to someone for a little while."

Tom: "Fine. What would you like to talk about?"

Karen: "Well, I just got a phone call from home saying that my grandmother died and I guess I just needed someone to talk to."

Tom: "Yeah, I know how you feel. I had a grandmother who died about eight years ago. She was the neatest lady I have ever known. Why, when I was a kid she used to bake cookies for me every Saturday. We used to go to the park on weekends for picnics. She sure was fun to be with."

Karen: "I'm sure you had a good time, but I sort of wanted to talk about my grandmother."

Tom: "Oh, sure. Well, what was she like?"

Karen: "Well, she was a good lady, but . . ."

Tom: "Yeah, I guess all grandmothers are pretty good."

Karen: "I guess so, but . . ."

Tom: "You know, it's been a long time since I thought about my grandmother. I'm really glad you came in today."

Karen: "Yes, well, I guess my break is about over so I'd better get back to work."

Tom: "Okay. It's been nice talking to you. Stop by anytime."

Karen: "Sure."

A number of factors may account for a person's focus on himself or herself rather than on the other person. Defensiveness is a common reason. People who feel that they must defend their position usually feel threatened. They feel that, in general, people are attacking them and their ideas and they develop the habit of defending themselves. Sometimes people who are championing a specific cause—women's rights, the elderly, peace, black equality—develop this attitude. They stand ready to respond to the least provocation and they tend to find fault with other people.

In the interview that follows, the supervisor demonstrates a defensive attitude and is consequently unable to listen to or empathize with the employee. The supervisor is the director of operations in a social service agency. He has arranged this appraisal interview with the employee because he is evaluating her performance as a community organizer.

Supervisor: "As you know, after sixty days we evaluate each new employee. That's why I've asked you to come here today. Here is the evaluation form I have filled out. Please read it."

Employee: *(after reading)* "I don't understand why you have marked me so low in dependability."

Supervisor: "Because you always ask so many questions whenever I tell you to do something."

Employee: "But the reason I ask questions is that I don't understand exactly what you want me to do. If I didn't ask the questions, I wouldn't be able to perform the task because your instructions are usually not clear to me."

Supervisor: "I marked you low in that area because you require so much supervision."

Employee: "It's not supervision I need, it's clear instructions, and I don't feel it's fair for you to mark me low in this area when I am not."

Supervisor: "It doesn't really matter what you think because I'm doing the evaluation."

Employee: "Don't I have anything to say about it?"

Supervisor: "No. Now that you've read it, will you please sign here?"

Employee: "Definitely not. I feel that is unfair and inaccurate."

Supervisor: "Then check the box that indicates you are not in agreement with the evaluation. All your signature means is that you have read it, not that you agree with it."

Employee: "This is the most ridiculous evaluation I have ever had in my entire life."

Supervisor: "That's unimportant at this point. If you don't have anything else to say, that will be all."

The defensive verbal behavior by the supervisor clearly interfered with his ability to listen to and empathize with his employee. Defensiveness usually interferes with our ability to listen and to empathize.

Another reason for self-focus is known as *experiential superiority*. People who have lived through a variety of experiences sometimes express this attitude toward people who have had less experience. Professors often cannot listen or empathize with students who are explaining why an assignment was not completed on time; they assume that the particular student will offer an excuse they have heard before. Parents sometimes fail to listen to their children's problems or to empathize with them: they feel that from their own past experience with the problem, they can just give a pat answer.

A variation of experiential superiority occurs in long-term relationships. People have a good deal of experience in the relationship and feel they can predict the other person's statements. Husbands may respond with an occasional "uh-huh" over the newspaper at breakfast; wives may repeat, "Sure, honey," while daydreaming about other matters. The characters in the Hagar cartoon on page 138 typify people who no longer listen to each other—probably as a result of a long relationship.

Another reason people focus on themselves is simple egocentrism. *Egocentrism* is the tendency to view yourself as the center of any exchange or activity. A person who is egocentric is overly concerned with himself or herself, and pays little attention to others. This person appears to be constantly asking, "How do I look? How do I sound? How am I coming through to you?" instead of responding to how the other person looks, sounds, and is coming through.

One place you can observe egocentric people is at a party. Egocentric people usually make a number of attention-getting moves which place them at the center of the stage. They may arrive late, talk loudly, dress flamboyantly, and stand in the center of the room to make others focus on them. They also move from person to person or group to group, but they do not give their full attention to the people with whom they are talking. They look around the room, glancing from one person to another. Rarely do they focus on anyone for more than a moment and, even then, they do not concentrate on the other person's message.

Our Perception of the Other Person

A third set of factors involves our perception of the other person. Preconceived attitudes—such as status or stereotypes—interfere with our listening to another person. If we believe that the other people have status, we accept what they say easily, rather than listening carefully and critically. We usually do not listen with care or critically when the speaker is an M.D., a professor, a Supreme Court justice, or a visiting expert. If we think that the other person has low status, we often do not listen to their statements at all, nor do we retain their messages. Seniors seldom listen to freshmen about study habits, and attractive people rarely take advice from people they consider unattractive. We dismiss state-

ments made by people of lesser status. Thus, we do not listen carefully to persons whom we perceive to have either a higher or lower status than we.

Our stereotypes also affect our ability to listen. If another person belongs to a group we respect—Democrats, beer drinkers, Volvo owners, or joggers—we believe what they say. If they belong to a group of people for whom we have little regard—highbrows, college dropouts, football players, or flirts—we reject their messages.

Status and stereotypes affect our ability to listen and to empathize. In order to demonstrate this for yourself, ask two people what they make of a presidential address or of a statement made by a labor leader, a member of Congress, or the governor. If you ask two people who have different perceptions of the status of the person and different stereotypes of the groups the person belongs to, you will probably end up with two entirely different versions of the same address or statement.

Sources of Interference with Listening and Empathy

In order to determine if you understand the various types of interference with listening and empathy, complete the following exercise. Mark each of the statements as follows:

M & O—FD	Message and occasion—Factual distraction
M & O—SD	Message and occasion—Semantic distraction
M & O—MD	Message and occasion—Mental distraction
M & O—PD	Message and occasion—Physical distraction
S—D	Self—Defensiveness
S—ES	Self—Experiential superiority
S—E	Self—Egocentrism
O—S	Other—Status
O—St	Other—Stereotype

1. "I guess you're right; after all you're a teacher." *O-S*

2. "I know that my point of view is correct. If you don't like the way I handle things, you can look somewhere else for a job. *S-D*

3. "I know what you're going to say—I was a student once, too, you know." *S-ES*

4. "Did you use the term *late bloomer*? You know, I really think people use that term carelessly, and often inaccurately." *M+O-SD*

5. "I'm sorry I didn't hear what you said. By the way, what do you think of my hair?" *S-E*

6. "If you think you've got problems, let me tell you what it was like when I was your age!" *S-ES*

7. "Did you use the word *gargoyle*?" *M+O-SD*

8. "What did you say? I was thinking about the guy I went out with last night."   *M+0 – M*

9. "It was really difficult to hear the lecture—the plumbers upstairs were making so much noise."   *M+0–P*

10. "I know you said I should get my hair cut shorter, but you're my mom. No offense, but mothers always say that."   *0–SJ*

11. "You don't have to say one word. I know just what you're going to say."   *E+S*

12. "Those were interesting statistics, Dr. Nelson, but what was the point of today's lecture?"   *M+0–FS*

13. "I'm so worried about my finals that I didn't hear you. What did you say?"   *M+0–M*

14. "Yes, I guess that—Oh no, I broke a nail. That really looks bad, doesn't it? What were you saying?"   *M+0–P ; B*

15. "I know that you don't agree with me, but I have a reputation to protect. If you only wish to attack my decision, I'm afraid our discussion is over."   *S–D.*

Improving Our Ability to Listen and to Empathize

Just as we can identify factors that interfere with our ability to listen and empathize, we can also identify ways of improving those abilities. Let us consider the three sets of factors that interfere with our listening and empathizing and suggest methods of overcoming each. The distractions that occur in the message and in the environment are factual, semantic, mental, and physical.

We can remove factual distractions by *focusing on the main ideas* that the other person is presenting, remembering that we can ask later for facts and details. It is far less offensive to another person to be asked for particular numbers, specific locations, or to spell a particular name than it is to be asked, "What in the world are you talking about?"

Semantic distractions can be minimized if we keep in mind that *words are arbitrary symbols*. They have no inherent or natural meaning that is shared by everyone. If another person uses a word that confuses us, the appropriate response is to *ask the meaning of the word or to ask how she or he is using the word*. If we cannot overcome our emotional reaction to a specific word, it is essential that we explain the word's negative associations to the person using it.

Instead of allowing mental side trips to distract us from other people's messages, we should use the time to *focus on their intent, as well as the content of their message*. By refusing to consider unrelated matters, we will find that our listening and our understanding can be greatly increased.

Physical distractions like noise, bright lights, unusual odors, or provocative surroundings can usually be handled easily. In most cases, a simple *move to another room or another location* will solve the problem.

The distractions that result from self-focus are created by defensiveness, experiential superiority, and egocentrism. The habit of focusing on ourselves rather than on the other person is difficult to break, however. Nonetheless, we need to alter this behavior if we hope to listen to someone else, and, in turn, understand that person.

Focusing on the meaning and experiences that we share is helpful if we find that we usually react defensively to other people's messages. Other persons may be attacking one of our pet beliefs or attitudes, but they may also be defending it from another perspective. Regardless of their point of view on the single issue, we can find a number of points of agreement. Maximizing our shared attitudes, values, and beliefs and minimizing our differences results in improved listening and better communication. In addition, if we do not react defensively to other people's disagreements with us, we may find ourselves being persuasive and encouraging them to agree with us.

If experiential superiority is the problem that interferes with listening and empathizing, *give the other person a full hearing*. Impatience with a person who has no experience with a particular problem and the poor listening which accompanies this attitude can result in a breakdown in communication. Listening to and empathizing with them will result in improved communication. You may even learn something new.

People who are continually concerned with their self-image and how that image is perceived by others have difficulty listening and empathizing. Egocentrism is an ingrained attitude that is extremely difficult to change. Perhaps the wisest suggestion to a person with this problem is, *attempt to concentrate on the other person*. There are advantages to concentrating on the other person that should appeal to someone who is egocentric. Concentrating on other people when they are speaking will probably cause them to focus on you when you are speaking. Even more important, you will "come across" better if the other person perceives you to be a good and empathic listener. No amount of make-up, clothing, or other adornments will make you as attractive to others as the ability to listen and to empathize.

In order to overcome problems related to our preconceptions of other people, we need to *learn how to suspend judgment*. Rather than assuming that their messages are acceptable or unacceptable without listening to them, we need to wait until we have heard them out. As we saw in chapter 3, we can make grave errors by assuming that a person who belongs to a particular group is like all of the other members of that group. Bernard Gunther said: "Take a chance on getting slapped, you might get kissed!"

We can also overcome these problems if we *focus on the other person as a source of feelings and thoughts, ideas, and information*. When we categorize other people, we can easily dismiss them. When we view them respectfully as valuable human resources, we find that our listening and our empathizing improve.

Listening with Empathy

In order to improve your ability as a listener, try this exercise. With a small group of people, discuss a controversial topic. Before each person can speak, he or she must state, without using notes, what the person who spoke just before said— and to that person's satisfaction. If the summary is inaccurate or incomplete, the previous speaker is asked to clarify the message. The next person to speak must again attempt to state the previous speaker's message.

When your group becomes successful at stating the content of the previous speaker's message, have each person state the previous speaker's intent. Now each person is explaining what the previous person said and what was intended by the remarks. Again, the previous speaker must agree that the content and the intent are accurate and complete before the discussion can continue.

Did you find that your task was easier or more difficult than you anticipated? Were particular people better able to restate another person's ideas? Why were they successful? How can you improve your own ability to listen for understanding?

Summary

In this chapter we considered the importance of understanding other people when we communicate with them. By improving two related and basic skills— listening and empathy—we can improve our ability to understand another person. Listening was defined as the process of receiving and interpreting aural stimuli. Empathy was defined as the ability to perceive the other person's view of the world as though that view were your own.

A number of factors interfere with our ability to listen and to empathize. These factors fall into three categories: those related to the message and the occasion, such as factual, semantic, mental, and physical distractions; those related to ourselves, including defensiveness, experiential superiority, and egocentrism; and those related to the other person, such as status and stereotypes.

We can overcome these obstacles, however, and improve our ability to listen and to empathize with others. Among the suggestions made were focusing on the main ideas; keeping in mind that words are arbitrary symbols; focusing on the intent, as well as the content, of a message; moving when physical factors interfere; focusing on the meaning and experiences that are shared; giving the other person a full hearing; concentrating on the other person; suspending judgment; and focusing on the other person as a source of feelings and thoughts, ideas, and information. Understanding another person is a difficult but worthwhile goal for each of us.

New Terms

Listening	Semantic distractions	Experiential superiority
Hearing	Mental distractions	Egocentrism
Empathy	Physical distractions	Status
Neutrality	Regionalisms	Stereotypes
Sympathy	Defensiveness	Suspended judgments
Factual distractions		

Additional Readings

Bach, George R., and Wyden, Peter. *The Intimate Enemy: How to Fight Fair in Love and Marriage.* New York: Avon Books, 1968.
The focus of the book is on conflict within marriage and other intimate relationships, but the guidelines and principles of conflict resolution are applicable in any context. The book treats conflict as natural and constructive to a relationship if the proper "rules" are observed. Good examples make the book interesting and instructive.

Berne, Eric. *Games People Play: The Psychology of Human Relationships.* New York: Grove Press, Inc., 1964.

*In a popular introduction to
transactional analysis, Berne describes
the games that we play in our
relationships with others. The games are
seen to be destructive. Good examples
provide insights into the games that we
play without being aware of them.*

————. *What Do You Say After You Say
Hello?* New York: Grove Press, Inc.,
1972.
A sequel to Games People Play. *An
exploration of game playing in more
depth and of the scripts that can
potentially control our life. Insights into
how to avoid gameplaying and take
control of your own behavior.*

Egan, Gerard. *Interpersonal Living: A
Skills/Contract Approach to Human
Relations Training in Groups.* Belmont,
Calif.: Wadsworth Publishing Co. Inc.,
1976.
*A detailed discussion of communication
skills necessary for effective
interpersonal relationships. Empathy,
feelings and thoughts, self-disclosure,
concreteness, and descriptiveness are
discussed in depth; each skill is broken
into specific, easily understood behavior.
Excellent introduction to the effective
application of communication principles
and concepts to actual behavior.*

*Fromm, Eric. *The Art of Loving.* New
York: Harper & Row, Publishers, 1956.
*Though written over twenty years ago,
the ideas presented are far from out-of-
date. Fromm discusses the love of self
and others as an active process involving
the whole personality and tells us that
love must be practiced by developing a
sensitivity to ourselves and to others.*

Harris, Thomas A. *I'm OK–You're OK:
A Practical Guide to Transactional
Analysis.* New York: Harper & Row,
Publishers, 1969.
*A student of Eric Berne, Harris explains
transactional analysis and applies the
concepts to an exploration of human
behavior. An easily read discussion of
games people play and the influence of
our attitude toward ourselves and others
on our communication. The basic
premise is that we must consider
ourselves and others as OK if we are to
have effective relationships.*

Rogers, Carl E., and Farson, Richard E.
"Active Listening." In *Readings in
Interpersonal and Organizational
Communication,* edited by Carl E.
Rogers and Richard E. Farson. Boston:
Holbrook Press, Inc., 1969.
*A detailed discussion of the techniques
and benefits of active listening, the book
provides guidelines for developing active
listening skills and ways to overcome
barriers to active listening. A concise
and easily understood discussion.*

Shostrum, Everett L. *Man, the
Manipulator.* New York: Abingdon
Press, 1967.
*Shostrum describes man as a person who
manipulates himself, others, and things
in self-defeating ways. Discusses various
manipulation strategies and offers
suggestions about how to become
"actualized," i.e., to manipulate
creatively and constructively.*

*Indicates more advanced readings.

Notes

1. See, for example, Edward J. J. Karmar and
Thomas R. Lewis, "Comparison of Visual
and Non-Visual Listening," *Journal of
Communication* 1 (November 1951): 16-20;
James I. Brown, "The Objective
Measurement of Listening Ability,"
Journal of Communication 1 (May 1951):
44-48; Paul W. Keller, "Major Findings in
Listening in the Past Ten Years," *Journal
of Communication* 10 (March 1960): 29–38;
S. Duker, *Listening Bibliography* (New
York: Scarecrow Press, 1964); and S.
Duker, ed., *Listening; Readings* (New
York: Scarecrow Press, 1966).
2. Ralph Nichols and Leonard Stevens,
"Listening to People," *Harvard Business
Review* 35 (1957), no. 5.

3. P. T. Rankin, "The Measurement of the Ability to Understand Spoken Language," *Dissertation Abstracts* 12 (1926): 847.

4. D. Bird, "Teaching Listening Comprehension," *Journal of Communication* 3 (1953): 127–30.

5. See, for example, Miriam E. Wilt, "A Study of Teacher Awareness of Listening as a Factor in Elementary Education," *Journal of Educational Research* 43 (1950): 626; D. Bird, "Have You Tried Listening?" *Journal of the American Dietetic Association* 30 (1954): 225–30; and B. Markgraf, "An Observational Study Determining the Amount of Time that Students in the Tenth and Twelfth Grades are Expected to Listen in the Classroom" (Master's thesis, University of Wisconsin, 1957).

6. Arthur P. Bochner and Clifford W. Kelly, "Interpersonal Competence: Rationale, Philosophy, and Implementation of a Conceptual Framework," *Speech Teacher* 23 (1974): 289.

7. Carl R. Rogers, *Freedom to Learn* (Columbus, Ohio: Charles E. Merrill Publishing Company, 1969), p. 237.

8

The Interview and the Small Group Discussion

An Application of the
Principles of Interpersonal Communication

Objectives

After study of this chapter you should be able to do the following:

1. Define and give examples of open and closed, neutral and leading, and primary and secondary questions

2. Develop and organize a series of interview questions organized in accordance with the funnel, inverted funnel, and tunnel approaches

3. Distinguish the purpose of the informational, persuasive, and employment interview

4. Prepare and conduct an informational, persuasive, and employment interview

5. Discuss the differences between a small group and a collection of people

6. Identify and give examples of social functions and task functions in small group discussion

7. Identify the four main principles of brainstorming; use brainstorming to create a list of topics for a small group discussion

8. Write questions of fact, policy, and value, and discuss the purpose of each type of question

9. Discuss the characteristics of good questions for discussion

10. List three ways of discovering information about a topic

11. State three questions that you should ask about the quality of information gained from primary sources

12. State three questions you should ask in evaluating information gained from secondary sources

13. List the steps in Dewey's method of reflective thinking

14. List the characteristics of leaders and compare these characteristics with the ways of deciding who is the leader of a small group discussion

15. Discuss the functions of leadership and compare these functions with the characteristics of leaders

16. Prepare, research, organize, and conduct a small group discussion on a specific topic with others in your class

These three cartoons introduce us to two types of interpersonal communication: the interview and the small group discussion. The first cartoon depicts an informational interview; the second illustrates a number of small groups; the third states one purpose of small group discussion. Each of us participates in interviews from time to time. We are interviewed by employers, doctors, instructors, friends, counselors, parents, and people making surveys. We interview our peers, our customers, our neighbors, and the people with whom we do business. We also participate in small group discussions. Some of these discussions are about problems that we share with others or are for the purpose of sharing information. Sometimes we communicate in small groups as a sociable way to spend time.

In this chapter, we will consider the interview and the small group discussion as types of interpersonal communication. The same principles of effective interpersonal communication that we have identified in previous chapters are essential to success in the interview or in small group discussion. In addition, we

must understand the specific features of these two forms of interpersonal communication if we wish to be competent interviewers, interviewees, or small
group discussants. We shall focus on some of the unique characteristics of the
interview and the small group discussion in this chapter.

The Interview

Interviewing is more formal than the conversations in which we engage, but less
formal than other types of communication—small group discussions and public
speaking—that are covered in this text. Interviews are generally planned, have a
specific purpose, and are organized. Almost all interviews involve the asking
and answering of questions. Most often, interviews occur between two people,
and are thus defined as *dyadic communication*. The term *interviewing* may be
defined as "a process of dyadic communication with a predetermined and serious purpose designed to interchange behavior and usually involving the asking
and answering of questions."[1]

Questions and Questioning

Nearly all interviews, thus, involve the asking and answering of various types of
questions. In planning an interview, the interviewer must determine the most
appropriate kinds of questions for the purpose. Questions fall roughly into three
categories: open or closed; primary or secondary; and neutral or leading.

Open or Closed   Open questions are broad and generally unstructured. They
often simply suggest the topic under discussion. The respondent, or interviewee,
is offered a great deal of freedom in answering. Examples of open questions are
"How do you feel about Jimmy Carter?" "What is Chicago really like?" "What
are your feelings on reverse discrimination?" and "What is your problem?"

Open questions do not allow for a yes-or-no answer. They allow other
people to see that you are interested in them. They generally create a supportive
communication climate and allow the interviewer to establish good rapport with
the interviewee.

Closed questions are restrictive. They offer a narrow range of answers;
often, all of the possible answers are included in the question. Sometimes, the
possible answers are limited to yes and no. Examples of closed questions include, "Do you attend the university at this time?" "Do you plan to drop out of
school if you get this job?" "What is more important to a social worker—the
ability to relate to people or the administrative experience which allows him to
handle a large number of cases?" and "Have you the time to do the work necessary to complete this class?"

Closed questions are useful if you wish a specific response. If the closed

question is threatening, the interviewee may become defensive; if it is without threat, a short answer is easy to give. Closed questions are appropriate when the interviewer has sufficient information about the respondent and his point of view, when the question contains or permits an appropriate response, and when the respondent has information, an opinion, or a point of view about the matter under discussion.

Primary or Secondary   Primary questions introduce a topic or a new area within a topic under discussion. Examples of primary questions include: "Shall we turn to the topic of summer employment?" "Could we begin the interview by discussing your experience in welding?" and "Let's go back to your grades for a minute—how's your algebra?"

   Secondary questions are used to follow up primary questions. When an interviewee does not answer fully or completely, the interviewer asks another question to secure the desired information. Secondary questions are often short: "Shall we go on?" "Can you tell me more?" "How did you feel then?" and "Is there anything you would care to add?"

Neutral or Leading   Neutral questions do not contain any correct or preferred answer. They do not suggest any particular response or direction. They are usually open. Examples of neutral questions are "What did you do last summer?" "How did you like your last job?" "What kind of music do you listen to?" and "How do you spend your weekends?"

Leading questions suggest a preferred answer—they ease the way for one answer and make any other answer difficult. Examples of leading questions can be created from the neutral questions above: "I suppose you worked last summer. What at?" "Even if you liked your last job, there's no harm trying to better yourself, is there?" and "I guess you play a lot of ball weekends, like most young men. What is your game?"

Leading questions are very useful in persuasive interviews, as when you are attempting to convince people that they do want an additional insurance policy, that they do want to enroll in a particular course, or that they are prepared to accept your religious beliefs. But leading questions can create a defensive climate when the interviewer is not attempting to persuade the interviewee and assumes an inaccurate response. For example, you and your wife expect to go bowling, but you meet a friend who says: "You and your wife would like to go to the symphony tonight with me and my husband, wouldn't you?" Or you go to your professor's office to drop the class, but before you can ask, you hear: "You really do enjoy my class, don't you?" Both the friend and the professor make you defensive by asking a leading question instead of a neutral question.

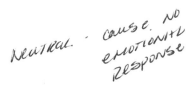

Neutral - cause. No emotional response

In the exercise below you can test your own ability to distinguish among open and closed, primary and secondary, and neutral and leading questions.

Types of Questions

To determine whether you understand the three categories of questions, complete the following exercise. Mark each question in this interview O or C for open or closed; P or S for primary and secondary; and N or L for neutral or leading.

		Open/ Closed	Primary/ Secondary	Neutral/ Leading
Interviewer:	"Hi, I was wondering if you could help me out?"	O	P	L
Interviewee:	"Sure, what do you need?"			
Interviewer:	"I'm looking for a good running shoe; what do you suggest?"	O	P	N
Interviewee:	"For jogging, a thicker sole will give you longer wear and more comfort."			
Interviewer:	"Would Adidas or Pumas be better?"	C	S	N
Interviewee:	"I'd recommend the Adidas."			
Interviewer:	"But Pumas are good shoes, aren't they?"	C	S	L
Interviewee:	"Yes, but their thinner soles make them better for racing than for recreational jogging."			
Interviewer:	"Let me get this straight, the thicker soled Adidas are better for jogging and the thinner soled Pumas are preferred for racing?"	O	S	L
Interviewee:	"Right!"			

Organizing the Interview

The interview may be organized in a number of ways, but the most common methods are known as the funnel approach, the inverted funnel approach, the tunnel approach, and the various combinations that can be created by using two or more of these approaches in a single interview. An interviewer using the *funnel approach* begins with broad, general, open questions, becomes increasingly restrictive with narrower open questions and concludes with closed questions. This approach is suggested when the interviewer has little advance preparation or knowledge of the interviewee or the topic under discussion. The *inverted funnel approach* begins with closed questions and becomes increasingly

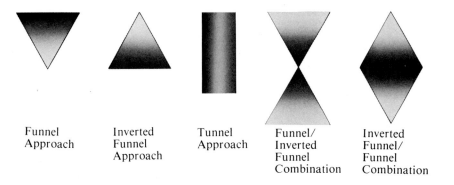

Figure 8.1   Organizational patterns of the
interview.

more general and unrestrictive as the interviewer switches to open questions. This approach is appropriate when we have a great deal of information about the interviewee and the topic. The *tunnel approach* involves the use of a set of similar questions, all of which are open or closed. It is most appropriate for the interviewer who wishes to gain information about attitudes or for the interviewer who plans on analyzing the information statistically. Combinations of these approaches are also used.

Purposes of Interviews

People engage in interviews for a variety of purposes. Among the most common reasons are to collect information, to persuade someone to buy or believe something, or to find employment. We will consider the informational interview, the persuasive interview, and the employment interview.

Informational Interviews   We enter into informational interviews when we are collecting information, opinions, or data about a specific topic.

The short excerpt that follows is a portion of an informational interview in which the interviewer is seeking information about job satisfaction at a particular company. The interview has a funnel-inverted funnel structure. It begins with an open question, switches to a series of closed questions, and concludes with the same open question with which it began. The notation in the left-hand column indicates whether each question is open (*o*) or closed (*c*), primary (*p*) or secondary (*s*), and neutral (*n*) or leading (*l*).

Interviewer: "We are conducting a study of job satisfaction at this company.
  c/p/n   We are particularly interested in why people came to work here
              originally, and why they stay for such a long time. How long
              have you been with us?"

Interviewee: "About four years, I guess."

Interviewer:	"Why did you choose this company?"
o/p/n	
Interviewee:	"Gosh, that was quite a while ago. Let me think."
Interviewer:	"Yes, it was some time ago. Who were you working for before
c/p/n	you joined us?"
Interviewee:	"Midwest Machines."
Interviewer:	"Why did you leave that company? Were you dissatisfied?"
o/p/n	
c/s/l	
Interviewee:	"It really wasn't a very pleasant place to work."
Interviewer:	"Did they offer a pension plan, a job rotation plan, training for
c/p/n	automation, a family health plan, or any other special benefits?"
Interviewee:	"No, they didn't have any of those things."
Interviewer:	"Did your wife think that you should continue to work for Mid-
c/p/n	west Machines?"
Interviewee:	"No, she was the one who suggested I try to get another job."
Interviewer:	"Did you hear about our plant through the paper or from
c/p/n	someone you knew?"
Interviewee:	"I spent a lot of time looking at the ads in the paper."
Interviewer:	"Why did you finally choose us?"
o/p/n	
Interviewee:	"It is a progressive company. It has a lot of personnel policies
	that I like. My wife is satisfied that it's the best job for me."

The importance of asking effective questions is apparent in the lines spoken by the interviewer. Because the interviewer's intention is to find out whether the employee is satisfied with the company, the questions focus specifically on why the employee may or may not be satisfied. The employee's answers are nearly all declarative, but in an informational interview, the interviewer has to be careful not to invite the desired answers. In this interview, for instance, the interviewer may be perceived by the interviewee as part of the company's management. The interviewee may know at the outset that employees are being questioned about their job satisfaction or he may get the drift of the interview by listening carefully to the questions. Reporters, government employees, survey takers, and others who interview other people regularly should realize that many interviewees will simply tell them what they think they want to hear. Is there any way that we could determine, for instance, that the employee being interviewed in the excerpt above was worried about his job and was simply giving the interviewer the answers that he thought were the "right" ones? In other words, is it possible that the interviewee interpreted as leading questions some that we coded as neutral?

Persuasive Interviews   We engage in persuasive interviews when our object is to sell a particular idea, product, or service, or when someone else is trying to sell us something.

In the short persuasive interview that follows, a person is trying to persuade

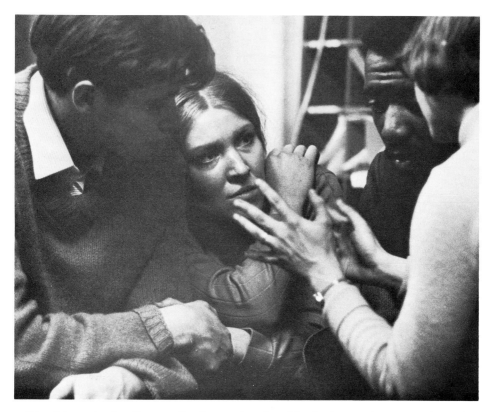

a friend to go to the theatre. Both emotional and logical appeals are used. **Notice** the tunnel organization.

Interviewer: "There's a hit comedy at the Cumberland County Playhouse.
   c/p/n   Would you like to go to see it Friday or Saturday night?"
Interviewee: "Oh, I don't know. I don't like plays too much."
Interviewer: "Tickets are $4 each, but I can get them through the Athletic
   c/p/l   Club for $3. I think you would enjoy it, don't you?"
Interviewee: "Well—what's it about?"
Interviewer: "It's a musical comedy starring Broadway actor David Holland
                 and a local performer, Gloria Baranowski. You know who Gloria
   c/p/l   is, don't you?"
Interviewee: "Yes, I know who Gloria Baranowski is. She's gotten herself
                 quite a reputation for acting."
Interviewer: "We could go out some place afterward and have a couple of
   c/p/l   drinks if you want. What do you say?"
Interviewee: "That sounds great! What time shall we go?"

    The interviewer is a skilled persuader. First, a choice of evenings is offered. Then comes an economic argument: we'll save money by buying the tickets through an organization. The play is then linked to a local celebrity. The enticement of drinks afterward clinches the sale. Notice that all the questions are closed and primary. With the exception of the first question, all are leading questions, as well. Closed and leading questions are the tools of the persuasive interviewer.

Employment Interviews   Employment interviews have the purpose of selecting people for employment and placing them in certain positions or jobs.

In the employment interview that follows, emphasis is on the background, experience, training and other interests that the applicant may have. In this situation, an application for the position has been previously submitted. The interviewer in this situation uses a tunnel approach of organization.

Interviewer: *c/p/n*	"Good morning Bob; Bob Johnson, is that correct?"
Interviewee:	"Yes, that's correct."
Interviewer: *c/p/n*	"I'm Dave Selking, employment interviewer here at the company. Come over here and have a seat. Do you smoke, Bob?"
Interviewee:	"No, thank you, I've never had the urge to start."
Interviewer:	"Well, I think you used good judgment in regard to your health and well-being, according to all recent medical reports.
c/p/n	"I see by your application that you have some college training. Are you currently enrolled?"
Interviewee:	"Yes, but only part-time now."
Interviewer: *c/s/n*	"What are you studying?"
Interviewee:	"Industrial management. I have twenty-one hours in the program."
Interviewer: *c/s/n*	"Do you enjoy this field enough to continue and complete the program?"
Interviewee:	"I enjoy the studies so far, but I met some students who are enrolled in a supervision program. I'm going into that some more because I think I would do well working with people. I'm more at ease with the human rather than the technical side of industry. And my credits would count toward a supervision degree."
Interviewer: *c/p/n*	"Have you had any experience either in technical work or in a supervisory position?"
Interviewee:	"Not really; I haven't been out of high school that long. However, I led a Boy Scout troop for five years and really enjoyed working with people. After becoming aware of the supervision courses, I feel that would suit me better."
Interviewer: *c/s/n*	"Have you had any other leadership positions?"
Interviewee:	"Not really in *leading* people, but I coach Wildcat Baseball teams every year and help to schedule the year's games."
Interviewer: *c/p/n*	"Do you enjoy working in community affairs?"
Interviewee:	"Yes, but I need a job, and that doesn't help me in getting one."

Interviewer: "It doesn't hurt your situation any, let me assure you! Our or-
               ganization, like every other industrial plant, exists in a commu-
               nity. We encourage our employees to participate and to show an
               interest in community projects."

Interviewee: "In that case, I would like to point out that I helped form and
               organize the Decatur Youth Center and helped secure the use of
               the old County Building for our activities. We canvassed for
               funds and assistance in remodeling the interior to meet our needs.
               Oh, yes, I also helped organize girls' softball three years ago. We
               had four teams then, and last summer we had sixteen full teams
               in the league with full sponsors. That took a lot of work, but it
               was rewarding. That's about all I helped to start."

Interviewer: "This has been a highly informative interview. We are not hiring
               at present, but when we do, I assure you you'll be given every
               consideration. Thank you for your time, Bob. I appreciate your
               promptness in coming in when we called you."

The interviewer in the employment interview tries to draw out as much information as possible from the applicant. Notice how the interviewer reinforces
the applicant every time he discloses additional information about his activities.
The result is that the applicant feels good about telling the interviewer even
more about his experience.

In general, the applicant should try to anticipate the questions. In this interview, the interviewer had to work to get the applicant to supply relevant leadership experience. Perhaps the interviewee was interpreting neutral questions as
leading questions and was reluctant to disclose information that might hurt his
opportunity for future employment with the company. It is essential to answer
questions as openly and fully as possible in the employment interview situation.

The Small Group Discussion

Before we define small group discussion, we need to clarify the terms we are
using. *Small* alludes to the number of participants in group discussions—generally three to twenty people, most often four to seven. The word *group* is also
used in a special way. In speech communication classes, it means a small
number of individuals who share a common interest or goal, who communicate
with each other regularly, and who all contribute to the functioning of the group.
We discount small numbers of people who do not have shared interests, do not
communicate regularly or with each other, and who do not all contribute to the
functioning of the group. In the cartoon, Momma is using the word *group* the
way most people use the word; we shall use the word more specifically in this
chapter. *Small group discussion* is defined as communication among approximately three to twenty people who share a common interest or goal, who meet
regularly, and who all contribute to the functioning of the group.

Momma

By Mell Lazarus

As small group discussion is a form of interpersonal communication, all the members have opportunities for verbal and nonverbal exchanges. The specific skills related to effective verbal and nonverbal communication in a dyad or in an interview are equally important in small group discussion. Self-awareness, self-disclosure, listening, and empathy all contribute to the success of the small group discussion.

The Function of Small Group Discussion

Small groups serve a variety of functions. They can satisfy the need that people
have to be with each other. They can provide an emotional outlet for people who
are concerned about a particular problem. Small groups allow people to meet the
need they feel to belong to something. Small groups can share information or
tackle important and difficult problems. In general, we can identify the function
of most small groups as either social or task.

Small groups that have a *social function* include lunch groups, coffee parties, beer busts, cocktail parties, family reunions, and similar gatherings. The

function of these groups is to provide time for companionship. They present an opportunity for individual interaction with a number of other people. Ritualized or ceremonial small groups, such as people at presidential teas, annual picnics, and even powwows are small social groups.

Small groups that have a *task function* include committees, church groups, community councils, task forces, book or literary clubs, parent-teacher associations, and business conferences. The task of such groups may be to share information or to solve a problem. In this chapter, we shall limit our consideration to small groups that have a task to perform.

Social, Task, or No Small Group at All?

Identify each of the groups listed below as a small social group (a group which allows people time to share pleasant companionship), a small task group (a group which has the purpose of sharing information or solving a problem), or as a group of people who do not fit our definition of a small group (approximately three to twenty people who have a shared interest or goal, who meet regularly, and who all contribute to the functioning of the group). Mark each statement with an S for a social group, a T for a task group, and an N if it does not fit the definition.

1. A group of people in an elevator. *N*
2. Weight Watchers' weekly meeting. *T*
3. A bridge group. *S*
4. A group of Elks out for a night on the town. *S*
5. The people who are riding on a city bus. *N*
6. The monthly company meeting. *T*
7. Four or five clerks in a department store who are gossiping about a new employee. *S or N*
8. The people assembled in a huge stadium to hear Billy Graham. *N*
9. A consciousness-raising group at a weekly meeting. *T*
10. A university committee meeting. *T*

The Process of Small Group Discussion: Preparation and Presentation

In the speech communication class in which you are enrolled, you will very likely be asked to present a small group discussion of an information-sharing or problem-solving nature. In order to assist you in the successful completion of this assignment, we shall describe the steps essential to the preparation and presentation of the small group discussion. Our focus is on the discussion in a problem-solving group because it incorporates the essential elements of the information-sharing group discussion and includes additional steps. The

problem-solving discussion tends to be more complex. If you are able to understand and carry out the suggestions for this form of group discussion, you should
have no difficulty adapting the suggestions to an information-sharing discussion.

Selecting a Topic   The first step in preparing for a group discussion is to select a topic. The method most often recommended is brainstorming. *Brainstorming* is a technique in which you list or name as many ideas as you can
within a stated period of time. Alex Osborn, who introduced the technique
nearly a quarter of a century ago, wrote that four rules govern brainstorming: (1)
don't criticize any ideas; (2) no idea is too wild; (3) quantity is important; and (4)
seize opportunities to improve or add to ideas suggested by others.[2]

Wording the Question to be Discussed   After you have selected a topic, the
next task is to word the question to be discussed. The wording of the question is
very important: it can lead to a fruitful or a wasted group discussion. The question clarifies the purpose of the discussion, suggests the avenues of research,
and largely determines the agenda.

    Categories of discussion questions. In general, questions to be discussed
can be placed into one of three categories. *Questions of fact* deal with truth and
falsity. They are concerned with the occurrence, the existence, or the particular
properties of something. Examples of questions of fact include, ''Does the
United States have enough water to meet normal needs?'' ''Are small amounts
of marijuana harmful to the human body?'' ''Do women have equal opportunities for employment in the United States?'' and ''Has Consolidated Edison New

York taken measures sufficient to forestall another blackout in the next five years?"

Questions of value require judgments of good and bad. Such questions are grounded in the participant's motives, beliefs, and cultural standards. Desirability and satisfaction are often central to questions of value. Examples of questions in this category are, "Is a college education desirable for everyone?" "Are older people discriminated against?" "Are beauty contests desirable?" and "Do we need to reform tax laws in the United States?"

Questions of policy concern future action. The purpose of a policy question is to determine a course of action to be taken or supported in a specific situation. The word *should* often appears in a question of policy. Examples of questions of policy include the following: "Should rules against nepotism be dropped?" "Should seniority systems be eliminated?" "Should students be required to take specific courses?" "Should the possession of small amounts of marijuana be legalized?"

Identify the Category of Each of These Questions for Discussion

Place the following questions into one of the three categories of discussion questions. Mark each question *F* for fact, *V* for value, or *P* for policy. *research – future (should)*

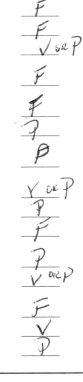

1. Does Laetrile cure cancer?   *F*
2. Is the U.S. facing a drought?   *F*
3. Should pornography be prohibited?   *V or P*
4. Do X-rays of the head or neck cause cancer of the thyroid gland?   *F*
5. Is a person's social standing directly related to his or her wealth? *F*
6. Should we spend less money on weapons?   *P*
7. Should employees determine their own work schedules?   *P*
8. Should women retain their unmarried names when they marry?   *V or P*
9. Should military academies be coeducational?   *P*
10. Does regular exercise lengthen your life?   *F*
11. Should the federal government regulate the use of energy?   *P*
12. Should everyone have the right to get married?   *V or P*
13. Does unemployment fall disproportionately on the young?   *F*
14. Are abortion laws too liberal?   *V*
15. Should right-to-work laws be repealed?   *P*

Characteristics of good discussion questions. All discussion questions should meet a minimum set of standards. Among the characteristics of good discussion questions—whether they are questions of fact, value, or policy—are that they should be simple, objective, and controversial. By *simple,* we mean that the question should be written with the fewest number of words, easily understood. The question should be understandable to all who read or hear it. The questions should be concise, not wordy. In addition, the question should be appropriate for the time available, the research available, and the persons who will be discussants. A question for discussion, "Do most people anticipate the advent of androgyny vis-à-vis the economic structure?" does not meet the criterion of simplicity. This question is lengthy, esoteric and obtuse.

A discussion question should be written objectively. It should not imply "correct" answers. Persons reading the question should be able to suggest alternative answers. The question, "Should the current national tax structure, which favors the rich and discriminates against the poor, be changed?" does not meet the criterion of objectivity. The only possible answer to this leading question is "Yes."

The discussion question should be controversial. It should not be a question the answer to which has already been determined. Nor should it concern a matter for which the group has an agreed-upon solution. The question should be timely—of current international, national, or local concern; interesting to the group members; and worthwhile to those involved. The questions that follow are not suitable. "Should the E.R.A. be passed?" is out of date for many Americans. "Should homosexuals be allowed to marry?" may be irrelevant to the members of a particular discussion group. "Should students be given more course selection in their higher education?" would probably receive a unanimous "yes" from a group of college students.

Researching the Topic   After you have identified the topic of your discussion and worded the question, the next task is to research the topic. You must *discover the information,* and then you must *evaluate it.* Among the sources that you should consider for securing information are (1) interviews with people close to the problem, (2) surveys of the people involved, and (3) secondary sources available in the library. Interviewing was discussed earlier in this chapter. Surveys and library research are discussed in chapter 11; read ahead to familiarize yourself with them. You may choose one or more avenues of research. The nature of your question will dictate the kind of research that is necessary.

It is equally important, in research, to evaluate the information you find. Too often, we assume that simply collecting information concludes the research task. An abundance of unevaluated information may be worthless.

Evaluating Primary Research   We evaluate *primary research*—interviews, surveys, and personal experience—differently from *secondary research*—infor-

mation we find in books, magazines, and similar sources. Three questions should be asked about our primary research: (1) Are eyewitness accounts confirmed? (2) Is the authority competent? (3) Is the source unbiased?

Are eyewitness accounts confirmed? In chapter 2 we discussed the role of perception in communication. We stated that people can observe the same phenomena but have greatly divergent perceptions and draw entirely different conclusions. Consensual validation—checking our observations with others—was suggested as a remedy. When we engage in primary research, we should validate the perceptions of one person with the perceptions of others.

Is the authority competent? In other words, is the person a recognized expert? Do others agree that he or she is knowledgeable and experienced about the question under consideration? We should keep in mind that people can be experts in one area, but may know little about other areas. The football player who testifies to the quality of women's clothing may be out of his league.

Is the source unbiased? Sometimes people have a vested interest in a particular point of view. They may realize some real or intangible gain if others can be convinced to see things in a certain way. For instance, a speech teacher would very likely believe that speech should be a required course. Experts in college administration or alumni would be better sources because they are less likely to be biased.

PRINTED

Evaluating Secondary Research   A different set of questions should be
asked if we are evaluating *secondary research*—information from books, magazines, and similar sources. Among them are (1) Is the information consistent? (2)
Is the information current? (3) Is the information complete?

Is the information consistent? Two types of consistency are important in
evaluating secondary research. Is the information internally consistent? Does
the author suggest two or more conflicting conclusions? Do the conclusions
follow logically from the material reviewed? Second, is the information consistent with other sources? Does it agree with other findings? Are there startling
conclusions that violate previously known facts? Differences between one author's point of view and another's do not render the information inaccurate or
the conclusion false, but you must consider why the disagreement exists.

Is the information current? The publication date of a source may be unimportant or crucial. In some cases, the date can resolve conflicts of evidence.

Is the information complete? The reference should be complete in two
senses. The source should not take information from other sources out of context or report someone else's work only partially, in order to make a point. The
reference work should be an examination of the entire problem or area under
consideration, rather than a tangential view. In other words, the secondary
source should include the comprehensive statement or conclusion offered by
another and should cover all of the ground that is promised.

Respectable

Organizing the Discussion   For many years, John Dewey's method of reflective thinking was considered the only way to organize a group discussion.
Discussants followed this organizational plan:

1. *Recognize the problem.* Acknowledge that a problem exists and that the group members
   are concerned about that specific problem.
2. *Define the problem.* Identify the nature of the problem and define the critical terms.
3. *Analyze the problem.* Suggest the cause of the problem, the extensiveness of the
   problem, and the limits of the problem.
4. *Establish criteria for evaluating solutions.* Decide by which criteria a solution will be
   evaluated. The group determines if the solution must solve the problem entirely or
   whether a partial solution will be acceptable. It decides whether the efficiency of the
   solution is an important criterion, and makes other similar decisions.
5. *Suggest solutions to the problem.* By brainstorming or other techniques, the group lists
   possible solutions to the problem.
6. *Select the best solution.* After many solutions have been offered, group members
   subject them to the previously established criteria (Step 4). They select those solutions
   that best fit the criteria. They consider combining two or more possible solutions.
   Finally, they identify the best solution.
7. *Test the solution.* The final step in the Dewey method of reflective thinking is testing the
   solution, which is often done by trying out the solution in practice. Decisions can then
   be made about the effectiveness of the solution.

More recently, authors have suggested that a strict adherence to this organizational pattern results in planned performances rather than decision-making processes. These authors have demonstrated that many questions are not susceptible to solution by Dewey's method of reflective thinking. However, you may find Dewey's method helpful in arranging your problem-solving discussion.

A number of alternative organizational patterns have been created for the use of small groups. Most of them include the following stages:

1. Identifying and specifying a particular question.
2. Collecting and analyzing relevant information.
3. Determining the strengths and weaknesses of various answers to the question.
4. Selecting the most appropriate answer.
5. Testing the answer.

At base, all problem-solving discussions must include two questions: (1) What is the nature of the problem? and (2) How can we solve it? Subsidiary questions can be added to this most simple organizational pattern to meet the group's needs.

A group may find that the problem it is considering requires a very loosely structured pattern. Or group members may find that they require a very prescriptive pattern of organization. The appropriate organizational pattern will depend on the nature and composition of the group as well as on the nature of the problem. Regardless of what specific organizational pattern seems appropriate, it is essential that the discussion be organized.

Leadership   In the past, this section on preparing for group discussion might have been entitled "Choosing a Leader." Earlier writers and researchers stressed the importance of identifying one person who would serve as the leader of the group rather than considering leadership as a process in which the entire group engages. *Leadership* is defined as behavior that aids in the clarification and achievement of group goals. Leadership is synonymous with influence. A *leader*, then, may be defined as an influential person, one who helps the group to

ANIMAL CRACKERS

clarify and attain its goals, or else as one who is selected or designated as the leader of a particular group. Leadership is generally shared by the members of a group; often, more than one person acts as the leader, depending on the definition that is used.

A number of qualities are associated with effective leaders of group discussion. Among these characteristics are the following:

1. An ability to communicate clearly and effectively.
2. An ability to listen for the content and the intent of the other group members' comments.
3. An ability to think quickly—to follow closely what is being said and to think ahead of the group.
4. Knowledgeability about the topic under discussion.
5. Knowledgeability of group process.

In a group discussion, the ideal situation is to have a number of people who can perform leadership functions and who are able and willing to share leadership. In addition, it is also important to identify one person as the chosen or designated leader. This person generally exhibits a number of leadership qualities, but also performs a number of procedural functions. Brilhart suggests five general functions that designated discussion leaders should serve. They include:

1. *Guiding.* The designated leader initiates the discussion, keeps the discussion orderly and organized, and encourages participation by all members.
2. *Stimulating both creative and critical thinking.*
3. *Promoting clear communication.*
4. *Promoting cooperative interpersonal relations.*
5. *Helping the group and its members to develop.*[3]

The leadership of a small group discussion is generally shared, but the designated leader has the responsibility of ensuring that all the leadership functions are performed. Effective leadership is essential to successful problem solving in small group discussion.

ANIMAL CRACKERS

Summary

In this chapter we explored two forms of interpersonal communication: the interview and the small group discussion. We stated that interviews generally have a specific purpose, and that they are planned and organized. Interviews are more formal than conversations and less formal than most small group discussions and public speaking. Interviews generally involve questions and are usually limited to two people. The questions can be categorized as open or closed, primary or secondary, and neutral or leading. A variety of approaches can be used in organizing the interview, including the funnel approach, the inverted funnel approach, the tunnel approach, a combination of the funnel and inverted funnel, and a combination of the inverted funnel and funnel. Among the reasons people engage in interviews are to collect information, to find employment, and to persuade.

We defined a small group as consisting of about three to twenty people who share a common interest or goal, who meet regularly, and who all contribute to the functioning of the group. Small groups serve a variety of functions, but most functions can be classified as social, which means that the group's purpose is to share time with agreeable companions, or task, which means that the group has the purpose of sharing information or solving a problem.

We considered the preparation and presentation of the problem-solving small group discussion in detail. Essential steps in problem solving include selecting a topic, wording the question to be discussed, researching the topic, organizing the discussion, and agreeing about leadership and selecting a leader. The success of both the interview and the small group discussion depends on the ability of the participants to communicate with each other effectively.

New Terms

Interviewing	Persuasive interview	Secondary research
Dyadic communication	Employment interview	Dewey's method of reflective thinking
Open question	Small group discussion	Problem-solving discussion
Closed question	Group	
Primary question	Small	Leadership
Secondary question	Social function	Leader
Neutral question	Task function	Designated leader
Leading question	Brainstorming	Leadership functions
Funnel approach	Fact question	Leadership characteristics
Inverted funnel approach	Value question	
Tunnel approach	Policy question	
Informational interview	Primary research	

Additional Readings

Beach, Dale S. *Personnel: The
Management of People at Work.* 3d ed.
New York: Macmillan Publishing Co.,
Inc., 1975. Pages 273–87.
*Beach outlines the purposes and
problems of the employment interview
from the perspective of the employer.
Good suggestions for planning the
interview and communicating with the
interviewee for best results.*

Bormann, Ernest G., and Bormann,
Nancy C. *Effective Small Group
Communication.* 2d ed. Minneapolis:
Burgess Publishing Company, 1976.
*A practical approach to learning the
skills of effective small group
communication, including task,
leadership, message preparation,
research, and discussion techniques.
Understandable, good introductory
reading.*

Brilhart, John K. *Effective Group
Discussion.* 3d ed. Dubuque, Iowa: Wm.
C. Brown Company Publishers, 1978.
*A practical approach to researching,
organizing, and discussing problems in a
small group. Contains specific
guidelines for improving discussion and
leadership skills.*

*Cathcart, Robert S., and Samovar, Larry
A. *Small Group Communication: A
Reader.* 3d ed. Dubuque, Iowa: Wm. C.
Brown Company Publishers, 1978.
*An excellent collection of the important
writings on small group behavior,
including a discussion of models,
interpersonal dynamics, leadership,
conformity, and group decision making.
Excellent source of material for term
papers or in-depth study of small group
processes.*

*Davis, James H., *Group Performance.*
Reading, Mass.: Addison-Wesley
Publishing Company, 1969.
*A report on the research into individual
performance in groups, the influence of
social interaction on decision making,
group size, cohesiveness, and structure.
Becomes a bit technical at times.*

*Shaw, Marvin E. *Group Dynamics: The
Psychology of Small Group Behavior.*
New York: McGraw-Hill Book
Company, 1971.
*A classic treatment of the variables
affecting small group processes.
Especially good chapters on group
formation, leadership, and interpersonal
dynamics as they affect the group's
ability to complete a task and make
decisions.*

Stewart, Charles J., and Cash, William B.
Interviewing: Principles and Practices.
2d ed. Dubuque, Iowa: Wm. C. Brown
Company Publishers, 1978.
*A discussion of informative, persuasive,
employment, appraisal, and counseling
interviews, with insightful examples of
each type. The principles of effective
communication in the interview context
and the writing and organizing of
questions for the interview are also
covered.*

Thomas, Coramae, and Howard, C.
Jeriel. *Contact: A Textbook in Applied
Communications.* Englewood Cliffs,
N.J.: Prentice-Hall, Inc., 1970. Pages 38
–48.
*The authors answer common questions
about an employment interview: what to
wear, what information to give, how to
prepare for the interview, and how to
behave verbally and nonverbally to make
the best impression.*

Zelko, Harold P., and Dance, Frank E.
X. *Business and Professional Speech
Communication.* New York: Holt,
Rinehart and Winston, Inc., 1965. Pages
142–59.
*A concise and helpful description of the
procedures for conducting a successful
interview. Step-by-step advice on setting
up the interview, planning the questions,
and conducting, recording, and closing
the interview.*

*Indicates more advanced readings.

Notes

1. Charles J. Stewart and William B. Cash, *Interviewing: Principles and Practices,* 2d ed. (Dubuque, Iowa: Wm. C. Brown Company Publishers, 1978), pp. 5–6.

2. Alex F. Osborn, *Applied Imagination: Principles and Procedures of Creative Thinking* (New York: Charles Scribner's Sons, 1953), pp. 300–301.

3. John K. Brilhart, *Effective Group Discussion,* 3d ed. (Dubuque, Iowa: Wm. C. Brown Company Publishers, 1978), pp. 170–82.

Public Communication

Public communication is the process of understanding and sharing that occurs in the speaker-to-audience situation. Public communication, like interpersonal communication, is a transaction in which people simultaneously give and receive meaning from each other.

Our exploration of public communication begins with the audience. Chapter 9, "Understanding Your Audience," reveals how to analyze an audience for information of value to the speaker. Chapter 10, "Sharing Yourself: Source Credibility," focuses on the speaker and answers the questions: what is credibility, what can a speaker do to enhance it, and what other aspects of the communication are affected by it? Will credibility, for example, help your audience to learn more? Will it help change attitudes or opinions?

Chapter 11, "Understanding Through Topics, Research, and Evidence," is a practical consideration of selecting a topic, doing research, and evaluating evidence. Chapter 12, "Sharing Your Message Through Organization," is a survey of the various patterns of organization for a public speech. "Sharing Yourself Through Delivery," chapter 13, is a discussion of the vocal and bodily aspects of speaking in public—including voice, eye contact, gestures, and movement. Chapter 14 is a study of the informative speech, containing practical advice for developing this type of speech. The last chapter, 15, is a study of the persuasive speech that describes strategies for altering the audience's attitudes and behavior.

9

Understanding Your Audience

Objectives

After study of this chapter you should be able to do the following:

1. Discuss the importance of learning public speaking skills; list opportunities you have already had to give a speech and describe situations that may require you to speak in public in the future

2. Discuss the importance of audience analysis to effective public speaking

3. Differentiate between captive and voluntary audiences and give examples of each

4. Identify the kinds of information available from a demographic analysis and ways of acquiring that information

5. Explain the importance of ascertaining the audience's interest in and knowledge of a topic, and describe ways of gathering that information

6. Differentiate among attitudes, values, and beliefs and describe ways of measuring them

7. Differentiate among observation, inference, and questionnaires as ways to analyze an audience; discuss the uses and limitations of each

8. Suggest ways in which you can adapt yourself and your message to an audience. Base your answer on your audience analysis

9. Speak on a specific topic; name the topic and analyze your classroom audience to predict its response

*"That's not me. I wouldn't want to stand up in front of twenty people and give a
speech."*

*"It's not so hard to deliver a speech after you've learned how to prepare one
and after you've given a few."*

*"That speech class was one of the best courses I took in college. I think
everyone should take it."*

Few students want to deliver a speech. At first, speaking before an audience
seems like one of the most difficult assignments a college student is asked to
complete. In schools where a speech course is required, students in large numbers skillfully avoid the course for years in the vain hope that it will go away.
Most students, however, seem to develop through the steps indicated in the quotations cited above. They gradually learn to like public speaking.

"That's not me." The words remind us of our earlier study of self-concept.
Many students cannot see themselves delivering a speech. They have difficulty
visualizing the situation and have a hard time imagining themselves giving a
speech. If you feel that way about public speaking, you are probably normal.
One study indicated that the Number One fear, the most widespread fear in our
country, is the fear of speaking in public.[1]

If speaking in public is so frightening, why do so many people learn how to
do it? At first, you may be encouraged to develop public speaking skills because
someone else wants you to learn them. Groups to which many adolescents belong, such as 4-H, FFA, Junior Achievement, and citizenship and sales groups,
encourage their members to cultivate public speaking. After an initial exposure
to public speaking in school or in organizations, you might learn to deliver
speeches because other people want to hear your ideas.

Successful people are public speakers. The successful athlete speaks at
sports banquets, the successful business person at luncheons, the successful
student at graduation, the successful scholar at professional meetings, and the
successful salesperson at sales meetings. As students you are asked to speak in
public about class reports or projects. As a responsible adult, you may be asked
to deliver speeches to inspire, entertain, inform, or persuade other people because you are educated, knowledgeable, or articulate.

You may learn how to prepare and deliver public speeches because there is
a demand in our society for people with that ability. A recent large-scale study
of the business community showed that one of the greatest needs of American
business and industry is employees who can express themselves well orally and
in writing, for people who can communicate with others, for people who can
employ language skillfully, accurately, and correctly.[2]

Perhaps even now you may think that you will never deliver a speech outside the classroom. You might think that because you do not plan to be a teacher, a minister, a lawyer, or a business person, you will never need to deliver a speech. But even more ordinary people are often pressed to give public speeches. The school board is going to start a new program with which you disagree; the zoning commission is going to permit a factory to be built on your block; your co-workers are lagging behind in production; your religious views are so important that you wish to share them; or your college is going to raise its tuition fees again. Your position on these issues will not be heard unless you speak out. These and many other circumstances lead us to communicate with others by speaking in public.

You may discover, after delivering a few speeches, that the experience is unworthy of being called "the most widespread fear in our country." Indeed, many students would admit that there is some pleasure in having the attention of twenty or more people at once. Students who have taken a course including public speaking are often among the first to insist that others share the same experience. At Iowa State University, the students majoring in business were asked, several years after graduation, which courses they found most useful in their everyday life. They did not rank the business courses first: they said that courses in speech and English, in oral and written communication, were of most importance to them.[3]

The remaining chapters of this book are intended to help you learn how to prepare, deliver, and evaluate speeches. The audience, the receiver of your message, is of first concern. In subsequent chapters, we shall talk about selecting a topic, choosing materials to support your argument, and the organization and delivery of speeches. In this chapter on audience analysis, you learn about the levels of audience analysis, about the methods of audience analysis, and about how to adapt yourself, your topic, your supporting materials, your verbal and nonverbal codes, and your style of delivery to an audience.

Four Levels of Audience Analysis

Creating a speech for an audience is similar to the situation faced by auto producers when creating cars for the American public. Automobile companies, especially their designers and engineers, may have their own ideas about what kinds of cars the public needs, just as speakers feel that they know what their audiences should hear. But both the auto producer and the public speaker are limited, by practical constraints, in what they can present. The auto producer's creation can be limited by the amount and cost of materials; the speech by what the speaker knows or can learn about the topic. Both the speaker and the auto producer also have to create something that the public wants, needs, or is willing to accept.

The engineers and designers have to ask: Will the public buy small, gas-conserving models this year? Or do they want flashy designs with vivid colors and racing stripes? The speaker has to find out: Does the audience need more information about this subject? Are they ready to accept the changes I shall propose? The key to success for both the auto producer and the speaker lies in effective audience analysis. But audience analysis is a combination of art and science. Automakers still occasionally produce cars that do not sell, and speakers still occasionally deliver speeches that their audiences will not accept. Nonetheless, audience analysis tends to reduce errors and promote effectiveness.

To begin our study of audience analysis, we will survey four levels of audience analysis. The categories are called *levels* because the first is relatively easy and the last is the most difficult to understand and to use. In that sense, the levels are like grade levels in school; the ideas and concepts increase in difficulty. The four levels begin with the distinction between voluntary and captive audiences.

Level 1: Captive and Voluntary Audiences

A *captive* audience, as the name suggests, is an audience that cannot get away, an audience that did not choose to hear a particular speaker or speech. It might look like the audience in the drawing on page 176. The teacher of a required class addresses a captive audience. A disc jockey who broadcasts commercial announcements between the songs that you want to hear addresses a captive audience. The administrator who speaks at a mandatory orientation session, the preacher who addresses a mandatory chapel, the student who addresses fellow students in a required speech class are all addressing captive audiences.

Why should a public speaker distinguish a captive from a voluntary audience? One reason is that a captive audience did not choose to hear from you or about your subject—you may have to motivate it to listen. Another is that captive audiences are characterized by their heterogeneity, by the wide variety of differences among the individuals. This means that the speaker must adapt the topic and the content of the speech to a wider range of information and to more disparate attitudes toward the subject. One of the advantages of a captive audience is that it gives the speaker an opportunity to present ideas to people who, under ordinary circumstances, might never have heard the information or the point of view embodied in the speech.

The voluntary audience chooses to hear the particular speaker or speech. The most important characteristic of the voluntary audience is that the partici-

Figure 9.1

pants have some need or desire to hear the speech. The people who go to listen
to a politician are usually sympathetic to the speaker's politics. The students
who stop to hear a traveling evangelist speak on the campus lawn are usually
curious about, or perhaps even committed to, the speaker's religious beliefs.
The advantage is that the speaker addresses an audience that is more homoge-
neous. To return for a moment to the automaker: addressing a captive audience
is like attempting to attract new customers to the product; addressing a voluntary audience is like attempting to please customers who have purchased the
product before. Both automaker and speaker are helped by knowing whether the
audience is voluntary or captive, because the nature of the audience affects the
topic, the rationale, the approach, and the goal.

The task of determining the character of an audience is far from simple. A
specific example can demonstrate its complexity. At first, you might guess that a
congregation is a voluntary audience: people chose to attend that particular
church to hear that particular minister. But what about the children in the congregation? Did they choose to hear the sermon or did their parents make them
go to church? What about some of the husbands and wives? How many people
are there because their spouses wanted them to come along? To what extent did

social pressures persuade them to attend church? Did they really know what the minister was going to say, or are they captives of the message that he is delivering? Even this first level of audience analysis is more challenging than it appears. The minister of a congregation addresses an audience that is in some ways voluntary and in some ways captive and must adapt the message to those differences.

How can you, in your speech class, make the distinction between the voluntary and the captive audience? You may find that your audience is more captive than voluntary: the members of the audience did not enroll in the class to hear you or your speech. On the other hand, they are there to learn how to give and listen to speeches. You may have to adapt to your student audience by insuring that they know why *you* are speaking to *them* about *this* particular subject. You will actually find yourself more dependent than most speakers on the other kinds of audience analysis covered in this chapter. Most public speakers work with voluntary audiences. They know, from experience and investigation, what their audience wants to hear and what they can do. You will probably have to learn about your audience through the methods suggested in this chapter.

Can you tell the difference between a
captive and a voluntary audience?
Categorize the following audiences:

		Captive	Voluntary
1. A cub scout troop hearing a presentation on artificial respiration		captive	
2. You in your freshman English class		captive	
3. A book club hearing a speech by an author			voluntary
4. A modern-dance class learning how to dance		captive	
5. Small boys in junior choir			voluntary
6. Students at a pep rally			voluntary

Level 2: Demographic Analysis

Demographics literally means "the characteristics of the people." This method of analysis is based on the kind of characteristics that used to be put on forms: name, age, sex, home town, year in school, race, major subject, religion, and organizational affiliations. Such information can be important to public speakers because it can reveal the extent to which they will have to adapt themselves and their topics to that audience. A closer examination of just one factor might dem-

Figure 9.2

onstrate the importance of information about the audience. Let us see what the effect might be of the major subject that people in your audience have elected.

Suppose you plan to speak about the cost of littering in your state. Your audience consists of twenty-two students: seven have not chosen a major subject; three are mathematics majors; four are biology majors; six are majoring in business administration; and one is an English major. This information gives you no reason to assume that any of them knows much about littering, but you can assume that from nine to thirteen have a basic understanding of numbers. The six business majors may have a better understanding of costs than the others, and the students majoring in math and science may find the cost-benefit approach attractive as well. If you add to that small bit of information more demographic information, then you can find even more to guide you: Does your college attract students who are likely to be concerned about the expense of

littering? Is your audience likely to be knowledgeable about rural or urban littering? Do any students in your audience belong to organizations concerned
about conservation? Whatever your topic, the demographic characteristics of
your audience can imply its receptiveness to your speech.

Public speakers usually rely heavily on demographic information. Politicians send personnel ahead to find out how many blue-collar workers, faithful
party members, elderly people, union members, and hecklers they are likely to
encounter. They consult opinion polls, population studies, and reliable persons
in the area to discover the nature of a prospective audience. Demographic analysis of your own class can serve a similar purpose: it will help you to design a
speech that is better adapted to your audience.

Level 3: Audience Interest in and Knowledge of the Topic

As you advance up the levels of audience analysis, the information you are
asked to discover becomes increasingly difficult to find. On Level 3, your task is
to find out the degree of the audience's interest in your topic and its knowledge
of the topic. Another way to ask the same question about interest and knowl-

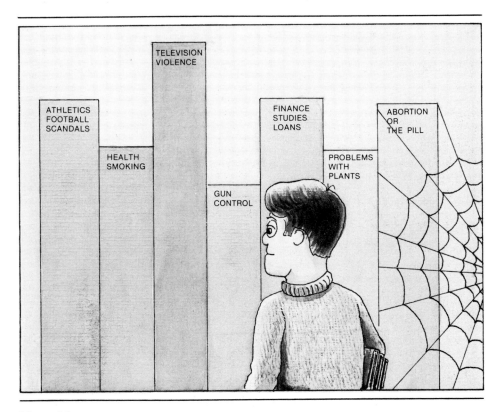

Figure 9.3

edge is "How familiar is your audience with the topic?" The question is important because, if your audience is uninterested or unfamiliar with your topic, you will have to generate that interest in your presentation.

One means of assessing an audience's interest in and knowledge of a topic is to consider the age of the topic. Age and familiarity are closely related because the longer a topic has been around, and the more recently it has gained importance, the more likely the audience is to have been exposed to it. Your classmates may know a great deal about a topic that has been a burning issue in the student newspaper, but they may not know about nuclear fusion, power satellites, or the latest fashions. A topic that is old to a middle-aged person can be new to a nineteen-year-old student. Addressing classmates of mixed ages, you would have to adapt to those persons who are familiar with the topic and to those who are not. Fortunately, old topics have new variations. Topics, like people, live, change, and die: some have long and varied lives; others pass quickly.

How can you gauge the audience's interest in and knowledge of your topic? One way to find out is to ask. You can ask demographic questions to help you assess audience interest in your topic. The audience members' ages, majors, year in school, and organizational commitments can suggest their familiarity with, knowledge of, and interest in your topic. Ask your fellow students before and after classes, in the hallways and in the cafeteria. Ask them in writing, through a questionnaire, if your teacher encourages that kind of research. You can even ask for some indication of interest during your speech, by asking your classmates to raise their hands in response to your questions.

Speech Topics

Consider with your teacher and your
classmates the appropriateness of some of
these subjects. The answers you receive
will tell you a lot about your classmates'
attitudes.

gun control *4*   sexual mores *3*   *NO*
birth control *2*   value of a college education *4*   swear words *GOOD*
abortion *3*   marriage *1*   street language
weapons *5*   divorce *3*   gambling *OK*
secret societies *1*   oil prices *5*   equal rights *NO GOOD*
                                                             GOOD.
                                                             gay liberation

Level 4: The Audience's Attitudes, Beliefs, and Values

An *attitude* is a predisposition to respond favorably or unfavorably to some person, object, idea, or event. The attitudes of members of an audience can be as-
sessed through questionnaires, by careful observation, or even by asking the
right questions. If your audience comes from a geographical area where many
attitudes, beliefs, and values are shared, you may have an easy task analyzing
that audience. A speech about birth control would be heard in some colleges
with as much excitement as one on snails, but at other colleges the same speech
could be grounds for dismissal. Attitudes toward politics, sex, religion, war, and
even work vary in different geographical areas and subgroups. Regardless of the
purpose of your speech, your audience's attitude will make a difference in the
appropriateness of your topic.

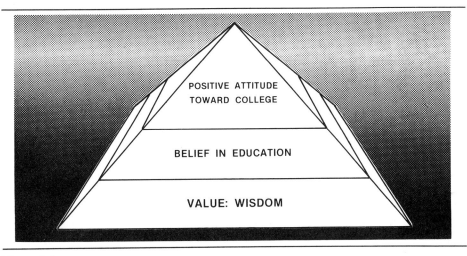

Figure 9.4

A *belief* is a conviction. Beliefs, or convictions, are usually considered more solid than attitudes, but our attitudes often spring from our beliefs. Your belief in good eating habits may lead to a negative attitude toward overeating and obesity and to a positive attitude toward balanced meals and nutrition. Your audience's beliefs make a difference in how they respond to your speech. They may believe in upward mobility through higher education, in higher pay through hard work, in the superiority of the family farm, in a lower tax base, or in social welfare. Or they may not believe any of these ideas. Beliefs are like anchors to which our attitudes are attached. To discover them we need to be inquisitive and we need to be astute observers.

Values are the deeply rooted beliefs that govern our attitudes. Our beliefs and attitudes can usually be traced to some value that we hold, sometimes unconsciously. Freedom, equality, and justice are values to many people; so are chastity, honesty, and courage. To know whether an attitude or belief is a value, you must know how it functions in a person's life. A value is an end, not a means. Money can be a means or an end: it can be regarded as something that we need to secure other things (a means) or it can be something we need to acquire for its own sake (an end). If money is a means, it is just something that we have a positive attitude toward; if it is an end, then it is one of our values.[4]

When people are asked to list their values in order of importance, they come up with surprisingly different lists. One researcher asked three groups of people to rank a list of values that included freedom and equality. One group consisted of people who had participated in political demonstrations; the second group was sympathetic to demonstrations; and the third group was unsympathetic to demonstrations. The figures below indicate how these three groups of people ranked freedom and equality.[5]

Value	Group 1 Participants	Group 2 Sympathetic	Group 3 Unsympathetic
Freedom	1	1	2
Equality	3	6	11

The people in Group 1, who had been participants in the demonstrations, ranked freedom first among the values listed; their sympathizers ranked it first as well; and the unsympathetic ranked it second. All three groups ranked freedom high. But the demonstrators ranked equality third, their sympathizers sixth, and the unsympathetic group eleventh. The more unsympathetic the groups were toward demonstrations, the less they valued equality.

To gain some idea of how values affect public speeches, rank the values in the exercise below. The values esteemed by your audience and the order in which it ranks them can provide valuable clues about their attitudes and beliefs. The speaker who addresses an audience without knowing its values is taking a risk that can be avoided by careful audience analysis.

Ranking Values

Rank these values yourself, in their order of importance to you.

If you can persuade some of your classmates, or the entire class, to do this as well, you will have information that will help you prepare your speech.[6]

Wisdom 5	Freedom 1	Wealth 8	Security 4
A comfortable life	Maturity 2	Leisure 7	Fulfillment 3
A world at peace	Equality 6		

How does your ranking compare to your classmates'? What other values might help you with your speech?

Three Methods of Audience Analysis

Method 1: Observation

Effective public speakers are often astute observers. An effective lawyer selects his or her audience by questioning prospective jurors. The lawyer asks questions that are designed to discover prejudice, negative and positive attitudes, beliefs and values. Later, as the witnesses testify, the lawyer observes their verbal and nonverbal behavior and calculates which arguments, which evidence, and which witnesses are affecting the jurors. Evangelists know, from their many addresses, which Bible verses, which stories, and which testimonials will bring sinners to the altar. People who speak on behalf of business associations, unions, political parties, colleges, and the underprivileged have usually spent years watching others and learning which approaches, arguments, and evidence are most likely to be accepted by an audience.

You can learn to do the same thing in your speech class. For every speech that you give, you might listen to twenty or twenty-five. You have a unique opportunity to discover what your classmates respond to. Do they respond well to speakers who come on strong and authoritatively, or to speakers who talk to them like equals? Do your classmates like or dislike numbers and statistics? Do they like speeches about work, leisure, getting ahead, or getting the most out of their education? Do they respond well to anecdotes and examples, graphs and posters, pictures and slides? Do they like a speaker to argue vehemently and forcefully, or do they dislike speeches that stir them up? As a listener in the classroom, you have a unique opportunity to observe your own and your class-mates' reactions and responses to a variety of speakers.

You can also observe some demographic characteristics of the audience: age, sex, race, group affiliations (athletic jackets, fraternity pins). You can see how it responds to a speaker who keeps his eyes on the audience and how it re-sponds to one who depends heavily on notes. You can observe whether you and the audience respond favorably when the speaker is deeply involved in the speech. Every speech you hear will, in some way, indicate the speaker's atti-tudes, beliefs, and values, and the response of the audience.

Even though your audience of fellow students may be more captive than most, you have an advantage over most public speakers. How many public speakers have an opportunity to hear every one of their listeners give a speech? Instead of sitting back like a passive observer when you are a member of the audience, take advantage of the situation by listening actively, by taking notes about the speaker's characteristics, and by recording the audience's responses. You can analyze your audience continually during a round of speeches, by careful observation.

Method 2: Inference

To draw an inference is to make a tentative conclusion based on some evidence, as the woman in the "B.C." cartoon does. We draw an inference when we see someone dressed in rags and we tentatively conclude that the person is poor. Our inferences are often accurate: we infer from his wedding band that a man is married, from the children tugging at his sleeve that he is a father, and from the woman holding his arm that she is his wife. We are basing these inferences on

thin data, but they are probably correct. You can base inferences on observed characteristics in your audience, on demographic information, and on question-naires.

Inferences may be true, accurate, or reliable, but they may also be untrue, inaccurate, or unreliable. The more evidence on which you base an inference, the more likely it is to be correct. You can draw inferences either indirectly or directly. An indirect way to draw inferences is by observation. For instance, you might be in a school where male students do not hold hands with female students (an observation). You infer that public displays of affection are discouraged by administrative edict, by custom, or by the students' own preference. You might also infer, from your limited data, that the prevailing attitudes militate against public disclosure of sexual mores, dating, courtship, and divorce.

A more direct way to gather data on which to base inferences is to ask questions of your classmates. You could ask them, either orally or in writing: How many students in the class have part or full-time jobs? How many are married, have families, have grown children? How many plan to become wealthy? How many were raised in urban or rural settings? How many have strong religious ties? The answers to these questions provide valuable information about your audience.

To illustrate how this method works, let us examine one question, one answer, and some inferences that could be drawn from the information. The question is: How many students have full or part-time jobs? The answer is that two-thirds, thirteen out of twenty students, are employed. The inferences that can be drawn from this data include: the students are probably older than the usual eighteen to twenty-one-year-olds who attend college; the students' or their parents' income is insufficient to allow them to attend school full time; the students are very ambitious or intelligent and can handle both jobs and classwork.

How can the inferences help you in preparing your speech? If the best-supported inference is that your classmates cannot afford to go to school full-time, then certain topics, lines of argument, examples, and approaches will be more attractive to them than others. Speeches on how to save money and how to manage time would probably be welcomed by this audience. On the other hand, speeches on yachting, owning your own racing horse, or taking a cruise might get you hooted out of the room.

Method 3: The Questionnaire

A more formal way to collect data on which you can base inferences is to ask your audience to fill out a questionnaire that you or others have developed. Demographic and attitudinal questions yield important information. A questionnaire can ask questions that require only that the people being questioned select the correct answer. This method of data collection makes it relatively easy to summarize the information. The questions would look like this:

_____ 1. I am *(a)* a freshman
               (b) a sophomore
               (c) a junior
               (d) a senior

_____ 2. I am *(a)* under 18
               (b) 18–19 years old
               (c) 20–21 years old
               (d) over 22

_____ 3. I am *(a)* single
               (b) married
               (c) divorced
               (d) separated

_____ 4. I have *(a)* no children
                 (b) one child
                 (c) two children
                 (d) more than two
                     children

The audience members do not have to identify themselves by name to provide this information. Keeping them anonymous (no blank for the name) encourages honest answers and does not reduce the value of the information.

The second kind of information, based on attitudinal questions, can be collected in at least two ways. One way is to ask questions that place audience members in identifiable groups, as these questions do:

_____ 5. I *(a)* am active in campus organizations
             (b) am not

_____ 6. I see myself as *(a)* conservative
                       (b) liberal
                       (c) independent

_____ 7. I see myself as *(a)* strongly religious
                       (b) moderately religious
                       (c) unreligious

A second method of gaining attitudinal information is to ask questions that assess people's values by asking them to rank values such as hard work; higher education; high pay; security. The answers that people give when they rank values can suggest additional information about their attitudes and beliefs.

Finally, to assess your audience's attitudes toward specific issues, you can list word-concepts that reveal attitudes. One way is to list the concepts along with an attitudinal scale like the one below:

Indicate, next to each word or phrase, your attitude toward it by writing in the appropriate number: (1) strongly favor; (2) mildly favor; (3) neutral; (4) mildly disfavor; or (5) strongly disfavor.

_3_	a.	Police	_N_	f.	Government controls	_3_	j.	Military
_3_	b.	Born-again Christians	_2_	g.	Professors	_5_	k.	Marijuana
_2_	c.	Gun control	_1_	h.	Abortion	_2_	l.	Religion
_3_	d.	Minority groups	_5_	i.	Welfare	_1_	m.	Individual rights
_5_	e.	Divorce						

The reactions to these and similar words or phrases can provide you with information that will help you to approach your audience successfully. If most persons in your audience are neutral to moderately favorable toward abortion, then your speech advocating it could be designed to raise their attitudes to moderately favorable to strongly favorable. If the responses are mixed, then you may have to work just to move your audience closer to a mildly unfavorable attitude or toward neutrality. The questionnaire will help you to learn about your audience's demographics, and its attitudes, beliefs, and values better than observation alone.

Adapting to the Audience

Analysis of an audience yields information about your listeners that enables you to adapt yourself and your verbal and nonverbal codes to that audience. A speech is not a message imposed on a collection of listeners: a speech is a compromise between speaker and audience that is designed to inform, entertain, inspire, teach, or persuade that audience. This compromise is based on your analysis of your audience.

Adapting Yourself

In the study of interpersonal communication, you learned about self-concept and about how people in pairs and groups adjust to each other. In public speaking, the speaker also has to adjust to information about the audience. Just as the senior who is preparing for a job interview adapts to the interviewer in dress, manner, and language, the public speaker prepares for an audience by adapting to its expectations. How you look, how you behave, and what you say should be carefully adjusted to an audience that you have learned about by observation, experience, and analysis. As you will discover in chapter 10 on source credibility, there are ways you can help an audience perceive you as a credible person.

Adapting Your Verbal and Nonverbal Codes

The language you employ in your speech, as well as your gestures, movements, and even facial expressions, should be adapted to your audience. Does your experience, do your observations, and does your analysis of the audience's attitudes indicate that your language should be conversational, colloquial, formal, cynical, or technical? Does your analysis indicate that your listeners like eye contact? Do your observations and the evaluations of your teacher and classmates indicate that you should pace the stage or stand still behind the lectern? Does your analysis indicate that you should not use taboo words in your speech lest you alienate the group, or does the audience like a little lively language? Your analysis of your audience provides the information that you need to make these strategic choices about verbal and nonverbal codes.

Summary

In this chapter we considered audience analysis first and foremost because the audience is related to you, your topic, your message, your organization, your language, and your delivery of a speech. Your decisions concerning all of these variables rest on what you have discovered about your audience.

We began by surveying some of the reasons why you and others learn to give public speeches. We discovered that the initial fear of public speaking is overcome, in part, by learning how to prepare and deliver a speech and by practicing public speaking in the classroom. We also discovered that public speaking becomes more valued after a person learns how to do it.

We examined four levels of audience analysis: Level 1 is distinguishing between voluntary and captive audiences; Level 2 is demographic analysis, in which the characteristics of the members of an audience are evaluated; Level 3 is analyzing the audience's interest in and knowledge about a topic; Level 4 is to determine the audience's attitudes, beliefs, and values—three indicators of an audience's predispositions that are important predictors of how listeners will respond to the speaker, the topic, and the message, as well as to the organization and delivery of the speech.

Three methods of analyzing an audience were described. The first is observation, which is based on watching your audience and learning from its behavior. The second is inference, in which incomplete data is used to draw tentative conclusions about an audience, conclusions that might make the audience's response more predictable. The third method of analysis is the questionnaire, which can be used to garner information about demographics, attitudes, and strength of belief.

We summarized the levels and the methods of audience analysis by indicating how they affect the speaker's adaptation to the audience. We found that audience analysis can help you to make strategic decisions about your own verbal and nonverbal behavior as a speaker. In the next chapter, audience analysis will be related to the credibility of the speaker.

New Terms

Audience analysis	Audience interest	Inference
Captive audience	Audience knowledge	Questionnaire
Voluntary audience	Attitude	Attitude scales
Heterogeneity	Belief	Adaptation to an audience
Homogeneity	Value	Strength of belief
Demographic analysis	Observation	

Additional Readings

*Becker, Samuel L. "New Approaches to Audience Analysis." In *Perspectives on Communication*, edited by Carl E. Larson and Frank E. X. Dance. Shorewood, Wisc.: Helix Press, 1970. Pages 61–77.
A complex and detailed look at approaches to audience analysis and selective exposure. Becker presents a model for analysis of audience attitudes.

Berquist, Goodwin F. *Speeches for Illustration and Example.* Chicago: Scott, Foresman and Company, 1965.
Sample speeches illustrating public speaking problems in presenting specialized material for specific audiences. Provides good insight into the application of audience analysis techniques in adapting messages.

Clevenger, Theodore, Jr. *Audience Analysis.* Indianapolis: Bobbs-Merrill Co., Inc., 1966.
Contains detailed discussion of techniques of measuring audience attitudes and knowledge, with specific discussions of the construction and uses of questionnaires, attitude scales, observational techniques, and information tests.

Cronkhite, Gary. *Persuasion: Speech and Behavioral Change.* Indianapolis: Bobbs-Merrill Co., Inc., 1969.
A thorough exploration of the effect of audience attitudes on the effectiveness of a persuasive message helps to clarify the purpose and techniques of audience analysis for the persuasive speech.

Hasling, John. *The Message, The Speaker, The Audience.* New York: McGraw-Hill Book Company, 1971.
Hasling's view is that the speaker's message is effective only if the audience understands and believes it, and he offers suggestions that help the speaker assist the audience in receiving the intended message.

Holtzman, Paul D. *The Psychology of Speakers' Audiences.* Glenview, Ill.: Scott, Foresman and Company, 1970.
A look at speakers and speeches from the audience's perspective. Holtzman discusses the audience's listening behavior, attitudes toward the speaker and the topic, and willingness to accept new ideas and values. He argues that the speaker must listen to the audience, i.e., audience analysis is a continuous process.

*Johannesen, Richard L. *Ethics and Persuasion.* New York: Random House, Inc., 1967.
An excellent presentation of the issues surrounding the use and misuse of public speaking in our society. Heavy reading, but contains stimulating ideas from Aristotle, Vance Packard, Karl Wallace, and others on the place of speech in a democratic society.

*Katz, Elihu. "On Reopening the Question of Selectivity in Exposure to Mass Communication." In *Speech Communication Behavior: Perspectives & Principles,* edited by Larry Barker and Robert Kibler. Englewood Cliffs, N.J.: Prentice-Hall, Inc., 1971. Pages 182–92.
Katz examines studies of selective exposure as they relate to mass communication and provides insights into the concept of captive and voluntary audiences and how selective exposure is used by an audience to select only desired messages.

*Indicates more advanced readings.

Notes

1. "What Are Americans Afraid Of?" *The Bruskin Report,* no. 53 (1973).

2. George Benson and Joseph Chasin, "Entry Level Positions," *Journal of College Placement* 37 (1976): 76.

3. Barbara A. Magill, Roger P. Murphy, and Lilian O. Feinberg, "Industrial Administration Survey Shows Need for Communication Study," *American Business Communication Association Bulletin,* no. 38 (1975), pp. 31–33.

4. Daryl Bem, *Beliefs, Attitudes and Human Affairs* (Belmont, Calif.: Brooks/Cole Publishing Company, 1970), p. 16.

5. Adapted, with permission, from Milton Rokeach, *Beliefs, Attitudes, and Values* (San Francisco: Jossey-Bass, Inc., Publishers, 1968), p. 170.

6. Adapted, with permission, from a list of values cited in Robert L. Heath, "Variability in Value System Priorities as Decision-Making Adaptation to Situational Differences," *Communication Monographs* 43 (1976): 325–33.

10

Sharing Yourself: Source Credibility

Objectives

After study of this chapter you should be able to do the following:

1. Define credibility and defend the position that it resides in the minds of the audience
2. Define and give examples of the four aspects of credibility
3. Explain how credibility is established before, during, and after a speech
4. Distinguish the influence of credibility on opinion from its influence on learning
5. Discuss and give an example of the "sleeper effect"
6. Give an example of how you might use co-orientation to establish common ground with your classroom audience
7. Suggest four variables that can affect your credibility during a speech
8. List and discuss variables that do not seem to affect credibility
9. Indicate how you might establish credibility in the classroom when you speak about a topic

"Too much sun will ruin your skin."

Little brother to sister

"Too much sun will ruin your skin."

Mother to daughter

"Too much sun will ruin your skin."

Physician to patient

The idea that *who* says something makes a difference is at least as old as Aristotle. Twenty-three hundred years ago Aristotle said that a speaker's "character may almost be called the most effective means of persuasion he possesses."[1] In all the centuries since that ancient Greek announced the importance of the source, and especially in this century, dozens of scholars have attempted to determine the importance of the source, or speaker. Several important ideas have emerged from their studies.

The first idea is that credibility is not inherent in the speaker. It is an estimation of value that is made by the audience. The individuals in an audience perceive a speaker as credible or not. As one pair of researchers on this subject wrote, "Credibility is in the eye of the beholder."[2] Credibility is not something a speaker possesses, like clothing. A speaker's credibility depends in part on who the speaker is, in part on the subject being discussed, in part on the situation, and in part on the audience. You may be more credible about some subjects than about others; you may be more credible in some situations than in others; and you may be more credible to some audiences than you are to others. The little bird in the "Peanuts" cartoon seems willing to do whatever is necessary to raise his credibility as a presidential contender.

A second important observation about credibility is that public speakers earn the right to speak, that they earn credibility through their own lives, their own experiences, and their own accomplishments. One saying that summarizes this idea is, "Before you express yourself, you need a self worth expressing." A person who has stood in line to collect unemployment compensation can speak

with conviction about the difficulties of the unemployed. The physician who has treated many alcoholics has earned the right to discuss the debilitating effects of alcohol on the human body and spirit. The student who has worked for four summers fighting forest fires can talk convincingly about carelessness with matches. We earn the right to speak—through our experience, our training, and our convictions.

To learn about credibility, we shall look first at four of its aspects. Then we shall summarize the research findings about credibility and derive from them some principles for you as a public speaker. A checklist of questions that can serve to enhance your own credibility as a public speaker concludes the chapter.

Four Aspects of Credibility

What does an audience perceive that gives it the idea that a speaker is credible? If credibility is based on judgments by individuals in the audience, then what is the basis for those judgments? On what will your classmates be rating you when they judge your credibility? Four of the most important aspects of credibility, according to recent studies, are competence, trustworthiness, dynamism, and co-orientation.[3]

Competence

The first aspect of credibility is *competence*. A speaker who is perceived as competent is perceived as qualified, trained, experienced, authoritative, expert, reliable, informed, or knowledgeable. A speaker does not have to live up to all these adjectives; any one, or a few, might make the speaker credible. The machinist who displays his metal work in a speech about modern technology as art is as credible as the Biblical scholar who is demonstrating her ability to interpret scripture. They have different bases for their competence, but both can demonstrate competence or expertise in their own areas of specialization.

Your own competence as a speaker is conveyed by your words, your visual aids, even your air of authority. What can you build into your speech that will help the audience to see and understand the basis for your air of authority? What experience have you had that is related to the subject? What special training or knowledge do you have? How can you suggest to your audience that you have earned the right to speak about this subject? The most obvious way is to tell the audience the basis of your authority or expertise, but a creative speaker can think of dozens of ways to hint, suggest, imply, and indirectly indicate competence without being explicit, without seeming condescending, arrogant, superior, and without lying.

Figure 10.1

Trustworthiness

The second aspect of credibility is *trustworthiness*. How honest, fair, sincere, friendly, honorable, and kind does the audience find the speaker? These descriptors are also earned. We judge a person's honesty both by past behavior and present estimates. Your classmates will judge your trustworthiness when you speak before them. How do you decide whether or not other speakers in your class are responsible, sincere, dependable or just? What can you do to help your audience perceive that you are trustworthy?

Dynamism

The third aspect of credibility is *dynamism*—the extent to which an audience perceives the speaker as bold, active, energetic, strong, empathic, and assertive.

Audiences value behavior that can be described by these adjectives. Perhaps when we consider their opposites—timid, passive, tired, weak, hesitant, and meek—we can see why dynamism is attractive. People who exude energy, who exhibit strength, and who show the spirit of their convictions impress others. Observe the public speakers on Sunday-morning television—the evangelists, the ministers, and the healers—and see how dynamic they look and sound. You can learn to do the same, and the evidence indicates that the audience's perception of your dynamic qualities will enhance your credibility.

Co-orientation

Co-orientation refers to the sharing of values, beliefs, attitudes, and interests. Audiences are drawn to speakers whose ideology is similar to their own. People flock to a speaker who can articulate their ideas and beliefs better than they could themselves. If our own views about a public issue coincide with his, William F. Buckley can state them better than we could. In the classroom, speakers can establish co-orientation by revealing to their audience the many ways in which they share their audience's orientation toward life, toward the issues, toward the information being presented, or toward the persuasive proposition. Thus we use the word *co-orientation* to indicate a vision possessed conjointly by audience and speaker.

A beginning speaker reading this formidable list of adjectives describing the four aspects of credibility might feel that establishing credibility is beyond the capability of the novice speaker. It is some comfort to know that you do not have to fit all the adjectives or even score well on all the aspects. Many highly credible speakers are not dynamic; in fact, all they may possess is their specialized knowledge. Some speakers may be thought to be credible simply because they exude sincerity, even though they lack knowledge and expertise and are not dynamic.

To continue our examination of source credibility, we turn next to some research findings. While explaining each finding we shall also try to suggest ways in which you can apply it to your own public speaking.

Some Ways of Increasing Credibility

Credibility can be achieved before, during, or after a public speech. A speaker can have a reputation before arriving at a hall; that judgment can be altered during the presentation; and the evaluation can change again, long after the speech has ended. You might think that Speaker X is a great person before you hear him. His dull presentation reduces his credibility. Then, in the weeks after the speech, your evaluation of Speaker X might rise again because you discover that his message has given you new hope. In other words, credibility is not static: it is always in flux, always changing, always alterable.

Nor is credibility, we should remind you, something that a credible speaker always possesses. It is contingent on topics, audiences, and situations. The interrelatedness of these variables makes the concept of source credibility a challenging one to public speakers. We intend these comments about the changing nature of credibility as a caution in interpreting the findings cited below. We shall examine those findings first by looking at some ways of increasing credibility and then by looking at some factors that are erroneously believed to influence credibility.

A Highly Credible Speaker Will Change an Audience's Opinion More than a Speaker of Low Credibility, but the Difference Diminishes in Time

A highly credible speaker is one who is perceived by the audience as competent, trustworthy, dynamic, or co-oriented. We might say that such a speaker has prestige before, during, and after the speech. Most of the studies that try to measure the effect of such a person's message on an audience indicate that highly credible speakers change opinions more than speakers whose credibility is poor.[4] At least initially, a person perceived as credible can seek more changes of opinions and achieve more changes.

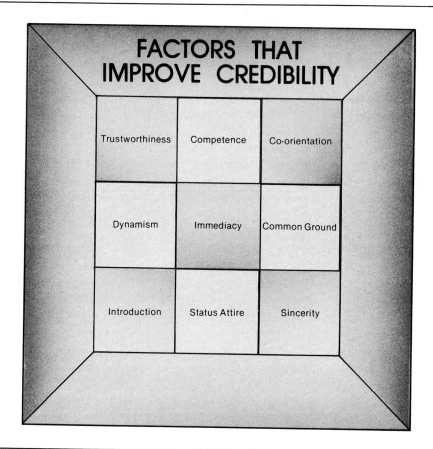

Figure 10.2

This finding demonstrates the importance of working for and earning an audience's respect as a source. In the speech classroom, it should make the speaker strive to become credible during the speech, since the speech is the main source of the audience's information about the speaker. Describing the origins of your authority, revealing to the audience how you relate to the topic and how you relate to them can help you become credible.

As our statement indicates, a highly credible speaker changes opinions when a speech is delivered.[5] However, as time passes, an interesting phenomenon occurs. Apparently the source of the speech and the message become separated in the listener's mind: "I don't remember who said this, but . . ." The result of this separation of source and message is that the effect of the credible speaker's message diminishes as the listener forgets who relayed it. The speaker with little credibility creates just the opposite effect. As time passes, the listener forgets the source of the information and the message tends to become more

effective. In one study, three or four weeks after a speech, a highly credible speaker and one with little credibility had pulled about even in respect to their ability to change opinions. Gains made by the less credible speaker are due to the "sleeper effect."[6]

The lesson for the public speaker is that the effect of credibility is short-lived. In most speech classes, several weeks or more may elapse between your presentations. In between, your classmates are exposed to other speakers and speeches. They need reminders of your credibility. We like to think that audiences remember us and our speeches, but in fact it is sometimes difficult for students to remember a speech they heard the day before yesterday. Intelligent speakers remind the audience of their credibility. Remind your audience about your major subject, your special interest in the topic, your special knowledge, or your special experience. Credibility decays in time and must be renewed if you want to have the maximum effect on your audience.

A Speaker Can Gain Credibility by Establishing Common Ground with the Audience

To establish common ground with an audience is to emphasize what you share with it—in the present situation, in your experience, in your ideas, or in your behavior. You can establish common ground by sharing the situation that you and your classmates have in common—you all have speeches to give and exams to take. You can share ideological common ground—values, beliefs, or ideas. One way to earn an audience's trust is to point out some of the important ways that you are like the audience. Revealing shared attitudes, beliefs, and values establishes co-orientation. You can address members of your audience as fellow students (common ground) or as people who believe that marks are destructive to learning or that bookstore prices are too high (co-orientation).

Some studies indicate that areas of agreement should be established early in a speech for maximum effect; others say that when it is established is not important, as long as it is established sometime during the speech. All the studies agree that speakers can enhance their relationship with the audience by talking about something they have in common with the audience. Some degree of commonality with voluntary audiences may be assumed, but it is necessary to be explicit to captive audiences. In the cartoon, it was probably the defense attorney who was wise enough to see that his client's position on conservation was conveyed to the jury.

Credibility Is Influenced by the Introduction of the Speaker, by the Status and Sincerity of the Speaker, and by the Organization of the Speech

The following generalizations and conclusions are based on a summary of nearly thirty years of studies of credibility.[7] *The introduction of a speaker by another person can increase the speaker's credibility.* The credibility of the person making the introduction is as important to the speaker's credibility as what is said in that introduction. A close friend introducing you can reveal information that could enhance or harm your status. To be safe, the speaker should always provide the introducer with information that could potentially increase credibility by showing the speaker's competence, trustworthiness, co-orientation, or dynamism. Your introducer can make evaluative statements about you that might sound self-serving from your own mouth. Your credibility may also be enhanced if the audience believes that your introducer is highly credible.

  The way you are identified by the person introducing you can affect your credibility. Students who are identified as graduate students are thought to be more competent than undergraduates. Graduate students are also seen as more fairminded, likeable, and sincere.[8] It is possible, therefore, that your identification as a sophomore, junior, or senior might contribute to your credibility with a student audience.

DUNAGIN'S PEOPLE

"WE FIND THE DEFENDANT GUILTY OF MURDER, CONSPIRACY, ROBBERY, ASSAULT, AND KIDNAPPING... BUT WE RECOMMEND LENIENCY BECAUSE HE WANTS TO SAVE THE REDWOODS."

The organization of your speech can affect your credibility. Students who listen to a disorganized speech think less of a speaker after the speech than they did before the speech.[9] This judgment by the audience may be based on its expectations: in the speech classroom, the students expect good organization, and when they perceive a speech as poorly organized they lower their evaluation of the speaker. The lesson from this study is relatively clear. The classroom speaker should strive for sound organization lest he or she lose credibility even while speaking.

The perceived status of a speaker can make a difference in credibility. In the study cited above, not only did audiences find graduate students more credible than undergraduates, their positive evaluation spread to several other areas as well. In another study, speakers of high status were consistently rated as more credible than speakers of low status. Even more striking was the finding that the listeners judged credibility and status during the first ten or fifteen seconds of the speech.[10] The probable explanation of this finding is that the audience receives a barrage of cues about the speaker at the very beginning of the speech: they see how the speaker is dressed; they see and make judgments about the speaker's appearance; they hear the speaker's voice; and they get an initial impression of the speaker's confidence, competence, trustworthiness, and dynamism.

Other interesting findings about credibility are related to delivery, fluency, and repetition. *A speaker whose delivery is considered effective, whose use of voice, movement, and gesture is effective, can become more credible during a speech.*[11] A payoff exists for the student who practices a speech and who learns to be comfortable enough in front of an audience to appear natural, confident, and competent. Nonfluencies, breaks in the smooth and fluid delivery of the speech, are judged negatively. Vocalized pauses such as *like, you know,* and *ahhh* are nonfluencies. Another kind of nonfluency is the repetitive use of certain words and phrases, such as *well, then,* or *now,* at every transition. These nonfluencies decreased the audience's ratings of competence and dynamism, but did not affect the speaker's trustworthiness.[12]

Factors That Do Not Affect Source Credibility

Some factors that appear to be related to credibility are not, according to studies. For instance, regardless of a popular myth, no evidence exists to show that sound organization increases credibility: the evidence indicates only that poor organization decreases credibility.[13] Other findings derived from studies include the following.

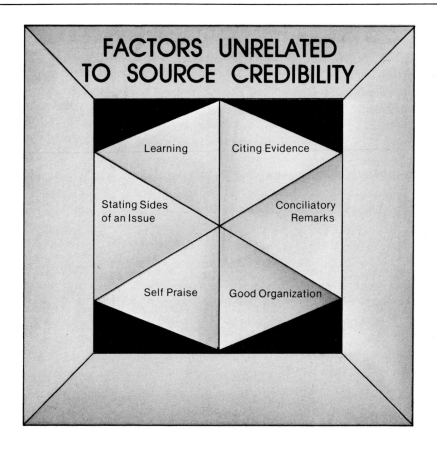

Figure 10.3

Credibility and Learning

Earlier we cited a finding that a credible speaker can create greater shifts of
opinion. That finding is based on measurements of attitudinal change. We are
now talking, not about changes in opinion or attitudes, but about learning. Andersen and Clevenger state, in their summary of the research: "There is not
enough evidence to suggest that the amount of information gained from exposure
to a message is related to the ethos [credibility] of the source—at least this lack
of relationship seems to be true of college populations."[14] A listener may be able
to recollect, recall, and recount information from a speech regardless of the
credibility of the source. Factors other than credibility of the source are more
closely related to learning—the listener's motivation, the speaker's selection of

material, the speaker's organization of the content, and the clarity of the presentation. An audience, in other words, can learn equally well from a highly credible source or a less credible source in the presence of one or more of these variables, but the person perceived as highly credible changes more opinions.

This finding should be reassuring to the classroom speaker who has many opportunities to build into the speech the factors that enhance learning. The speaker can include materials that encourage the audience to listen and help it to relate to the speaker and the topic. The speaker can select appropriate supporting materials, evidence, and examples. The speaker can organize the speech to make it clearer and deliver it in a manner that makes it easier for the audience to learn from it. The speaker can do all of these things to enhance learning. If persuasion or change of opinion is the purpose of the speech, then the thing to work on is credibility—not teaching.

Covering Both Sides of an Issue and Citing Sources

When we turn to the organization of a speech, in chapter 11, we shall find that presenting both sides of an issue can help to change opinions. But no evidence indicates that covering both sides of an issue will help or hinder a speaker's credibility.[15] In other words, there may be reasons for presenting one side or two sides or many sides of an issue, but the motivating force for such a decision should not spring from the speaker's desire to enhance credibility. As Andersen and Clevenger point out in their summary of research on credibility: "No evidence . . . supports the common belief that giving 'both sides' is a superior way to present controversial material."[16]

Nor is there any evidence that citing sources of evidence increases the persuasiveness of a speech. The citing of sources is encouraged in public speaking to preserve the integrity and the ethical basis of a public address. We tell an audience where we found supporting material so that we do not imply that it is our own. Footnotes may not make a speech more persuasive either, but the convention of presenting citations is one of the rules of scholarship that neither speaker nor writer should circumvent. We cite sources, not to increase our persuasiveness—we know it does not—but because it is a time-honored practice that listeners and readers expect a speaker or writer to follow.

Conciliatory and Self-Praising Remarks

Another commonly held belief that is unsupported by communication studies is that making conciliatory remarks increases credibility. Thus, speakers say: "It is a pleasure to speak to such an intelligent audience," or "You have been particularly responsive and attentive tonight," or "Few audiences would have been able to reach the level of understanding exhibited here." Common sense and

popular belief might tell you that such remarks would endear an audience to a
speaker; the studies indicate that they do not.[17]

    Self-praise is another technique often used to enhance credibility. Perhaps
all of us have heard speakers who drop names or who inform the audience how
special they are. Common sense tells the speakers that self-praise will enhance
their credibility; again, the studies do not agree.[18]

Instead of depending on self-praise to carry the day, speakers should describe their qualifications. They can help an audience to understand them and perceive them as credible by describing their qualifications, by revealing how and why special knowledge was acquired, and by establishing common ground with an audience. When speakers shade over into the self-evaluative area, they move from description to self-praise. Speakers can state or describe qualifications that will help an audience perceive their competence. A comment about how great a salesperson you are is not likely to increase your credibility, but a statement about how many years you have been employed as a salesperson might.

Strategies for Improving Your Credibility

Below is a checklist that you can use to make sure that you have considered the possible ways to improve your credibility.

Place a check in the blank on the right to indicate that you have considered the implications of the statement.

1. Have you selected a topic in which you are involved, so that you can be perceived as sincere, responsible, reputable, and trustworthy? _____

2. Have you considered the relationship between your apparent competence and your credibility by building into your speech cues that indicate your experience, training, skill, and expertise in the subject? _____

3. Have you considered the relationship between your apparent trustworthiness and your credibility by building trust through concern for your audience's welfare, through objective consideration of their needs, through friendly rapport, and through responsible and honest handling of the speech content? _____

4. Have you selected a means of delivery and content that will help the audience see you as dynamic—energetic, strong, empathic, and assertive? _____

5. Are you indicating in your speech one or more ideas, beliefs, attitudes, or characteristics that you hold in common with most of the people in your audience? _____

6. Can you ask your teacher or someone else who introduces you to say something praiseworthy about you or your qualifications? _____

7. Have you reminded your audience, descriptively, of your qualifications to speak on the subject? _____

8. Are you dressed appropriately for this audience? _____

9. Given the classroom situation, your class audience, and the topic you have selected, are you likely to be perceived as competent, trustworthy, dynamic, and interested in this audience's well-being? _____

10. Have you carefully pointed out how your topic is related to the audience, selected appropriate supporting materials, organized the content, and found a way to deliver your speech that will help your audience to learn and to retain what you say? _____

Summary

An effective speaker is constantly aware of his or her own impact on the speech and on the audience. We have examined four aspects of credibility: competence, trustworthiness, dynamism, and co-orientation. We have reviewed the results of many studies of the variables that influence credibility. Variables that improve credibility were identified. Some that are not related to credibility, although they are believed to be, were also identified. Our review contained ten questions to help you determine if you have considered all of the possible ways of improving your credibility.

New Terms

Credibility	Credibility is earned	Self-praise
Competence	Sleeper effect	Description
Trustworthiness	Common ground	Evaluation
Dynamism	Vocalized pauses	
Co-orientation	Conciliatory remarks	

Additional Readings

Berquist, Goodwin F. *Speeches for Illustration and Example*. Chicago: Scott, Foresman and Company, 1965. *A good chapter on source credibility and the effect of the speaker's trustworthiness, competence, and dynamism on the impact of the message. Excellent sample speeches and study questions help the student understand the techniques by which credibility is enhanced.*

Bettinghaus, Erwin P. *Persuasive Communication*. New York: Holt, Rinehart and Winston, Inc., 1968. *A look at the way credibility affects the persuasive message. Bettinghaus relates the concepts of credibility to message planning and audience analysis and also looks at speeches in various settings, including small groups and organizations.*

Cronkhite, Gary. *Persuasion: Speech and Behavioral Change*. Indianapolis: Bobbs-Merrill Co., Inc., 1969. *Information about the factors of source credibility and how they are related to the success of the persuasive speech. Credibility, an important variable, is also related to other factors of the persuasive speech.*

Hovland, Carl I., Janis, Irving J., and Kelly, Harold H. "Credibility of the Communicator." In *Dimensions in Communication: Readings*, edited by James H. Campbell and Hal W. Hepler. Belmont, Calif.: Wadsworth Publishing Co., Inc., 1970. Pages 146–69. *A discussion of the research on the effect of audience-rated source credibility on persuasiveness. A detailed exploration of the factors affecting the establishment of credibility to an audience and the manner in which credibility affects message acceptance.*

Swanson, Richard, and Marquardt, Charles. *On Communication: Listening, Reading, Speaking, and Writing*. Beverly Hills, Calif.: Glencoe Press, 1974. Chapter 8. *General strategies for changing attitudes. The credibility of the source as one method of proving an argument. A brief examination of credibility, but easy to understand and apply.*

*Thompson, Wayne N. *Quantitative Research in Public Address and Communication.* New York: Random House, Inc., 1967. Pages 31–94.
Though the research may be a bit outdated, these pages contain a summary of a vast amount of research into easily understood conclusions that serve as principles for constructing public speeches. An excellent treatment of the research into guidelines for credibility that is understandable, and useful to the student speaker.

Thonssen, Lester, and Baird, A. Craig. "The Character of the Speaker." In *Readings in Speech,* edited by Haig A.

Bosmajian. New York: Harper & Row, Publishers, 1971. Pages 118–28.
The authors discuss credibility as a source of proof, relate Aristotle's position on ethical proof to modern speeches, and list some ways in which speakers can enhance their credibility.

Walter, Otis M. *Speaking to Inform and Persuade.* New York: Macmillan Publishing Co., Inc., 1966.
In Chapters 6 through 8, Walter develops the concepts behind source credibility as a variable in persuasive speaking. The concepts are related to specific strategies available to the speaker. A bit superficial, but clearly written and covers major concepts of credibility.

*Indicates more advanced readings.

Notes

1. Aristotle, *Rhetoric,* trans. W. Rhys Roberts, ed. by Richard McKeon, in *The Basic Works of Aristotle* (New York: Random House, Inc., 1941), 1, 1356a, ll. 12–14.

2. Ralph L. Rosnow and Edward J. Robinson, eds., *Experiments in Persuasion* (New York: Academic Press, Inc., 1967), p. 18.

3. Derived from a study by Christopher J. S. Tuppen, "Dimensions of Communicator Credibility: An Oblique Solution," *Speech Monographs* 41 (1974), 253–60.

4. Rosnow and Robinson, p. 8. See also, Kenneth Andersen and Theodore Clevenger, Jr., "A Summary of Experimental Research in Ethos," *Speech Monographs* 30 (1963): 59–78.

5. Marvin Karlins and Herbert I. Abelson, *Persuasion* (New York: Springer Publishing Company, 1970), pp. 113–14.

6. Carl I. Hovland and Walter Weiss, "The Influence of Source Credibility on Communicator Effectiveness," in Rosnow and Robinson, p. 21.

7. Wayne N. Thompson, *Quantitative Research in Public Address and Communication* (New York: Random House, Inc., 1967), p. 54.

8. Andersen and Clevenger, pp. 59–78.

9. Harry Sharp, Jr., and Thomas McClung, "Effects of Organization on the Speaker's Ethos," *Speech Monographs* 33 (1966): 182–83.

10. L. S. Harms, "Listener Judgments of Status Cues in Speech," *Quarterly Journal of Speech,* 47 (1961): 168.

11. Thompson, p. 56.

12. Ibid.

13. Sharp and McClung, pp. 182–83.

14. Andersen and Clevenger, p. 77.

15. Thompson, p. 54.

16. Andersen and Clevenger, p. 78.

17. Ibid.

18. Ibid.

11 Understanding Through Topics, Research, and Evidence

Objectives

After study of this chapter you should be able to do the following:

1. Define the process of brainstorming; use this method to create a list of possible speech topics

2. Explain the personal inventory method of generating speech topics; use this method to create a list of possible speech topics

3. Discuss the importance of personal involvement in selecting a topic for a speech

4. Suggest the importance of personal knowledge in selecting a speech topic

5. Identify two ways of limiting a topic. Use one of them to identify and limit a specific topic

6. Discuss the types and uses of primary and secondary research; choose a specific topic and indicate where you might find primary and secondary research materials

7. Name the three types of secondary evidence and their uses

8. Discuss ways in which you should adapt your topic, your purpose, and your supporting materials to your audience

9. Select a topic and limit it for use in a classroom speaking assignment; research the topic from primary and secondary sources and adapt your speech to your audience

"I don't have the foggiest notion what I should talk about in my speech next Monday."

Beginning speech student

"I have found a topic that I really like, but I find that I know only enough about it to fill two minutes, certainly not five or ten. What am I supposed to do now?"

Intermediate speech student

"You did not provide any support for the main contention in your speech: no personal experience, no quotations from experts that you interviewed, and no information from authoritative sources. Furthermore, in the second proposition of your speech you told us the average but did not give us the range or median, which would have helped in interpreting the mean. Only at the end did you report the results of a national survey that supported your argument."

Advanced speech student

Once you have considered your audience and yourself, you need to choose a topic or subject for your speech. You have probably already written a paper for a high school or college class. Much of the agony in completing a writing assignment is selecting the topic. Some teachers make the assignment easier by assigning topics. But, usually, we try to find topics by paging through magazines or reading the newspaper, and we sharpen our pencils many times during our contemplation. The actual selection of a topic is often made uncomfortably close to the time the paper is due. Speech students also spend a disproportionate amount of time choosing a topic.

To assist you, we shall examine two methods of selecting a topic for a speech. Both methods make the task easier and allow more time for preparing the speech and adapting it to a particular audience.

Selecting and Limiting the Topic

Brainstorming

In chapter 8, in the section on small group discussions, under "Selecting a Topic," you learned the term *brainstorming*. This technique can also be used effectively in selecting a topic for a speech. The most important characteristics of brainstorming are that it can generate a large number of ideas and that the ideas are not being evaluated. Imagination can run riot. No one student will develop the same list as another because each will think of topics that relate in some way to himself or herself. You may end up with a list of possible topics that you can develop into speeches. You might want to try brainstorming, to find out if it works for you.

Brainstorming Exercise

Take out a pencil and paper. Give yourself five minutes to write down the ideas that come to mind. Use single words, phrases, or sentences, or any combination. The emphasis is on quantity. How many topics can you produce in five minutes? When you have completed this portion of the exercise, you may have as many as twenty-five or more ideas, or as few as five. The second step is to go over your list and select three that you find interesting enough to use for your speech. Last, select the one that appeals to you most. This can be the topic which you use for your speech *if* you know enough about the topic or can find out enough through research, and *if* you can figure out how to adapt the topic to your audience.

Personal Inventory

Another way to find a topic for your speech is to survey your own reading habits. Choosing one topic from thousands of possible topics requires some self-analysis.

You make choices every time you read something. When you sit down with the newspaper, you probably do not read the entire paper. You might read the headlines, a few articles on the front page, the comic strips, and the sports page. Another person might read the wedding announcements, the opinion page, and the obituaries. Even when you read a general newsmagazine like *Time, Newsweek,* or *U.S. News and World Report,* you probably choose certain parts to read. You might read the international news and the art news but skip the sections on music and books. What you do when you read a newspaper or newsmagazine reflects your own interests. To discover your own interests more systematically, you might try completing the next exercise.

Newspaper Inventory

Take the local newspaper and note down
which sections you read often (+),
sometimes (o), rarely or never (−).

__+__ Front-page news *18*

__O__ Comics *12*

MOTIVATE __−__ Sports *6*

__⁄__ Editorial page *4*

__⁀__ Letters to the
        editor

__+__ Obituaries *3*

__O__ Birth and wedding *4*   *rarely 10*
        announcements

__−__ Home and family *4*

__⁀__ Art and music *4*

__⁀__ Books *5*

__⁀__ Travel *1*

Newsmagazine Inventory

Or, take the newsmagazine of your own
choice and record which sections you
actually read (+), which sections you
occasionally read (*O*), and which sections
you rarely or never read (−). The

following sections are the ones ordinarily
published in *Time* magazine, but a similar
list could be compiled for any
newsmagazine.

__O__ Cover story

__⁀__ Essay

__⁀__ Art

__O__ Books

__+__ Cinema

__⁀__ Economy and
        business

__⁀__ Energy

__O__ Law

__⁀__ Letters to the
        editor

__⁀__ Living

__O__ Milestones

__⁀__ Nation

__O__ People

__O__ Religion

__−⊘__ Science

__−⊘__ Sports

__⁀__ World

The checklist of items that you read in the newsmagazine or newspaper
gives you a rough indication of your own interests. Another way is to list your
hobbies or leisure-time activities, the organizations to which you belong, the
books you have read recently, the movies you have seen recently, the television
shows you watch most frequently, and the magazines you most enjoy. Your
choice of college, major subject, and elective courses can also indicate your likes
and dislikes.

After you have completed a personal inventory of your own preferences,
you can more clearly identify the topics or subjects that are most appropriate for
you. Since you already know how to analyze an audience, you can determine
whether your topic is appropriate. You are now ready to assess your personal
involvement in the topic and your personal knowledge of the topic.

Involvement

After you have tentatively selected a topic area, you should evaluate the topic to see if you have the appropriate interest, knowledge, and experience to speak about that topic. The first step in evaluating the topic is to consider the importance of the topic to you.

The first question is, How strongly do you feel about the topic you have selected? An easy test of your feelings is a question: Would you feel that an attack on your speech is in some way an attack on you? For example, if you spoke about rock music and someone attacked the speech, would you view the critic's reaction as a personal affront? If a hypothetical attack on your speech does not make you feel defensive, that is a sign that the topic does not mean that much to you, that you are not highly involved in it.

A second question is, How much time and energy do you devote to the subject area or topic? When you are really involved in something, you usually expend time and energy on it. If you really want to become a secretary, retailer, lab technician, or forester, you will be committing your time and energy to learning the subject matter and the skills that will lead to success in that voca-

tion. And you will probably resent any implication that your chosen field is not worthy and will defend it.

Observation of your fellow students will probably reveal which speakers are involved in their topics and which are not. People who are involved in their topics speak with more conviction, passion, and authority. They give us many indications that they care about the subject. The person who has, by chance, selected a topic from a *Reader's Digest* article the night before usually cannot convey the sense of involvement that is so important in public speaking. When the president talks on television about one of his favorite plans, when Ralph Nader talks about consumerism, and when your professors discuss their favorite subjects, they usually show that they are involved, that the topic is important to them. You can display the same kind of involvement if you choose a topic that matters to you.

Knowledge

If you select a topic in which you are involved, you will probably know more about that subject than most of your classmates. This personal knowledge is something that students often forget to consider in their speeches. Speeches do not have to consist entirely of material looked up in the library. The speech will be better, in fact, if you add your own experience.

The importance of speaking from personal experience was demonstrated to the authors at a large university where over seven hundred students were invited to select the best speeches made in their individual speech classes. The winners delivered their speeches in a runoff contest, and the three best speakers gave their speeches to everyone taking the course. Those three speakers, selected by their classmates, were two black males and a handicapped white female—but, of the seven hundred competitors, very few were black and even fewer were handicapped. All three spoke about topics in which they were highly involved and to which they were committed: the two black men spoke about being black students in a predominantly white university, and the woman told what it was like to be a student confined to a wheelchair.

The black men told about being stared at in class, hearing classmates constantly asking them about being black, and being misunderstood. The handicapped woman told of having practically nobody speak to her no matter where she was, of people moving to the other side of the sidewalk when she approached, and of being considered an oddity. All three students had special knowledge and experience with the topic on which they based their speeches.

You may not be able to find an aspect of yourself that is that dramatic, but you probably can find a topic about which you have personal experience. You will find that you can strengthen your speech by taking advantage of your own knowledge of the topic.

Definition

Whether you employ brainstorming techniques, use a personal inventory, or simply feel you have a wide selection of possible topics, you have probably chosen a topic that is too broad for a short speech. One way of reducing that topic to more manageable proportions is to define the topic—make it more specific, less abstract, and more concrete. Suppose you realized that you have an interest in business. You read the business section of the newspaper, and several of your brainstorming topics were related to that category. Take the abstract category called *business* and shrink it by making it increasingly specific and concrete. For example:

Business

Getting a job in a business

Getting a job in a local business

Where to find jobs in local businesses

How to get job interviews with local businesses

How to get interviews for summer jobs with local businesses

The shrinking can continue, but at this point the topic is approaching the appropriate size for a five-to-ten-minute speech.

Another method is to take the broad category and think of as many particular smaller topics as you can that would fit under that heading. For example:

Sports

Special treatment of basketball recruits

Tutoring of athletes

Scholarships for athletes

Keeping score in wrestling

New opportunities for women in golf

Financing our athletic program

Is our proposed stadium worth the expense?

The new track program for women

Injury: The unpublicized problem in college football

What happened to our basketball stars?

The list could go on and on. All the topics are related to sports, and many are suitable for a five-to-ten-minute speech. Either of the methods we have suggested can be used to reduce the size and scope of the broader topics that result from brainstorming and personal inventories.

Supporting the Topic with Evidence

Once you have selected a topic and narrowed it sufficiently, you are ready to begin considering the content of your speech. The *content* of a speech consists mainly of evidence, illustrations, proofs, arguments, and examples. Finding these supporting materials is the subject of this section. The name of the specific activity is *research*, and it consists of two kinds of investigation. The first is *primary research*, the materials that you gather or know of at first hand. The second is called *secondary research* because it consists of information, ideas, or evidence gathered by other people. Most secondary research is done in the library.

Primary Research

Primary research results in evidence that you have garnered from first-hand experience. You can use occurrences in your own life or information that you have gathered by talking with other people. The types of primary research we are interested in now are your personal experience and information gained by interviewing.

A great deal of evidence exists in our personal experience. We can tell others how to make a dress from experience, or we can tell them how to assemble a simple electric motor, build an airplane model, or compose a business letter. We can use, as "proof," our own experience in the home, in the armed services, or on the job. If you selected a topic in which you are involved and to which you are committed, you will have a lot of personal evidence to offer in support of your claims.

You should not, however, use your own experience uncritically. Important questions should be asked about personal experience before you employ it as proof. Is your experience typical? If you are among the very few who had an unfortunate experience with a local bank, you should think carefully before you generalize and assume that many people have been treated similarly. You can ask some questions about your personal experience that will help you evaluate it as evidence of what you plan to say in your speech:

Was your experience typical?

Was your experience so typical that it will be boring or so atypical that it was a chance occurrence?

Was your experience one that this audience will appreciate or from which this audience can learn a lesson?

Does your experience really constitute proof or evidence of anything?

Not all personal experiences can be shared with an audience. Only a limited number of them can really be used as evidence.

Another question about your experience is whether it was firsthand or the experience of someone else. If the information is not firsthand, it is usually questionable. It may have been distorted in transmission. The old game of passing a message down a line of people illustrates the problem of getting a message intact from person to person. You might find yourself passing along a falsehood to your audience unless the experience is your own.

ANIMAL CRACKERS

A second kind of primary research is gaining information by talking with others. You can discover knowledge beyond yourself by consulting with other people who may know more about the topic than you. Sometimes these sources of information are fellow students; more often, they are faculty members or people in the town or city who have special knowledge of the subject. To prepare yourself for this kind of information gathering, you should review the information in chapter 8 on interviewing, where you learned and may have even practiced the very kind of research that is suggested for the public speaker.

You are likely to derive some benefits from interviewing people for your speech. You will meet people who share an interest in your subject. You will gain information that you can use yourself as well as in your speech. You may be able to enhance your own credibility by being knowledgeable, authoritative, and responsible. And you may increase your self-confidence by addressing an audience about a subject in which you are increasingly involved. Interviewing takes planning, time, effort and, sometimes, a little courage, but the benefits for you personally and for your speech make it a worthwhile method of research.

Secondary Research

Secondary research results in information derived from published sources, usually books, periodicals, microfilms, tapes, motion pictures, records, and

```
Marvin Karlins and Herbert I. Abelson, Persuasion
(New York: Springer Publishing Co., Inc., 1970),
pp. 128-29.
The authors state: "People are most persuaded by
a communicator they perceive to be similar to
themselves." P. 128.
They cite a study in which some discussion leaders
tried to be "liked" by their fellow discussants and
others tried to be disliked. They were more
successful in persuading the discussants when they
were liked by them. Pp. 128-29.
```

Figure 11.1 Index Card.

newspapers. The major source of secondary information is the library. You will find that the library has files and indexes which will lead you to information that you can use in your speeches.

One of the researcher's most important resources is the library's card catalog. The card catalog lists every book in the library by author, title, and subject. And the books are usually cross-indexed so that you can find them simply by looking at the cards collected under the subject heading. If you picked a subject in which you are involved and to which you are committed, you should not have to read a large number of books on the subject. On the other hand, if the subject is truly of interest to you, you may want to read some of them. Usually, it is sufficient to check out several of the best books on the topic and read them selectively for information that is most usable to you in your speech. As in interviewing, it is important to take good notes, to record the information accurately and precisely, and to credit the author of the book in your speech when you deliver it. An entry like the one below on an index card or a separate sheet of paper will usually help. Be sure to include author, title, publisher, place of publication, date of publication, and page reference, as well as the information.

Another reference work of great value is the *Reader's Guide to Periodical Literature*. This multivolume work lists all the articles that have appeared in magazines. You can look up a topic like marijuana and find a listing of all the articles that have appeared in popular magazines on the subject. If you want to explore the topic further, you can look up "key words" in the *Reader's Guide* that will lead you to still other sources. You could explore the subject of marijuana further by looking up key words like *drugs, law enforcement, international regulation, medicine,* and *juvenile delinquency.* It would be difficult to think of a topic that is not covered in the popular literature. As a student, you should learn how to use these reference works and sources to help you learn more about your topic and so improve your papers as well as your speeches.

   Some additional sources frequently used by speech students for finding information include:

1. Yearbooks and encyclopedias. Some frequently used yearbooks are the *World Almanac,* the *Book of Facts, Facts on File,* and the *Statistical Abstract of the United States.* These compendia contain facts and figures about a wide variety of subjects, from population to yearly coal production. The encyclopedias contain background material about many topics, and short bibliographies. Among the popular encyclopedias are the *Encyclopedia Americana* and the *Encyclopaedia Britannica.*
2. Sourcebooks for examples, literary allusions, and quotations include Bartlett's *Familiar Quotations,* George Seldes' *The Great Quotations,* and Arthur Richmond's *Modern Quotations for Ready Reference.*
3. Biographies of famous persons can be found in *Who's Who in America, Current Biography,* and the *Dictionary of American Biography* (deceased Americans).
4. Newspaper files are useful, especially if your college has the *New York Times,* one of the few newspapers that has an index.
5. Professional journals, which are also indexed, are collected by many libraries. You can find articles about speech, communication, psychology, sociology, economics, chemistry, mathematics, and many other subjects.
6. Many modern libraries own volumes of material on microfilm. Media resource centers on campuses have lists of slides, films, and other visual materials.
7. Your reference librarian is an expert at helping you locate materials.

Types of Evidence

Three types of secondary evidence deserve closer scrutiny because they are used so frequently in public speaking. One of the reasons for examining these three is that you need to know how to evaluate your own evidence before you use it in your speech. You will also be listening to many more speeches than you make, and the questions that need to be asked in evaluating evidence can help you to listen intelligently. The three types of evidence examined in this section are (1) surveys and studies, (2) testimonial evidence, and (3) statistics.

Surveys and Studies

Much of the evidence employed in speeches is "proof" that is secured by reading. Items that get into print are almost always more credible than personal experiences because someone—an editor, a screening committee, or a critic—

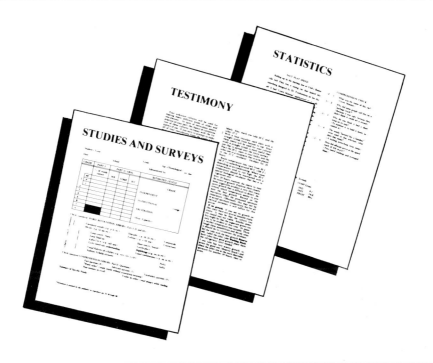

Figure 11.2

reads the material before it is printed. One person's experience with alcohol can have impact on an audience, but a survey that indicates how widespread the problem is can lend considerable credence to the speaker's argument. *Psychology Today, U.S. News and World Report,* newsmagazines, newspapers, professional journals, and books contain surveys and studies that you can use in your speech. Even *Playboy* and some of the less scholarly publications contain national surveys and studies that can support your arguments, claims, and propositions.

Just as with personal experience, there are some important questions that you should ask about the evidence that you find in these sources:

How reliable is the source that you used? A report in a professional journal of sociology, psychology, or speech is likely to be more thorough and more valid than one found in a local newspaper.

How broad was the sample used in the survey or study? Was it a survey of the entire nation, the region, the state, the city, the campus, or the class?

Who was included in the survey or study sample? Did everyone in the sample have an equally good chance of being selected or were volunteers asked to respond to the questions? *Playboy's* readers may not be typical of the population in your state.

Who performed the survey or study? Was it a nationally recognized survey firm like Lou Harris or Gallup, or was it the local newspaper editor?

(Continued)

Was it performed by professionals like professors, researchers, or management consultants?
Why was the study done? Was it performed for any self-serving purpose—to attract more readers—or did the government make it to help establish policy or legislation?

Testimonial Evidence

A second kind of evidence is information found in printed interviews, usually in the form of quotations or testimonial evidence. You may find that the words of others lend support to ideas that you wish to convey in your speech. The difficulty in using the words of others is that you must determine whether or not your audience will find the statements of these people as important as you did. Again, some questions should be asked about the sources of your evidence:

Is the person you quote an expert whose opinions or conclusions are worthier than most other people's opinions?

Is the quotation about a subject in the person's area of expertise?

Is the person's statement based on extensive personal experience, professional study or research, or another form of firsthand proof?

Will your classmates find the statement more believable because you got it from this outside source?

Statistics

A third kind of evidence derived from secondary sources is statistics. Statistics are a kind of numerical shorthand that can summarize large quantities of data for easy consumption by an audience. They must be used with care, however, because they can be deceiving. To assist you in your use of statistics both as a speaker and as a critical listener, you should have a brief vocabulary relating to statistics and numbers, and you should know some of the questions that can be asked about them.

The terms below are only a partial listing of words that are commonly used in describing statistics; along with each term is a brief explanation and some appropriate questions to ask about it.

Mean or Average   The term refers to the total of a list of numbers divided by the number of items. For example, given these six scores—4, 7, 7, 11, 13, and 15 —the mean would be 9.5, or the sum of the scores divided by the number of scores. Sometimes the average, or mean, is not a good indicator of central tendency. For example, if the scores were 1, 2, 2, 1, 14, 15, the average would be 5.8. But all the scores actually fell on the extremes and nobody received a score

even close to the average. The average grade in a class could be *C* if everyone were given an equal number of *A*'s and *F*'s. Two good questions to ask about the mean, or average, are: Does the average tell us where most of the numbers or scores are clustered? What was the range of the numbers?

Mode   The mode is the most frequently recurring number in a list of numbers or a distribution. If the mode on an examination were 7, it would mean that more people earned a 7 than any other score. However, the mode is not necessarily where most of the other numbers are clustered. The critical listener has to ask for several measures of central tendency: "What was the mean?" "Was the mode near the average?"

Percentage   The term *percentage* literally means "by the hundred" because it refers to the ratio or fraction of one hundred. Percentage can be expressed as a decimal: .56 means 56 percent or 56/100. Among the questions that can be asked about percentages are: What is the basis for the whole? That is, what is 100 percent? A 500 percent increase in sales, for example, can mean that the person sold one car last year and five cars this year. One hundred percent, then, represented one car. Percentages can be difficult for an audience to comprehend unless you make them palatable. It is easier for an audience to understand percentages stated as percentages than as decimals, although they mean the same thing. It is also easier for an audience to comprehend percentages that are rounded off than percentages that are stated too specifically. A number like 49.67 percent is easier to understand if it is rounded off to 50 percent.

Range   The highest and lowest numbers in a distribution are the *range* of that distribution. For example, the examination scores ranged from 5 to 25 out of a possible 30 points. The range does not reveal where most of the numbers are clustered; it simply tells the two end points in a distribution of numbers. All the remaining numbers or scores must fall between these two points, but exactly where they cluster is unknown unless you ask the right questions. Two questions that will give you a better idea of where the numbers cluster are: Where was the mean, or average? Where was the mode?

Raw Numbers   The term refers to specific numbers that are often cited in population, production, and other measures of quantity. Say that the number of teenagers in the state increased by 325,465 this year. The raw number is often difficult to absorb because it is so specific. Raw numbers are easier for an audience to understand if they are rounded off (over 325,000) or stated as a percentage of increase (a 15 percent increase). A good question to ask about a raw number is: What percentage of increase or decrease does that raw number represent? Another question worth asking is: What was the original number and what is the new total? Raw numbers are hard to interpret if you have no basis for comparison. If the speaker does not provide that basis, the critical listener must ask for additional information before the number can be understood. Listeners should not feel embarrassed about inquiring about statistics and numbers in speeches. They are often difficult to understand and interpret. As a speaker, you should strive to provide all the information necessary for interpreting numbers and statistics; as a listener you should ask for additional information when you need it.

Adapting the Topic, Purpose, and Supporting Materials to the Audience

In this chapter, we have investigated how your topic relates to you and to the audience. You discovered how primary and secondary research and various types of evidence can be employed in public speaking. You will now be asked to consider how your topic, your purpose, and your supporting materials relate to **an earlier subject—audience analysis.**

Adapting Your Topic

Public speakers should be permitted to speak about any topic that fits the assignment. In the classroom, at least, you should select a topic because of how it relates to you. But you also have to give your speech to an audience of classmates. Therefore, the topic you select must be adapted to them. Audience analysis is a means of discovering the audience's position on the topic. From information based on observation, description, and inference, you have to decide how you are going to adapt your topic to this audience.

Audience analysis can tell you what challenges you face. If you want to speak in favor of abortion and your audience analysis indicates that the majority of your listeners is opposed to that position, you need not conclude that the topic is inappropriate. But you may have to adapt to the members of your audience by starting with a position closer to theirs. Your initial step might be to make the audience feel less comfortable about its present position so that it is readier to hear your position. You might choose another tactic. Audience analysis can reveal the obstacles that you face with that audience.

Your analysis might indicate that the audience already has considerable information about the subject. The analysis, then, might require that you adapt by locating information that they do not have. You may want to deliver an informative speech about the latest world crisis, but analysis indicates that the audience is not only already interested but also that it has sufficient information of the sort that you planned to offer. You can adapt your topic by shifting to an area of the subject about which they are not so well-informed: What is the background of the conflict? What is the background of the personalities and the issues? What do the experts think will happen? What are the possible consequences of the confrontation? Your analysis can help you to adapt your topic to your particular audience.

Adapting Your Purpose

You should also adapt the purpose of your speech to your audience. Speech teachers often ask the student to state the purpose of a speech—what do you

DOONESBURY   **by Garry Trudeau**

want your audience to know, to understand, or to do? It may help you to think
of your speech as one part of a series of informative talks that your audience will
hear about your topic. It has probably heard something about the topic before,
and is likely to hear about the topic again. Your particular presentation is just
one of the audience's exposures to the topic.

Still, your immediate purpose is linked to some larger goal. The goal is the
end that you have in mind. In the "Doonesbury" cartoon, Ms. Slade's immediate purpose is to announce her candidacy for the United States Congress; her
larger goal is to be elected to office. Some examples of immediate purposes and
long-range goals will illustrate the difference. In an informative speech, the
immediate purposes and long-range goals might be:

Immediate Purpose	Long-range Goal
To help the audience remember three factors in adopting nuclear power plants as a source of energy.	To increase the number of people who will read articles and books about nuclear power as an energy source.
To teach the audience six expressions that are part of the "street language" used by urban blacks.	To help the listeners understand and appreciate the language employed by some black students.

In a persuasive speech, the immediate purpose and the long-range goal might be:

Immediate Purpose	Long-range Goal
To get the audience to remember three positive characteristics of the candidate for mayor.	To get some of the audience members to vote for the candidate at election time.
To reveal to the audience the nutritional value of two popular "junk foods."	To dissuade the listeners from eating junk food.

The more specific your purpose, the more able you will be to discover
whether you accomplished it.

In chapter 9, we explored a number of ways to analyze an audience. You
should employ audience analysis to help you discover whether your purpose is
appropriate. Suppose half the people in your class are going into fields where
knowledge of food and nutrition is important. They already know more than the
average person about nutritional values, and they know about the debilitating
effects of junk food. Consequently, it is probably not appropriate to deliver a
speech about junk food. It may also not be wise to speak to a group of athletes
about the importance of exercise. You adapt your purpose to the audience by
considering the level of their information, the novelty of the issue, and the other
factors that we talked about in chapter 9.

Adapting Your Supporting Materials

Your personal knowledge, your interviewing, and your library research should
have provided more material for your speech than you can use. Again, audience
analysis helps you select materials for this particular audience. Your analysis

might reveal that your classmates do not have much respect for authority figures. In that case, you might be wasting your time informing them of the surgeon-general's opinion about smoking: your personal experience or the experience of some of your classmates might be more important to them than an expert's opinion. On the other hand, if your audience analysis reveals that parents, teachers, pastors, and other authority figures are held in high regard, you may want to quote physicians, research scientists, counselors, and health-service personnel.

As a public speaker, you should always keep in mind that the choices that you make in selecting a topic, in choosing an immediate purpose, in determining a long-range goal, in organizing your speech, in selecting supporting materials, and even in creating visual aids are all *strategic choices*. All these choices are made for the purpose of adapting the speaker and the subject to a particular audience. The larger your repertoire of supporting arguments, the better your chances of having appropriate arguments. The larger your supply of supporting materials, the better your chances of having evidence, illustrations, and visual aids that the audience will respond to. Your choices are strategic in that they are purposeful. The purpose is to choose, from among the available alternatives, the ones that will best achieve your objectives with the particular audience.

Summary

The purpose of this chapter is to help you select a topic, find materials, evaluate supporting materials, and relate topic, purpose, and supporting materials to an audience. Brainstorming and personal inventory are two methods of topic selection. Involvement in and knowledge of the topic are two means of evaluating a topic. After a topic is selected, you are encouraged to pursue primary research through personal experience and interviews and secondary research through library sources such as reference works, books, periodicals, journals, and microfilms. Three types of secondary evidence bear close examination: surveys and studies, testimonial evidence, and statistics. The information in the chapter was synthesized by relating the topic, purpose, and supporting materials to adaptation to your audience by analysis of that audience.

New Terms

Brainstorming	Surveys and studies	Percentage
Personal inventory	Reliability	Range
Involvement	Sample	Raw numbers
Limiting the topic	Testimonial evidence	Audience analysis
Content	Statistics	Immediate purpose
Primary research	Mean, or average	Ultimate goal
Secondary research	Mode	

Additional Readings

Anastasi, Thomas E., Jr. *Communicating for Results.* Menlo Park, Calif.: Cummings Publishing Co., Inc., 1972. *An overview of public speaking skills via a step-by-step approach to planning, developing, and delivering the speech. In a good chapter on visual aids, Anastasi explains in detail the effective construction and use of graphics, handouts, and the various media.*

King, Robert G. *Forms of Public Address.* New York: Bobbs-Merrill Co., Inc., 1968. *Guidelines for developing speeches for specific occasions that may not be covered in the basic speech course. Campaign speeches, after-dinner speeches, and ceremonial speeches are discussed, and examples are analyzed.*

Kruger, Arthur N. *Effective Speaking: A Complete Course.* New York: Van Nostrand Reinhold Company, 1970. Pages 243–77. *The use of statistics, evidence, and visual aids in the speech is explained. Some workable techniques for researching the topic and recording the information for easy reference as you develop the speech are suggested.*

Mills, Glen E. *Message Preparation: Analysis and Structure.* New York: Bobbs-Merrill Co., Inc., 1966. Pages 1–46. *Topic selection is related to the type of speech to be presented and the characteristics of the audience. Subtypes of informative and persuasive speeches*

and methods of analyzing topics for each type of speech are defined. Contains helpful advice about finding information and improving your efficiency as a researcher.

*Newman, Robert P., and Newman, Dale R. *Evidence.* Boston: Houghton Mifflin Company, 1969. *Heavy theoretical reading, but an extremely articulate and thorough analysis of the types and uses of evidence. Includes tests for evaluating the validity and appropriateness of analogies, syllogisms, causal relationships, and other forms of evidence.*

Robb, Stephen. "Fundamentals of Evidence and Argument." In *Modcom: Modules in Speech Communication.* Chicago: Science Research Associates, Inc., 1976. *Easily understood presentation of the issues underlying the use of evidence. Excellent section on the analysis of evidence and inference making. Shows the relationship between evidence and argument.*

Verderber, Rudolph F. *The Challenge of Effective Speaking.* 3d ed. Belmont, Calif.: Wadsworth Publishing Co., Inc., 1976. Pages 185–218. *A good chapter outlining the basic issues of evidence and its uses. A simply written and easily understood pragmatic approach to evidence as support for reasoning and motivation.*

*Indicates more advanced readings.

12

Sharing Your Message Through Organization

Objectives

After study of this chapter you should be able to do the following:

1. Name the five purposes of an introduction
2. Prepare three different introductions for the same topic and discuss to what extent, and how, each introduction fulfills the five purposes of an introduction
3. Differentiate between the form and the function of organization
4. Name the three principles governing an outline
5. Outline a speech, using the principles identified in 4
6. Discuss the functions of organization and give examples of each function
7. Differentiate eight patterns of organization and give examples of topics for which they would be appropriate
8. Discuss the function and characteristics of transitions
9. Discuss the functions of a conclusion
10. Select a topic that you have researched; prepare an outline illustrating the introduction, body and conclusion; discuss the characteristics of your organization and the reasons you selected a specific organizational pattern

"I just can't get my act together. I don't know how to start a speech and I don't know how to end it."

"I have ten pages of material to present to the class, but I have only five minutes to do it."

"That's nothing. In my last speech on team sports, I forgot to tell the class that I'm a recreation major until the very end."

Each of these students is facing a problem in organizing a speech. The same problems are faced by every speaker inside and outside of the classroom. Anxiety about organizing the speech usually occurs after we have decided on a topic and after we have gathered some information that we wish to present. In this chapter, we will examine the three main parts of a speech: the introduction, the body, and the conclusion. The advice, the examples, and the explanations will help you avoid the problems faced by the students quoted above.

The Introduction: Gaining and Maintaining Attention

The purposes of the introduction to a speech are: (1) to help the audience to focus on the speaker; (2) to arouse the audience's interest in the subject matter; (3) to indicate the purpose of the speech; (4) to describe any qualifications that might improve your credibility; and (5) to begin to indicate any common ground with your audience.

A number of techniques can be used to attract the audience's attention. One is to begin the speech with an eloquent quotation from one of your sources. A person giving a speech on new life styles could begin his speech with a quotation such as this, from *Time* magazine:

> From time immemorial—or at least since the first U.S. census was taken in 1790—the head of household has been identified for every house, hovel, plantation, apartment, co-op, condominium, igloo and wigwam to which an intrepid census taker could wend his way.[1]

The speaker could then point out that the new life styles—unmarried men and women living together, women who earn more than men in the same family, and sometimes groups of people living together—have caused the Census Bureau to eliminate the designation "Head of Household" from the census forms. The quotation is appropriate, it introduces the topic in an imaginative way, and it will probably capture the audience's attention.

A second commonly used method of introducing a speech is to cite a striking statistic or fact. "People seem to be changing their eating habits to avoid heart attacks," the speaker might begin. "According to *U.S. News and World Report,* the consumption of poultry has gone up 16 percent in the last ten years, fish is up 20 percent, eggs are down 14 percent, and animal fats are down 31 percent. But we still eat too much: total consumption of food has increased by nearly 6 percent."[2] Or the speaker might start by stating that "School vandalism costs taxpayers $600 million a year in repairs; there are 70,000 assaults each year against teachers; and assaults against both teachers and students rose 58 percent in just four years."[3] Striking facts and statistics can arouse the audience's interest.

A third way to introduce a speech is to begin with some action. One woman who was giving a speech on self-defense started her speech by inviting a cohort to attack her from behind, whereupon she flipped him neatly on his rear. A chemistry student began by showing the class a brief experiment. A motorcycle lover brought his chromed beauty right into the classroom. These active introductions were difficult to ignore.

These are just three out of dozens of possibilities. You can begin a speech with a vivid description; with two conflicting views that invite resolution; with a brief or extended story or narration; with a personal experience related to the

Figure 12.1   Gaining attention.

topic; with emotional language of your own or from a source; with a statement of uncertainty that your speech will clarify; with a cause or effect that will be expanded in the speech; or with a statement that exploits an immediate concern or an unexpected development. There is no one pat way of starting a speech: every speaker should try to be creative and imaginative enough to invent ways of capturing and maintaining audience attention.

Some other suggestions can help you to plan your introduction. Remember that the time and effort that goes into composing an effective introduction is well worth the effort. We have already referred to research that indicates that audiences tend to make inferences about the speaker and the speech within the first 15 seconds.[4] Your first exposure may have a disproportionate impact.

Your attention-getting introduction should also be related to your topic. Banging on the lectern or writing SEX on the board to capture an audience's attention, when these actions have nothing to do with the topic in hand, is self-defeating.

Avoid being overly dramatic. One of our colleagues had a harrowing experience in class. She was still writing down some comments about the previous speech when the next student rose to deliver his speech. She heard a horrifying groan and looked up to see the student on the floor with his whole leg laid open and bleeding. The students in the class leaped up and surrounded the injured student while she ran to the office to call emergency assistance. The student planned to give a speech on first aid. He had gotten a plastic leg wound in living color from the student health center. He had a bag of simulated blood on his stomach which he squeezed rhythmically so it would spurt like a severed artery. Unfortunately for the student, his attention-getting action introduction was too **realistic. Instead of capturing the audience's attention, he managed to get so**

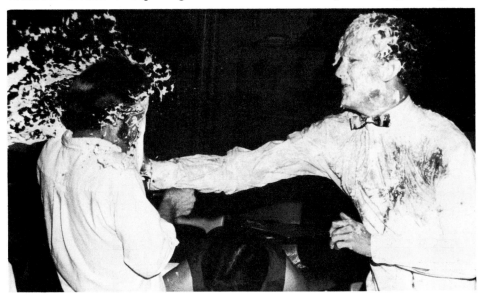

much adrenalin into their bloodstreams that they were in no mood to listen to any more speeches that day.

Another purpose of the introduction, in addition to assisting the audience to focus on the speaker and to arouse interest in the speech, is to state the purpose of the speech. Almost always, speakers should tell an audience what they want that audience to know, learn, or understand from the speech. Some exceptions to this general rule occur in persuasive speaking. When speakers face an audience with a proposition to which the audience is opposed, they are well advised not to reveal their purpose at the outset. Ordinarily, though, the speaker will state the purpose of the speech very explicitly:

Today I will show you the basic construction of a simple electric motor.

There are three main causes of the inflation that reduces the value of your money.

I will provide you with a new way of looking at welfare.

In speaking, as in teaching, the members of an audience are more likely to learn and to understand if they know what is expected of them.

The introduction is also the appropriate place to describe any special qualifications that you have. You can talk about your experience, your research, the experts that you interviewed, and your own education and training in the subject. You should be wary about self-praise, but you need not be reserved in stating why you can speak about the topic with authority.

Finally, you can begin to establish common ground with your audience in your introduction. You can point out that you are a student, a worker, a sophomore, or a poor person—like most of the audience. You can mention areas in which you believe you are in agreement: "Like most of you, I believe that student fees are too high," or "I think we would all agree that the cost of textbooks has gotten out of hand," or "Most of us are politically independent."

Your restricted time may make it impossible to achieve all of the purposes stated here. In an eight-minute speech, the introduction lasts only one or two minutes. You need to determine which of the purposes are most important to you.

Checklist for Your Introduction

Check the means you believe could be the most effective in developing the introduction to your speech.

1. Assisting the audience to focus on me as a speaker by:

    a. An introductory quotation from a magazine, book, or interviewee;   _____

    b. A striking statistic or fact about the topic; or   _____

    c. An action or demonstration related to the topic.   _____

    d. Other _____   _____

2. An example or illustration that will arouse the
   audience's interest in the topic.   _____

3. An explicit statement that reveals the purpose of my
   speech and my expectations of the audience.   _____

4. A description of my qualifications to speak about this
   subject.   _____

5. The establishment of common ground by stating
   characteristics or ideas that I hold in common with
   this audience.   _____

6. Other _____

   _____   _____

The Body of the Speech: Form

The most common way of organizing a speech is to outline it. If you have already learned how to outline in high school courses or freshman composition, you may want to read this section as a helpful review.

Principle of Subordination

Categorize

One of the first rules of outlining is known as the *principle of subordination,* which means that in outlining you must be able to distinguish among main headings, subheadings, points, and subpoints so that your audience will realize which statements are of greater or lesser importance.

Subordination Exercise

Examine the statements below and determine if you can classify them into a main heading and subpoints in the blank outline provided.[5]

1. More than 750 million in loans are overdue from students.

2. Defaults in the guaranteed-student-loan category alone stand at about $600 million.

3. Thousands of young Americans have not repayed federally backed student loans.

4. Delinquencies in direct loans amount to $151 million.

I. _3_ (Insert the number of the main heading).

A. _1_ (Insert the number of each subpoint).

B. _2_

C. _4_

   In the Subordination Exercise, statement no. 3 is the main heading. All the others are subpoints, and any order in which you placed them would be correct.

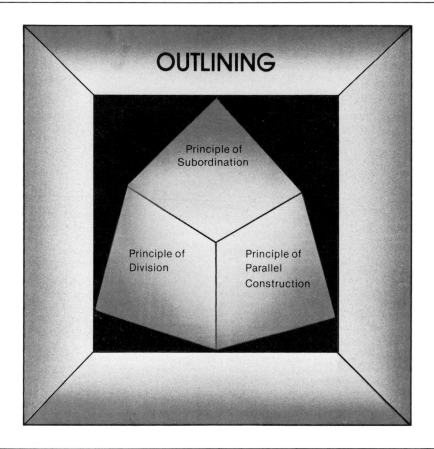

Figure 12.2

Principle of Division

A second rule of outlining is the *principle of division*. A main heading cannot be subdivided into less than two parallel parts. Your topic, then, is divided into two or more parts—main headings—which in turn can be divided into two or more subheadings. If a main heading or subheading cannot be divided, it stands alone. The result is an outline that looks similar to this basic form:

Title of Speech

I. Main heading
   A. Subheading
   B. Subheading

II. Main heading
   A. Subheading
   B. Subheading
   C. Subheading
III. Main heading

One can further divide subheadings into points and subpoints, using Roman numerals, capital letters, Arabic numbers, and small letters to clarify the organization. There are still two or more divisions of each heading, or none at all:

I. Main heading
   A. Subheading
      1. Point
         a. Subpoint
         b. Subpoint
      2. Point
   B. Subheading

Principle of Division Exercise

Try to determine two subheadings for the first two statements. Use the same kind of sentence structure each time.

I. There are two main reasons why young couples marry before the age of twenty:

   A. *Because of home life*

   B. *Because of pregnancy*

II. There are two solutions to the problem:

   A. *GOOD PARENT CHILD RELATIONS*

   B. *BIRTH CONTROL*

Try to think of an appropriate main point for the subpoints below.

1. _____

   a. Because the cheapest aspirin cures a headache just as well as the most expensive.
   b. Because additives like buffers do not improve aspirin's ability to cure a headache.

Principle of Parallel Construction

A third rule of outlining is the *principle of parallel construction*—that is, the forms used in the main heads, subheads, main points, and subpoints should be consistent and similar. In the Principle of Division Exercise, the two subpoints were both dependent clauses beginning with the word *because.* Some teachers may want you to compose a sentence outline because it requires more thorough and detailed planning, but others may be satisfied with a word outline, a phrase outline, or some other form. All instructors will probably expect you to employ the principle of parallel construction illustrated in the Parallelism Exercise.

Parallelism Exercise

Outline A—*Correct*

I. Three principles govern the composition of an outline.
   A. The principle of subordination dictates that the subheads and subpoints be less important than the main heads and subheads.
   B. The principle of division means that main heads and main points cannot be divided into less than two parts.
   C. The principle of parallelism states that sentence, clause, or phrase construction in an outline must be used consistently.
II. Outlines should be used as plans for a speech.

Outline B—*Incorrect*

I. Three outlining principles.
   A. The principle of subordination.
   B. Principle of division.
   C. Parallelism means the use of similar form used consistently throughout an outline.
II. Outlines should be used as a plan for a speech.

Can you determine why Outline A is correct and why Outline B is incorrect?

Organizing the Speech: Function

The examination of the outline in the Parallelism Exercise concentrates on form; another important aspect of speech organization is function. Whereas *form* pertains to how the speech looks in written form, *function* pertains to the content of the parts of the speech. The explanations normally included in an introduction of a speech are primarily functional because they specify the content of the introduction. Following that orientation, we are prepared to examine the function of organization in the body of the speech.

Some functions that were described in the introduction are in play throughout a speech. Below is a chronological list of the functions of the different parts of a speech. The comments reveal whether the function is a general one, in play throughout the speech, or a specific one, pertaining only to a specific part of the speech. The comments also indicate some functional differences between informative and persuasive speeches.

Functional Organization Pattern

Function	Comments
purpose I. Arousal (Steps A–D) The Introduction	Serves the function of gaining audience attention, showing relationships between speaker and topic, and between audience and topic. Includes the purpose, in most speeches.
A. Focus audience's attention on the speaker.	Important throughout the speech, but vital at the very beginning.

B. Arouse audience   Initiated in the introduction and maintained throughout.
    interest in the topic.

C. Statement of   Purpose stated near the beginning and also near the end.
    specific purpose.   Complex purposes often also stated in the body.
                            Exception: if audience not friendly and ready to be
                            persuaded, see II, C.

D. Description of   Credibility stated early, but additional statements can be
    speaker's   made throughout.
    qualifications.

II. Explanation (Steps   Arguments, explanations, and the main content of the
    A–D)   speech concentrated here.
    The Body.

A. Forecast of speech   An overview of the organization, usually a review of main
    development.   headings. Should appear in introduction or early in body.

B. Motivational   How the topic is related to the audience's needs: why
    materials or   they should listen and learn. (Motivational materials
    rationale for   should be used throughout speech, especially in
    intended change.   conclusion.)
                            Exposition in informative speech and rationale for change
                            in persuasive speech provided by main headings,
                            subheads, points and subpoints.
                            Evidence, visual aids, illustrations, and demonstrations.

C. Delayed revelation   For persuasive speakers facing unfriendly audience.
    of purpose   Preparation for persuasive proposition should precede
                            statement of purpose.

D. Action or   Persuasive speech: how audience should behave as a
    application.   result of adopting the new attitude or idea. Informative
                            speech: how the new information can be applied by the
                            audience.

III. Review and   Speech nearing end: indicated by language, tone,
     inspiration (Steps A   nonverbal behavior, and by summarizing content and
     and B)   exhorting the audience.
     The Conclusion.

A. Review of   Informative speech: speaker reviews by summarizing
    exposition.   what audience was expected to learn. Audience made to
                            focus sharply on content. Persuasive speech: speaker
                            reviews rationale for change, most compelling evidence,
                            best arguments. How audience would behave if
                            proposition accepted.

B. Finale.   Informative speech: speaker concludes with clever,
                            insightful, or memorable statement. Audience is pleased,
                            perhaps wants to hear more. Persuasive speech: speaker
                            concludes by rewarding audience with vision of a better
                            world through adoption of the new attitude or idea.

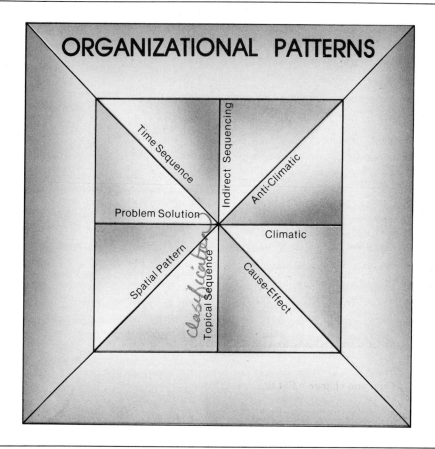

Figure 12.3

A Repertoire of Organizational Patterns

Many organizational patterns can be used in speeches. This section can be considered a source to consult when you are seeking an appropriate organization for a speech. Each entry consists of the name of an organizational pattern, a brief description of the pattern, a statement about the appropriate uses of that organization, and a brief example.

I. Time-Sequence Pattern
   A. *Description:* an organizational pattern that is used whenever chronology or time is the key factor in the speech.
   B. *Application:* Used in speeches that examine the past, present, and future of some idea, issue, group, plan, or project. Also appropriate when the speaker is telling the audience how to do something in which the sequence, chronology, or steps must be accomplished in a specific order. Recipes, formulas, and projects —from making a cake to figuring an equation to building a doghouse—require precision and careful attention to performing the steps in a specific order.

C. *Example:*
   When you change a flat tire you should:
   1. Drive the car on the shoulder as far as possible, set the emergency brake, put the gear into "park," and, if necessary, block the wheels so the car will not roll when you raise it.
   2. Find the jack and jack handle (which is usually a combination handle and wrench for removing the nuts from the wheel) in your trunk.
   3. Remove the hubcap and use your jack handle or wrench to loosen the nuts on the wheel of the flat tire before raising the car so that the wheel does not turn when you remove the nuts.
   4. Place the jack in the notch in the bumper or hook it close to the corner of the bumper nearest the damaged tire.
   5. Often the jack has a lever to raise or lower it. Set the jack so that when you move the handle up and down, the jack rises. Jack the car up until the damaged tire clears the ground or road.
   6. Remove the nuts and place them in the hubcap.
   7. Remove the damaged tire and place the spare tire on the bolts.
   8. Tighten the nuts as much as possible with the car elevated.
   9. Put the jack setting on "lower," and lower the jack until the tire is solidly on the ground.
   10. Tighten the nuts firmly, replace the hubcap, and lower the jack until it can be removed. Place it in the trunk.

II. Topical-Sequence Pattern
   A. *Description:* a speech addressed to advantages, disadvantages, qualities, or types.

B. *Application:* used to explain to an audience why you want them to accept a certain point of view. Most appropriate for speeches in which you have two to five points to make: three reasons why people should buy used cars, four of the main benefits of studying speech, five characteristics of a good football player. One of the most versatile patterns of all. Main headings carefully selected so most important arguments or points never appear in the middle. (See "climactic and anticlimactic organization," p. 244.) Strong beginnings and endings: start with strongest argument and end with second strongest, or vice versa. Or speaker moves from the strongest argument (anticlimax order) to the weakest, and then summarizes by moving from the weakest to the strongest (climax order). Specific pattern chosen with the purpose and the audience in mind.

C. *Example:*
   At most universities and colleges, four ranks of full-time teachers exist.
   1. The instructors, who are at the beginning of their teaching careers.
   2. The assistant professors, who usually have doctoral degrees and some experience in teaching.
   3. The associate professors, who have doctorates, have teaching experience, and have begun publishing scholarly works.
   4. The full professors, who have demonstrable competence in teaching and research.

III. Problem-and-Solution Pattern
   A. *Description:* the problem-solution speech describes a problem and proposes a solution to that problem. The main purpose is to present the solution. Usually easily divisible into two distinct parts with an optional third part in which the speaker meets any anticipated objections to the proposed solution. Frequently follows topical pattern within the two divisions (see example).
   B. *Application:* Decide, by analyzing audience, how much time and energy to devote to the two main parts of the speech and anticipated objections. Audience usually has at least passing acquaintance with problem, so less time is spent

presenting it, and most time is spent on solution, with which they are likely to be less familiar, and on objections to the solution. Occasionally, the audience may be familiar with both problem and solution, but not with objections to solution. Speaker always concentrates on what the audience needs to learn to understand —the problem, the solution, or the possible objections to the solution.

C. *Example:*
Young people should start a regular program of physical fitness through jogging.
   1. Many college students are in poor physical condition.
       a. Fewer colleges are requiring physical education courses.
       b. Increasing numbers of young people are overweight.
       c. Increasing numbers of youth are suffering from physical problems that can be cured by staying in good physical condition.
   2. Jogging is good for social, psychological, and physical reasons.
       a. People who jog together have time to get to know each other well.
       b. Joggers can take out some of their frustration, anxiety, and aggression on the track.
       c. Joggers can gain and maintain good physical conditioning through regular workouts.
   3. The main objections to jogging are the time it takes and the energy it requires.
       a. We should take time to care for our bodies just as we take time to develop our minds and our spirit.
       b. The effort that jogging takes is its main benefit, as it benefits our cardiovascular system.

There are many additional patterns of organization other than time, topical, and problem-solution patterns.

Spatial organization. The speech can be organized spatially, with emphasis on where the parts of a whole exist in space. Examples: description of a control panel from center to periphery, electrical transmission from energy source to the home, a dress design from top to bottom. Speech can be organized according to cause-effect design, described below.

Cause-effect organization. In a cause-effect organization the speaker explains the cause or causes and the consequences, results, or effect similar to problem-solution pattern. Examples: causes of inflation and some possible solutions to the problem. Ratio of cause to effect decided by audience analysis. If causes well known to audience, then more attention can be concentrated on the effect.

Climactic and anticlimactic organization. In a climactic organization, strongest or best information and arguments are stated last. In an anticlimactic organization, best or strongest arguments and evidence are presented early.

Indirect sequencing. Speaker first states the grounds for an argument or conclusion, then the generalization or conclusion based on that information.

Example:

Grounds:

1. Our present waste-disposal system is outdated, ineffective, and expensive.
2. Our present waste-disposal system does not permit the recycling of metals, glass, and paper.
3. Our present waste-disposal system does not allow for the burning of combustible waste products.

Conclusion:

Our present waste-disposal system needs to be replaced.

The indirect sequencing pattern uses an inductive method of arriving at a reasonable conclusion.

The foregoing list does not exhaust the possible patterns of organization that a speaker can employ. The possibilities for patterns of organization are somewhat like the possibilities for attention-getting introductions: they are limited only by the imagination and creativity of the speaker.

Transitions

One aspect of speech organization that is not readily apparent in the overall organization of the speech are the linkages between sections of the speech known as *transitions*. The purpose of a transition is to help the audience move from one point to another in a speech as smoothly as possible. Audiences appreciate forewarning, and a transition is a verbal indication of a move. Rarely is it appropriate to indicate blatantly that the speaker is moving from one point to another. We do not state: "This is my introduction," or "Now I am approaching my conclusion." Nonetheless, we do announce that we are going to present arguments favoring some proposition, and we do state, in transition, "My second point is ...," "To summarize my position on this subject ...," or, "The best argument in favor of legalized gambling is ..." Transitions are a way of telling an audience where you are going, of mapping the organization of your speech, and of summarizing what you have already covered.

The most important transitions are between the introduction and the body, between the main points of the body, and between the body and the conclusion of the speech. Many others can appear in a speech: between the main heading and the main points, between the main points and the subpoints, between examples, and between visual aids and the point being illustrated. Transitions consist of forecasts, or previews, of coming attractions; of internal summaries that inform listeners how far the speech has progressed; and of statements of relationship telling how the parts of the whole are related in the speech's organization. Transitions are the mortar between the building blocks of the speech. Without it,

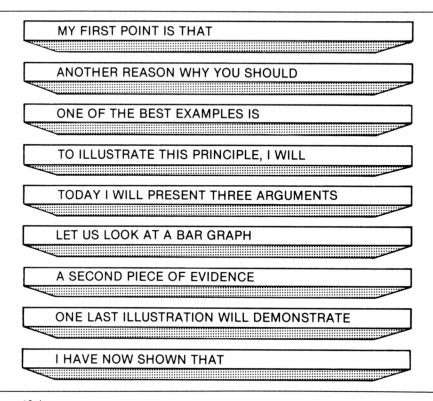

Figure 12.4

cracks appear and the structure is less solid. Examples of transitions are contained in the sample speech that follows.

**A Sample Organization:
Form and Function Unite**

Explanation	*Organization*
The topic	I. *Introduction:* One of the student's favorite scapegoats is the bookstore.
An anecdote arouses interest	A. A personal narrative about buying books for this session, with emphasis on the prices.
Common ground, or co-orientation	B. Our common plight as student consumers is that we have to pay high prices for required texts.
Source credibility and transition into the body	C. To investigate this topic, I interviewed the bookstore manager, compared prices of textbooks at two different colleges, and talked with two publishers' representatives who were on campus.
Authoritative source: interview material	II. *Body:* The bookstore manager told me how many books he sells, the number of books that students steal, and the discount he receives from the publishers.

Evidence from
authoritative source

Another authoritative
source, and visual aid
showing breakdown of
costs

Testimony from
authoritative source

Types of expenses
incurred by publishers

More testimony

Persuasive appeal—
purpose of speech
deliberately delayed

More evidence

Motivating change in
attitude and behavior

Summary of basic
information

Persuasive appeal—call to
action

Finale

A. The bookstore sells a large volume of books at prices that are not substantially above the wholesale cost.

B. Students and other customers steal books and supplies which have to be taken into account in pricing of the books.

C. The book companies' representatives told me how much the author makes on each book, and what the company pays for. They also explained why each new book is a gamble.

   1. Authors usually earn from 12-15 percent of the book's price.

   2. The company pays for the editing, the paper, the printing, the binding, the review copies, the advertising, and the sales personnel. These expenses account for most of the cost of the book.

   3. The profit on a textbook depends heavily on the sale of a large number of books.

D. We may have been unfairly blaming the bookstore for costs that are out of its control and for expenses that we directly affect.

   1. The cost of paper, printing, distributing, and selling books has escalated in recent years.

   2. The cost of stealing books and supplies from the bookstore is one that we students can reduce by changing our attitudes and our behavior.

III. *Conclusion:* We should think about the cost of producing textbooks and the costs that we ourselves are responsible for, the next time we complain about the price of books.

A. The class is encouraged to spread the word about why books are so expensive.

B. We tend to blame the bookstore for ripping us off when part of the problem is that we have been ripping off the bookstore.

This sample outline illustrates how form and function unite to make a speech. Next we will concentrate on ways of concluding a speech.

The Conclusion

Like the introduction and the body of a speech, the conclusion has certain functions. Complex speeches frequently conclude with a summary of main points from the body of the speech. Persuasive speeches frequently end with an appeal to the audience to think or behave in some manner that is consistent with the persuader's purpose. The means of ending speeches are numerous. The speaker can terminate a speech with a rhetorical question: "Knowing what you now know, will you feel safe riding with a driver who drinks?" Or with a quotation from some famous person: "As Patrick Henry said, 'Give me liberty or give me death.'" Or with a literary passage: "We conclude with the words of Ralph Waldo Emerson, who said, 'It is one light which beams out of a thousand stars; it is one soul which animates all men.'" Or perhaps with some action that demonstrates the point of the speech: the quickly assembled electric motor works for the class to see, the speaker twirls and does a split in one graceful motion, the experiment is completed and the mixture of soda and vinegar boils and smokes.

Introductions and conclusions—getting started and drawing to a close—are often difficult for beginning speakers. Because of this, these two parts of the speech should be rehearsed so they will be presented as planned. The speaker who fails to plan a conclusion may near the end with nothing more to say.

Audiences need to be warned by your words, your tone, or your actions that the speech is nearly completed. Otherwise, you might end your speech with the audience dangling in the wind as you head for your seat. Audiences appreciate a sense of closure, a sense of completeness, and a sense of finality in the conclusion of a speech. Speakers who ignore this expectation risk offending the very people that they seek to influence.

In concluding, as in beginning, it is possible to be overly dramatic. At one big Midwestern college, the speech classes were taught in a block-long building that held several thousand students every class hour. On the third floor of this building, students were giving their final speeches. In one room, a student was delivering a speech about insanity. As the speech progressed, the class became increasingly aware that the young man delivering the speech had a few problems. At first, it was difficult to understand what he was saying: words were run together, parts of sentences were incoherent, pauses were too long. Near the end of the speech, the young man's eyes were rolling and his jaw had fallen slack. At the very end of the speech, he looked wildly at the audience, ran over to the open window, and jumped. The class was aghast. Teacher and students rushed to the window expecting to see his shattered remains. Far below, on the ground, were twenty fraternity brothers holding a large fireman's net with the speaker waving happily from the center.

A better idea is to conclude your speech with an inspirational statement, with words that make the audience glad they took the time and energy to listen

Figure 12.5   The end.

to you. One student that I heard over ten years ago came up with a single line at the end of his speech on automobile accidents that summarized his speech and gave his audience a line to remember: "It is not who is right in a traffic accident that really counts," he said, "it is who is left." That conclusion was clever, was a brief summary of the speech, and was an intelligent and safe way to end a speech.

Summary

In this chapter, we studied ways of introducing a speech, developing the body of a speech, and of concluding a speech. We learned that the introduction can serve any of several functions, including (1) getting the audience to focus on the speaker; (2) arousing the audience's interest in the subject matter; (3) indicating the purpose of the speech; (4) describing the speaker's qualifications; and (5) indicating common ground with the audience.

To help us organize the body of a speech we investigated the outline and found that it follows the principles of subordination, division, and parallel construction. We also examined the functions of the body of the speech: to forecast the development of the speech; to provide information or to motivate an audience to act, believe, or think in some manner consistent with the speaker's purpose; and to provide a rationale for any such change. To help you select an organizational pattern appropriate to your audience and situation, we reviewed eight organizational patterns that are commonly employed in speeches, including the time-sequence pattern, the topical-sequence pattern, and the problem-solution pattern. Transitions, the linkages among the main sections of a speech and among the many subsections, were discussed. We examined a sample outline whose sections were labeled to show how form and function unite in a speech, and we ended with a discussion of the functions of conclusions.

New Terms

Introduction	Forecast	Spatial organization
Arousal	Body	Cause-effect organization
Statement of purpose	Delayed revelation	Climactic organization
Common ground	Review and inspiration	Anticlimactic organization
Principle of subordination	Review of exposition	Indirect sequencing
Principle of division	Finale	Transition
Principle of parallel construction	Time-sequence pattern	Forewarning or previews
Form of organization	Topical-sequence pattern	Conclusion
Function of organization	Problem-and-solution pattern	

Additional Readings

Connolly, James E. *Public Speaking as Communication.* Minneapolis: Burgess Publishing Company, 1974. Pages 35–47.
Provides insights into patterns of organization: chronological, spatial, cause-effect, problem-solution, and so forth. Also contains a rationale for organizing messages so the audience can process the information more readily.

Ellingsworth, Huber W., and Clevenger, Theodore, Jr. *Speech and Social Action: A Strategy of Oral Communication.* Englewood Cliffs, N.J.: Prentice-Hall, Inc. 1967. Pages 56–103.
An inventive and insightful examination of organization. The authors show how context affects meaning and discuss the elements of organization as ways in which to provide the best context for the information to be presented. Interesting and worthwhile reading.

Kruger, Arthur N. *Effective Speaking: A Complete Course.* New York: Van Nostrand Reinhold Company, 1970. Pages 201–42.
Kruger suggests ways to analyze topics in order to discover their subpoints, presents organization as a means of thinking through a speech, and views organization as a process by which to develop the subject rather than as an end in itself.

Mills, Glen E. *Message Preparation: Analysis and Structure.* Indianapolis: Bobbs-Merrill Co., Inc., 1966. Pages 47–69.

Purposes and kinds of outlines are discussed. General principles of outlining are presented with examples of correct and incorrect outlines. Organizational patterns are related to the informative and the persuasive speech.

Oliver, Robert T.; Zelko, Harold P.; and Holtzman, Paul D. *Communicative Speaking and Listening.* 4th ed. New York: Holt, Rinehart and Winston, Inc., 1968. Pages 112–32.
The authors relate the principles and techniques of outlining to audience involvement. Organization makes the message clearer to the audience and helps the audience respond in a manner consistent with the speaker's purpose.

Thomas, Coramae, and Howard, C. Jeriel. *Contact: A Textbook in Applied Communication.* Englewood Cliffs, N.J.: Prentice-Hall, Inc., 1970. Pages 193–211.
A discussion of principles of outlining in an easy-to-understand format. Examples of subordination and division are given. Excellent help in understanding and improving your outlining skills.

Walter, Otis M. *Speaking to Inform and Persuade.* New York: Macmillan Publishing Co., Inc., 1966. Chapters 2, 3, and 4.
Walter develops the principles of introductions and conclusions. A straightforward style clearly identifies the basic elements of good organization for informative speaking. Walter also describes the use of internal summaries and transitions to carry the speech from one point to another.

Notes

1. "Headless," *Time,* July 18, 1977, p. 21.
2. "Tomorrow," *U.S. News and World Report,* July 18, 1977, p. 8.
3. "American Youth," *U.S. News and World Report,* July 18, 1977, p. 19.
4. L. S. Harms, "Listener Judgments of Status Cues in Speech," *Quarterly Journal of Speech* 47 (1961): 168.
5. "Time of Reckoning for Student Deadbeats," *U.S. News and World Report,* July 18, 1977, p. 21.

13

Sharing Yourself Through Delivery

Objectives

After study of this chapter you should be able to do the following:

1. Differentiate four modes of delivery and discuss the uses, advantages, and disadvantages of each
2. Define seven aspects of vocal delivery and discuss how they influence the effectiveness of your speech
3. Discuss the uses of gestures, eye contact, and movement in delivering a speech
4. Specify the methods of improving your vocal and bodily delivery
5. Explain the relationship between delivery and effective public speaking; defend the position that the content of the speech is more important than its delivery
6. Discuss the importance of effective delivery in persuasive and informative speaking
7. Deliver an extemporaneous speech to your classroom audience demonstrating effective vocal and bodily delivery

"Reverend Heathweather was so good today. I just loved his sermon. He is such a fine speaker."

"What was it that he said that impressed you so much?"

"Well, I don't know. He just has such a way with words."

The response to the Reverend Heathweather's sermon is not uncommon among listeners who have heard a skilled public speaker. Sometimes a speech is presented with such skill that the listener misses the message and focuses instead on the delivery.

What is delivery and how does it fit into the process of public speaking? *Delivery,* in the field of communication, is a broad term that includes a large variety of behavior that is related to how we enrich the verbal content with nonverbal messages. Delivery includes the paralanguage discussed in chapter 4, on nonverbal communication. The meaning of a speech is conveyed only in part by the words. The speaker delivers the words in tones that convey conviction, irony, sarcasm, happiness, or anger. The voice is an important instrument for evoking meaning. The speaker also conveys messages with the body: facial expressions, bodily movement, gestures, and eye contact help the audience to interpret the words. These features of public speaking—the vocal and the bodily aspects of delivery—are the subject of this chapter. We shall survey four modes of delivery and their appropriateness in various public communication situations. Then, we shall examine both the vocal and the bodily aspects of delivery.

paralanguage.

Four Modes of Delivery

Four modes of delivery are possible choices for the public speaker: the reading of papers or manuscripts; the delivery of memorized speeches; extemporaneous speeches; and impromptu speeches. We shall look at each and point out the appropriate circumstances for selecting them.

script = entire speech plain Reading.

Manuscripts and Papers

① Look at script Not audience ② Can't adapt to reactions

Speakers who have to be very careful about what they say and how they say it choose to present manuscripts. In other words, the speaker has a script of the entire speech. The advantage of this mode of delivery is that the speaker is never at a loss for words: they are all right there. The disadvantage of a manuscript speech is that it is often mere reading of the words, that it invites the speaker to attend to the script instead of the audience, and that it discourages the speaker from adapting to the reactions of the listeners.

The most appropriate time to read a manuscript is when there is a compelling need to have every word, phrase, and sentence stated precisely. The consequences of a misstatement can be very serious, as when the president makes an important address. He may appear to be speaking without any notes at all, but he is actually reading his speech off a teleprompter that permits him to read every word while looking directly at the television camera or his audience. Many ministers write out their sermons so that their main points are correctly documented with Biblical references. College teachers often work from a manuscript so that they give the same lesson to each section that they teach. Students may be asked to deliver a manuscript, but usually the emphasis for beginning speakers is on the next mode which we will consider, the extemporaneous mode of delivery. *Only use when must be precise.*

The Extemporaneous Speech

prepared but spontaneous

① FREEDOM FROM NOTES ② eye contact ③ adapt easier to audience

Extemporaneous speeches are the most common in the classroom where students are learning how to prepare and deliver speeches. The extemporaneous speech is carefully prepared and researched, but it appears to be spontaneous in its delivery. The extemporaneous mode of delivery does not have the disadvantages of the manuscript speech. While reading a manuscript invites dependency on the script, reduces eye contact, and makes adaptation difficult, extemporaneous delivery invites freedom from the notes, encourages eye contact, and makes adaptation easier. The speaker who employs the extemporaneous mode delivers the speech from key words, an outline, or a list of main points. Because much of the speech is composed in the speaker's head as the speech is being delivered, it appears to be done "on the spur of the moment," the literal Latin root of the term *extemporaneous.*

uses out line + key words.

The Impromptu Speech *NO NOTES NO planning*

The impromptu speech is delivered without notes and without planning or preparation. The term *impromptu* comes from Latin and French roots meaning "in
readiness." You have undoubtedly already delivered impromptu speeches.
When you answer a question in class, you are giving an impromptu answer.
When someone asks you to explain something at a meeting, your presentation is
usually impromptu. When you are asked to introduce yourself, to say a few
words about yourself, or to reveal what you know about some subject, you are
probably making an impromptu presentation. You may be prepared for the
speech in the sense that you do have something to say, but you did not prepare
to give a speech the way you would prepare for an extemporaneous speech.
Some teachers give students an opportunity to practice impromptu speaking by
having each student introduce himself or herself; others have students draw
topics out of a hat for an impromptu performance. One of the advantages of this
mode of delivery is that you learn how to think on your feet without benefit of
notes. A disadvantage is that this mode of delivery does not encourage audience
analysis, research, and prior adaptation to the audience.

(1) think on feet.
(2) No research, or analysis, or adaption.

The Memorized Speech *comitted to memory.*

The *memorized speech* is simply one that the speaker has committed to memory.
The speaker achieves this goal either by rote memory or by delivering it so many
times that it is imprinted on the mind. This type of delivery is common in ora-

① minimul spontenaity to audience ③ sound memorized.
② HELPS THINK OF DELVERY.   ③ good eye contact
                                 ④ no search FOR WORDS

tory contests, on the lecture circuit, and at banquets. It is appropriate both on ceremonial occasions and at ritualistic events where a minimum of spontaneous adaptation to the audience occurs. Many politicians have a stock speech that they have committed to memory so that it can be used wherever the politically faithful might gather. The main advantage of a memorized address is that it permits the speaker to concentrate on delivery. Eye contact can be continuous, searching for words is eliminated. The main disadvantage is that the memorized address permits little or no adaptation during the presentation. The speaker runs the risk of having a speech that sounds memorized. However, in some formal situations there may be little need for adaptation: some speakers have delivered the same speech so many times that they even know when the audience is going to applaud, and for how long.

Different speakers prefer different modes of delivery. Whereas the impromptu mode teaches students very little about preparing a speech, both the reading of manuscripts and the delivery of memorized speeches require a great deal of time. The extemporaneous mode is favored in the public speaking classroom because it is versatile, because it is efficient, because it allows for maximum adaptation to the audience before and during the speech, and because it helps students learn how to prepare a speech.

Nonetheless, the mode of delivery does not determine the effectiveness of a speech. In a study to determine whether the extemporaneous or the manuscript mode of delivery was more effective, two researchers concluded that the mode of delivery simply did not determine effectiveness. The ability of the speaker was more important: some speakers were more effective with extemporaneous speeches than with manuscripts, but others used both modes with equal effectiveness.[1]

Vocal and Bodily Aspects of Delivery

Delivery, as we have already observed, concerns paralanguage, the effect of factors beyond the words or language of the speech. We turn now to two aspects of delivery: vocal and bodily.

Vocal Aspects of Delivery

Studying the vocal aspects of delivery is like studying the music that comes from the notes. Musical notes are like the words of the speech. The music that results is like the paralanguage we hear when someone says the words. Different musicians can make the same musical notes sound quite different; different speakers can evoke different interpretations of words and produce different effects on the audience. We shall examine the music we hear when someone delivers a speech

by defining the different vocal characteristics, by referring to relevant studies, and by offering some suggestions about your delivery. The seven vocal aspects of delivery are: pitch; rate; pauses; volume; enunciation; fluency; and vocal variety.

Pitch is the highness or lowness of the speaker's voice, its upward and downward inflection, the melody produced by the voice. Pitch is what makes the difference between the "Ohhh" that you utter when you earn a poor grade in a class and the "Ohhh" that you utter when you see something or someone really attractive. The "Ohhh" looks the same in print, but when the notes turn to music the difference between the two expressions is vast. The pitch of your voice can make you sound animated, lively, and vivacious, or it can make you sound dull, listless, and monotonous. As a speaker you learn to avoid the two extremes: on the one hand, you avoid the lack of change in pitch that results in a monotone; on the other hand, you avoid repetitious changes in pitch that result in a singsong delivery. The best public speakers employ the full range of their normal pitch.

Some studies indicate that control of pitch does more than make a speech esthetically pleasing. One study indicates that changes in pitch, together with some other variables, can actually help an audience retain information.[2] Another scholar found that voices perceived as "good" were characterized by a greater range of pitch, more upward inflections, more downward inflections, and more pitch shifts.[3] Certainly, one of the important features of pitch control is that it can be employed to alter the way an audience will respond to the words. Many subtle changes in meaning are accomplished by changes in pitch. The speaker's

Question determination
doubt, irony.
surprise

pitch tells an audience whether the words are a statement or a question, whether the words are sarcastic or ironic, and whether the speaker is conveying doubt, determination, or surprise.

Pitch control, whether in baseball or speech, is learned only by constant practice. An actor who is learning to utter a line has to practice it many times and in many ways before he can be assured that most people in the audience will understand the words as he intended. The public speaker rehearses a speech before a sympathetic audience to get feedback on whether the words are being understood as intended. Sometimes we sound angry or brusque when we do not intend to; sometimes we sound cynical when we intend to sound doubtful; and sometimes we sound frightened when we are only surprised. We are not always the best judge of how we sound to others, so we have to place some trust in other people's evaluations. Practicing pitch is a way of achieving control of this important vocal aspect of delivery. *Speed of delivery 125–190*

Rate, the second characteristic of vocal delivery, is the speed of delivery. The normal rate for American speakers is between 125 and 190 words per minute. But our minds can comprehend many more words per minute than that. That is why some medical schools are recording professors' lectures in a compressed form. Mechanically speeding up the lecture allows the student to hear a one-hour lecture in forty-five minutes. However, there is some question about what public speakers should conclude from this information. Perhaps information gleaned from studies on the subject of rate, listenability, and comprehension will help us to decide.

An early study of students who won collegiate oratory contests indicated that they spoke an average of 120 words per minute.[4] That rate is slightly below the average speaking rate for Americans. In oratorical contests, there may be some advantage to a slow delivery. There have also been studies of the relationship between rate and listenability. Can the audience understand the speaker when the rate varies? One scholar used recorded stories and found no differences in listenability when they were played back at 125, 150, 175, and 200 words per minute.[5] Notice that only the 200-word-per-minute instance exceeds the normal range of 125-190 words per minute, and that it exceeds the normal rate only slightly. We may safely conclude from this study that, with recorded stories at least, a rate within the normal range does not adversely affect listenability.

How does rate relate to comprehension or understanding of the content of a speech? One study indicated that comprehension at 282 words per minute, well above the normal range, was only 10 percent less than it was at 141 words per minute, near the middle of normal range.[6] Given the rather large increase in rate, the loss in comprehension was relatively small. Another study related to rate and comprehension indicated that with just ten minutes of practice, students could learn to listen to double the amount without a loss of comprehension.[7]

These research findings seem to indicate that speakers can talk faster than normal without adversely affecting the listenability or intelligibility of a speech, and without affecting the audience's comprehension. Indeed, one study showed that when students shortened their pauses and raised their speaking rate from 126 words to 172 words per minute, neither the audience's comprehension nor their rating of the speaker's delivery was affected.[8] It appears, then, that the human mind can understand information delivered at a faster rate than we normally speak and that rapid delivery can increase the amount of material covered without adversely affecting the audience's rating of the speaker's delivery. Then why do winners of oratory contests speak even more slowly than most speakers? Perhaps because speech teachers more often tell their students to slow down than to speed up. Many speakers betray their anxiety by speeding up, which is not pleasant to an audience. Then again, perhaps the studies are not conclusive. One of them demonstrated that increasing the speed of recorded stories did not reduce listenability, but all but one speed was well within the normal range. Stories are among the easiest verbal material to comprehend, anyway. In another study, the speed was increased from 126 to 172 words per minute without a reduction in comprehension or the audience's evaluation of delivery. But both speeds are within the normal range. One study that included a rate well beyond normal resulted in a 10 percent loss of comprehension. Instead of reading the studies as an indication that faster is better, it turns out that a speaker need only to stay within a normal range of rates.

The essential point, not revealed in the studies, is that speaking rate needs to be adapted to the audience and the situation. A grade-school teacher does not rip through a fairy tale: the audience is just learning how to understand words. The public speaker addressing a large audience without a microphone might speak slowly and distinctly to enhance the audience's comprehension of the words. If audience and situation need to be taken into account in determining appropriate rate, so does content. Whereas stories delivered at a relatively fast rate may be easy to understand, a string of statistics may have to be delivered slowly and repetitively to be fully understood. The rate may depend on what kind of effect you are seeking. Telling a story of suspense and intrigue would be difficult to do at a high speed. Effective public speakers adjust their speed according to the audience, the situation, the content of the speech, and the effect they are trying to produce.

A third vocal characteristic is the *pause*. Speeches seem to be meant for a steady stream of verbiage, without silences. Yet pauses and silence can be used for dramatic effect and to get an audience to consider content. The speaker may begin a speech with rhetorical questions: "Have you had a cigarette today? Have you had two or three? Ten or eleven? Do you know what your habit is costing you in a year? A decade? A lifetime?" After each rhetorical question a pause allows each member of the audience to answer the question in his or her own mind.

On the other hand, vocalized pauses are nonfluencies that adversely affect an audience's perception of the speaker's competence and dynamism. The "ahhhs," "nows," and "you knows" of the novice speaker are anathema to the public speaking teacher. Unfortunately, even some highly experienced speakers have the habit of filling silences with vocalized pauses. At least one group teaches public speaking to laypersons by having members of the audience drop a marble into a can every time a speaker uses a vocalized pause. The resulting punishment, the clanging of the cans, is supposed to break the habit. A more humane method might be to rehearse your speech before a friend who signals you every time you vocalize a pause, so that you do it less often when you deliver your speech to an audience. One speech teacher hit on the idea of rigging a light to the lectern so that every time the student speaker used a vocalized pause, the light went on for a moment. Perhaps we should be less afraid of silence: many audiences would prefer a little silence to vocalized pauses.

One way to learn how to use pauses effectively in public speaking is to listen to how your classmates use them. You should also listen to professional speakers. Paul Harvey, the radio commentator, practically orchestrates his

pauses. His delivery of the ''Page Two'' section of his news broadcast helps make him unique. Oral Roberts, Billy Graham, or any of a dozen radio and television evangelists use pauses effectively.

A fourth vocal characteristic of delivery is *volume,* the relative loudness of your speech. We are accustomed to speaking to people at a relatively close distance, about an arm's length in conversation. In order to speak effectively in front of a class, a meeting, or an auditorium full of people, we have to speak louder or project our voices so that all may hear. Telling speech students to speak so that all may hear might sound like very elementary advice, but many beginning speakers see those people in the first few rows and speak only to them. We project our voices by making sure that the most distant people in the room can hear what we say. Even when practicing in an empty room, it is a good idea to project your voice so that someone sitting at the rear could hear with ease.

Volume is more than just projection. Variations in volume can convey emotion, importance, suspense, and subtle nuances of meaning. We whisper a secret and we use a stage whisper in front of an audience to signal a furtive intent. We may speak loudly and strongly on important points and let our voices carry our conviction. An orchestra never plays so quietly that the patrons cannot hear, but the musicians vary their volume. Similarly, a public speaker who considers the voice an instrument learns how to speak softly, loudly, and everywhere in between to convey meaning.

Enunciation, the fifth vocal aspect of delivery, is the pronunciation and articulation of words. Because our reading vocabulary is larger than our speaking vocabulary, we may use, in our speeches, words that we have rarely or never heard before. It is risky to deliver unfamiliar words. One student in a speech class gave a speech about the human reproductive system. During the speech he managed to mispronounce nearly half the words used to describe the female anatomy. The speaker reduced the audience's view of his competence, and thereby his credibility. Rehearsing in front of friends, roommates, or family is a safer way to try out your vocabulary and pronunciation on an audience.

The best way to avoid pronunciation problems is to find the words in a dictionary. Every dictionary has a pronunciation key. For instance, the entry for the word *belie* in the *Random House Dictionary of the English Language* looks like this:

> be •lie (bǐ-li′), v.t., -lied, -ly •ing. 1. to show to be false; contradict: His trembling hands belied his calm voice. . . .[9]

The entry indicates that the word *belie* has two syllables. The pronunciation key says that the ǐ should be pronounced like the *i* in *if,* the *u* in *busy,* or the *ee* in *been.* The ī, according to the pronunciation key, should be pronounced like the *ye* in *lye,* the *i* in *ice,* or the *ais* in *aisle.* The accent mark (′) indicates which syllable should receive heavier emphasis. You should learn how to use the pronunciation key in a dictionary, but if you still have some misgivings about how to pronounce a word, you should ask your speech teacher for assistance.

Another way to improve your enunciation is to learn how to prolong syllables. This makes you easier to understand, especially if you are addressing a large audience, an audience assembled outside, or an audience in an auditorium without a microphone. The drawing out of syllables can be overdone, however. Some radio and TV newspersons hang onto the final syllable so long that the practice draws attention to itself. In general, a student speaker can improve pronunciation, articulation, and the audience's understanding by learning how to increase the duration of syllables.

Pronunciation and articulation are the important components of enunciation. Poor *articulation,* poor production of sounds, is so prevalent that there are popular jokes about it. One adult remembers hearing in Sunday School, a song about Willie the cross-eyed bear. The song was "Willing the Cross I Bear." Some children have heard the Lord's Prayer mumbled so many times that they think that one of the lines is "hollow be thy name."

The problem of articulation is less humorous when it happens in your own speech. It occurs in part because so many English words are spelled differently and sound alike and because people often fail to articulate carefully. In consequence, their words are conveyed inaccurately. A class experiment will illustrate this problem. One student whispered a phrase from a presidential address, and a line of students whispered the message from person to person. The phrase was,

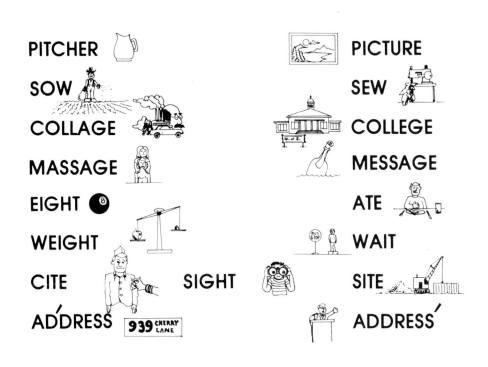

Figure 13.1

"We must seek fresh answers, unhindered by the stale prescriptions of the past." By the time the message left the third person, it was "When we seek stale answers to the prescription." The eighth person heard the message, "When the snakes now answer the question." Similar problems can occur in a public speech if a speaker does not take care to articulate words properly.

The sixth vocal characteristic of delivery is *fluency*—the smoothness of delivery, the flow of the words, and the absence of vocalized pauses. Fluency is difficult because it cannot be achieved by looking up words in a dictionary or by any other simple solution. Fluency is not even very noticeable. Listeners are more likely to notice errors than to notice the seemingly effortless flow of words in a well-delivered speech. It is possible to be too fluent. A speaker who seems too glib is sometimes considered "slick," "smooth as a used car salesman," or "so greasy that you could tap him for oil." The importance of fluency is emphasized in a study which showed that audiences tend to perceive a speaker's fluency, the smoothness of presentation, as a main ingredient of effectiveness.[10]

To achieve fluency, public speakers must be confident of the content of their speeches. If the speakers know what they are going to say and have said it over and over in rehearsal, then disruptive repetition and vocalized pauses are reduced. If speakers master what they are going to say and concentrate on the overall rhythm of the speech, their fluency will improve. Speakers must pace, build, and time various parts of the speech so that they all fit together in a coherent whole.

The seventh vocal aspect of delivery—one that summarizes many of the others—is *vocal variety*. This term refers to voice quality, intonation patterns, inflections of pitch, and syllablic duration. Vocal variety is encouraged in public speaking because the studies indicate that it improves effectiveness. Charles Woolbert, in a very early study of public reading, found that audiences seem to retain more information when there are large variations in rate, force, pitch, and voice quality. More recently, George Glasgow studied an audience's comprehension of prose and poetry and found that it decreased 10 percent when the material was delivered in a monotone. A third study indicated that audiences understood more when listening to skilled speakers than when listening to unskilled speakers. They also recalled more information immediately after the speech and at a later date. The skilled speakers were more effective, whether or not the material was organized, disorganized, easy, difficult. Good vocalization was also found to include fewer but longer pauses, greater ranges of pitch, and more upward and downward inflections.[11]

Bodily Aspects of Delivery

There are three *bodily aspects of delivery*—nonverbal indicators of meaning—that are important to the public speaker. In any communication, speakers indicate how they relate to the material and the audience by posture, facial expression, and bodily movements. When we observe two persons busily engaged in conversation, we can judge their interest in the conversation without hearing their words. Just so, in public speaking, the nonverbal bodily aspects of delivery reinforce what the speaker is saying. Researchers have found that audience members who can see the speaker comprehend more of the speech than audience members who cannot see the speaker.[12] Apparently, the speaker's visible behavior conveys enough meaning to improve the audience's understanding of what is being said. Among the important bodily aspects of delivery are gestures, eye contact, and movement.

Gestures are movements of the head, arms, and hands that we use to describe what we are talking about, to emphasize certain points, and to signal an advance to another part of the speech. We rarely worry about gestures in a conversation, but when we give a speech in front of an audience, arms and hands seem to be bothersome appendages. Perhaps we feel unnatural because public speaking is an unfamiliar situation. Do you remember the first time you drove a car, the first time you tried to swim or dive, or the first time you tried to kiss your date? The first time that you give a speech you might not feel any more natural than you did then. Nonetheless, physically or artistically skilled people make what they do look easy. A skilled golfer, a talented painter, an excellent runner, and a graceful dancer all perform with seeming effortlessness. The beginners, the novices, are the ones who make a performance look difficult. The paradox is that human beings have to work hard to make physical or artistic feats look easy.

What can you do to help yourself gesture naturally when you deliver your speech? The answer lies in involvement and rehearsal. Angry farmers and angry miners appear on television to protest low prices and poor working conditions. These orators have not spent a lot of time practicing, but they deliver their speeches with gusto and a lot of determined gestures. They also look very natural. The main reason for their natural delivery may be their involvement in the issue they are discussing. They are upset, and they show it in their words and actions. They are mainly concerned with getting their message across. The student of public speaking can also deliver a speech more naturally if his or her attention is concentrated on getting the message across. Self-conscious attention to our own gestures is often self-defeating: the gestures look studied, rehearsed, or slightly out of synchronization with our message. Selecting a topic that you

find involving can have the unexpected side benefit of improving your delivery, especially if you concentrate on your audience and your message.

Another way of learning to make appropriate gestures is to practice a speech in front of friends who are willing to make constructive criticisms. Indeed, constructive criticism is also one of the benefits you can receive from your speech teacher and your fellow students. Actors spend hours rehearsing lines and gestures so that they will look spontaneous and unrehearsed on stage. Public speakers appear before many audiences until they learn to speak and move naturally. In time and after many practice sessions, they learn which arm, head, and hand movements seem to help and which seem to hinder their message. You too can learn, through practice, to gesture naturally—in a way that reinforces your message instead of detracting from it.

Another physical aspect of delivery that is important to the public speaker is _eye contact_. This term refers to the way a speaker watches the audience. Studies and experience indicate that audiences prefer maintenance of good eye contact,[13] and that it enhances source credibility.[14] Eye contact is one of the ways we indicate to others how we feel about them. We are wary of persons who, in conversation, will not look us in the eye. Similarly, in public speaking, eye contact conveys our relationship with our audience. The public speaker who rarely or never looks at the audience may appear uninterested in the audience, and the audience may resent it. The public speaker who looks over the heads of audience members or scans them so quickly that he does not really establish contact may appear to be afraid of the audience. The proper relationship between audience and speaker is one of purposeful communication. We signal that sense of purpose by treating members of the audience as individuals with whom we wish to communicate. The appropriate way to treat people with whom we wish to communicate is to look at them for responses to our message.

How can you learn to maintain eye contact with your audience? One way is to know your speech so well that you have to make only intermittent references to your notes. The speaker who does not know the speech well is manuscript-bound. Delivering an extemporaneous speech from key words or an outline is a way of encouraging yourself to keep an eye on the audience. One of the purposes of extemporaneous delivery is to enable you to adapt to your audience. That adaptation is not possible unless you are continually monitoring the audience's behavior to see if the individuals understand your message. Other ways of learning to use eye contact include scanning or continually looking over your entire audience, addressing various sections of the audience as you progress through your speech, and concentrating on the head nodders. In almost every audience there are some individuals who overtly indicate whether your message is coming across. These individuals usually nod "yes" or "no" with their heads, thus the name, _nodders_. Some speakers find that it helps their delivery to find friendly faces and positive nodders who signal when the message is getting through.

A third physical aspect of delivery is *movement,* what the speaker does with the entire body during a speech presentation. Sometimes the situation limits movement. The presence of a fixed microphone, a lectern, a pulpit, or some other physical feature of the environment may limit your activity. The length of the speech can also make a difference. A short speech without movement is less difficult for both speaker and audience than a very long one. Good movement for the public speaker is appropriate and purposeful movement. The "caged lion" who paces back and forth to work off anxiety is moving inappropriately and purposelessly in relation to the content of the speech.

Because of the importance of eye contact, the speaker should always strive to face the audience, even when moving. Some other suggestions on movement relate to the use of visual aids. The speaker who writes on the blackboard during a speech has to turn his or her back on the audience. This can be avoided either by writing information on the board between classes or by using a poster instead. Some speakers move during transitions in the speech to give a visual indication of advancement in the speech; others move forward on the points that they regard as most important. The college classroom is a laboratory for the student who wants to learn movement. The college student can watch professors, lecturers, and fellow students when they deliver public speeches. You can learn through observation and practice what works for others and what works for you.

Effective delivery has many advantages. Research indicates that effective delivery, the appropriate use of voice and body in public speaking, contributes to the credibility of the speaker.[15] Indeed, student audiences characterize the poorest speakers by their voices and the physical aspects of delivery.[16] Poor speakers are judged to be fidgety, nervous, and monotonous. They also maintain little eye contact and show little animation or facial expression.[17] It has also been found that good delivery increases the audience's capacity for handling complex information.[18] Thus, public speakers' credibility, the audience's evaluation of them as good or poor speakers, and their ability to convey complex information may all be affected by the vocal and physical aspects of delivery.

Summary

After reading this chapter on delivery, you might have the impression that what you say is less important than how you say it. You might believe that delivery is so important that the person who is fluent, who pauses appropriately, who speaks at the best pitch and rate, and who gestures and moves well does not have to worry much about the substance of the speech. You should be wary about drawing this conclusion from the evidence presented here. Eye contact, gestures, and enunciation are important, but content may be even more important. The very same researcher who found that poor speakers are identified by their voices and by the physical aspects of their delivery also found that the best speakers were identified on the basis of the content of their speeches.[19] Two other researchers found that more of an audience's evaluation of a speaker is based on the content of the speech than on vocal characteristics such as intonation, pitch, and rate, and still another pair of researchers found that a well-composed speech can mask poor delivery.[20] Finally, one researcher reviewed all of the studies on informative speaking made prior to 1963 and reported that, while some research indicates that audiences that have listened to good speakers have significantly greater immediate recall, other findings show that the differences are slight. His conclusion: the influence of delivery on comprehension is overrated.[21]

What is the student of speech supposed to do in the face of these reports that good delivery influences audience comprehension positively but also that the influence of delivery on comprehension is overrated? What is the student of speech supposed to do when one study says that poor vocal characteristics result in evaluation as a poor speaker and another says that good content can mask poor delivery? Perhaps we all tend to oversimplify problems by not recognizing degrees of importance. If we recognize degrees of importance, then we may be able to resolve the apparent conflict—at least until more evidence comes in. The studies cited in this chapter emphasize the importance of delivery. The researchers who challenge those findings do not say that delivery is unimportant; instead, they say that in evaluating the relative importance of delivery and substance, or content, there is reason to believe that content may be more important than delivery. However, the jury is still out on this question. Additional studies may modify what we think and believe at this time. For the moment, the safest position for the speech student is to regard both delivery and content as important in public speaking. What you say and how you say it are both important—and in that order.

New Terms

Delivery of a speech	Rate	Intelligibility
Modes of delivery	Pause	Vocalized pauses
Manuscript mode	Volume	Projection
Extemporaneous mode	Enunciation	Pronunciation
Impromptu mode	Fluency	Articulation
Memorized mode	Vocal variety	Gestures
Paralanguage	Listenability	Eye contact
Pitch	Comprehension	Movement

Additional Readings

*Black, John W., and Moore, Wilbur E. *Speech: Code, Meaning, and Communication.* New York: McGraw-Hill Book Company, 1955. Chapters 2, 3 and 4.
A rather technical explanation of the mechanics and uses of voice to produce intelligible speech. A good resource book for the student who may have problems developing good vocal delivery techniques.

Bradley, Bert. *Speech Performance.* Dubuque, Iowa: Wm. C. Brown Company Publishers, 1967.
An exploration of various aspects of delivery, including modes of delivery, movement, poise, use of the microphone, appearance, and adaptation of delivery to the setting and the audience. Ways of reducing or controlling stage fright are suggested.

DeVito, Joseph A.; Giattino, Jill; and Schon, T. D. *Articulation and Voice: Effective Communication.* Indianapolis: Bobbs-Merrill Co., Inc., 1975.
The physiological bases of speech and hearing and the role of correct vocal techniques in effective communication are explained. Excellent exercises for improving articulation and vocal quality. Excellent resource for the nonclinical improvement of vocal delivery.

Kruger, Arthur N. *Effective Speaking: A Complete Course.* New York: Van

Nostrand Reinhold Company, 1970. Pages 21–150, 355–76.
The vocal production of sounds is explained with advice and exercises to help improve vocal delivery. Poise, movement, and gestures are also discussed, with some suggestions about effective ways to practice the speech and reduce nervousness.

Weaver, Andrew T., and Ness, Ordean G. *An Introduction to Public Speaking.* New York: Odyssey Press, 1961.
Contains an excellent discussion of delivery techniques, including gestures, movement, and posture. Good delivery must be direct, animated, and have vitality.

Winans, James A. "Conversing With an Audience." In *Selected Readings in Public Speaking,* edited by Jane Blankenship and Robert Wilhoit. Belmont, Calif.: Dickenson Publishing Co., Inc., 1968. Pages 163–81.
Winans argues that public speaking does not differ significantly from conversational speech and suggests clear, workable guidelines for developing a direct, communicative delivery. Thinking about what you want to say, rather than how you are going to say it, is the key to effective delivery.

*Indicates more advanced readings.

Notes

1. Herbert W. Hildebrandt and Walter Stevens, "Manuscript and Extemporaneous Delivery in Communicating Information," *Speech Monographs* 30 (1963): 369–72.
2. Charles Woolbert, "The Effects of Various Modes of Public Reading," *Journal of Applied Psychology* 4 (1920): 162–85.
3. John W. Black, "A Study of Voice Merit," *Quarterly Journal of Speech* 28 (1942): 67–74.
4. William N. Brigance, "How Fast Do We Talk?" *Quarterly Journal of Speech* 12 (1926): 337–42.
5. Kenneth A. Harwood, "Listenability and Rate of Presentation," *Speech Monographs* 22 (1955): 57–59.
6. Grant Fairbanks, Newman Guttman, and Miron S. Murray, "Effects of Time Compression upon the Comprehension of Connected Speech," *Journal of Speech and Hearing Disorders* 22 (1957): 10–19.

7. John B. Voor and Joseph M. Miller, "The Effect of Practice upon the Comprehension of Time-compressed Speech," *Speech Monographs* 32 (1965): 452–54.

8. Charles F. Diehl, Richard C. White, and Kenneth W. Burk, "Rate and Communication," *Speech Monographs* 26 (1959): 229–32.

9. From *The Random House Dictionary of the English Language*. Copyright © Random House, Inc. Reprinted by permission of Random House, Inc.

10. Donald Hayworth, "A Search for Facts on the Teaching of Public Speaking," *Quarterly Journal of Speech* 28 (1942): 247–354.

11. Charles Woolbert, "The Effects of Various Modes of Public Reading," *Journal of Applied Psychology* 4 (1920): 162–85; George M. Glasgow, "A Semantic Index of Vocal Pitch," *Speech Monographs* 19 (1952): 64–68; Kenneth C. Beighley, "An Experimental Study of the Effect of Four Speech Variables on Listener Comprehension," *Speech Monographs* 19 (1952): 249–58 and 21 (1954): 248–53; John W. Black, "A Study of Voice Merit," *Quarterly Journal of Speech* 28 (1942): 67–74.

12. Edward J. J. Kramer and Thomas R. Lewis, "Comparison of Visual and Nonvisual Listening," *Journal of Communication* 1 (1951): 16–20.

13. Martin Cobin, "Response to Eye-Contact," *Quarterly Journal of Speech* 48 (1962): 415–18.

14. Steven A. Beebe, "Eye Contact: A Nonverbal Determinant of Speaker Credibility," *Speech Teacher* 23 (1974): 21–25.

15. Erwin Bettinghaus, "The Operation of Congruity in an Oral Communication Situation," *Speech Monographs* 28 (1961): 131–42.

16. Ernest H. Henrikson, "An Analysis of the Characteristics of Some 'Good' and 'Poor' Speakers," *Speech Monographs* 11 (1944): 120–24.

17. Howard Gilkinson and Franklin H. Knower, "Individual Differences Among Students of Speech as Revealed by Psychological Tests—I," *Journal of Educational Psychology* 32 (1941): 161–75.

18. John L. Vohs, "An Empirical Approach to the Concept of Attention," *Speech Monographs* 31 (1964): 355–60.

19. Henrikson, pp. 120–24.

20. Roland J. Hard and Bruce L. Brown, "Interpersonal Information Conveyed by the Content and Vocal Aspects of Speech," *Speech Monographs* 41 (1974): 371–80; D. F. Gundersen and Robert Hopper, "Relationships between Speech Delivery and Speech Effectiveness," *Speech Monographs* 43 (1976): 158–65.

21. Charles R. Petrie, Jr., "Informative Speaking: A Summary and Bibliography of Related Research," *Speech Monographs* 30 (1963): 81.

14

The Informative Speech

An Application of the Principles of Public Communication

Objectives

After study of this chapter you should be able to do the following:

1. Define the informative speech
2. Name and give examples of the five behavioral purposes of informative speeches
3. Discuss information hunger and indicate ways of creating it in an audience
4. Define information relevance and discuss methods of enhancing the relevance of a topic
5. Define extrinsic motivation
6. Describe the findings about selecting information for an informative speech
7. Discuss the importance of organizing an informative speech and state some guidelines
8. Define and discuss the purpose of the document as a step in the preparation of an informative speech
9. Prepare and deliver an informative speech and justify the decisions you made about the purpose, content, adaptation to the audience, organization of the material, and presentation of the speech

"Speech is the mirror of the soul: as a man speaks, so is he."

                                                                    Syrus

"It is with narrow-souled people as with narrow-necked bottles; the less they have in them, the more noise they make in pouring out."

                                                            Alexander Pope

"Nothing is so firmly believed as what we least know."

                                                        Michel de Montaigne

As a student, you have already spent the better part of thirteen or fourteen years hearing informative speeches from teachers of American history, literature, grammar, music, art, math, physics, chemistry, social studies, typing, shop, home economics, health, and physical education. As an employee, you may have to tell others about products, sales goals, policies, and ways to sell, service, and salvage products. As a religious person, you may wish to explain scripture, doctrine, or ideals to groups of individuals. As a citizen, you may speak to others about domestic politics, foreign affairs, or impending legislation. Teachers inform students, lawyers inform clients, priests inform parishioners, fire fighters inform groups about safety, police inform citizens about protecting person and property, managers inform subordinates, and foremen inform workers. You, like all of these people, will likely find yourself informing others —in verbal reports, instructions, and speeches. This chapter focuses on the primary vehicle for informing others: the informative speech.

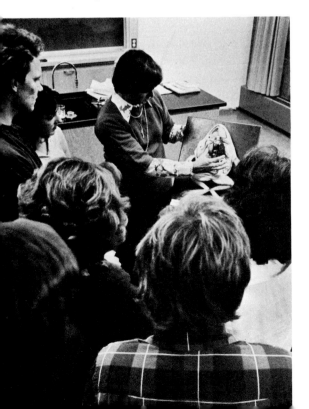

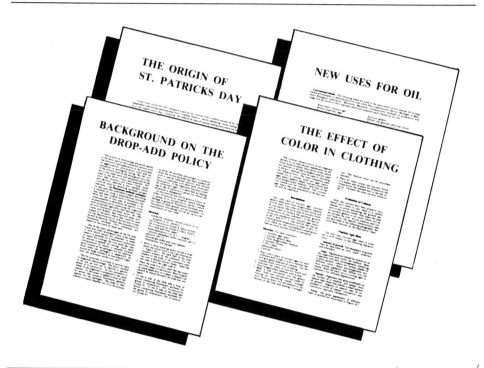

Figure 14.1 *understand, comprehend, learn, change, know more*

The Purposes of the Informative Speech

The informative speech is a means of getting an audience to understand, comprehend, learn, and even change its behavior. The main purpose of an informative speech, however, is to alter the cognition of an audience. In simpler words, you want the audience to know more, to understand more. You may want it to understand the causes of a disease, the uses of an instrument, the places where it can find something, the types of trees, the origins of language, the dangers of drugs, or the kinds of animals. The only way that we know that cognitive change has occurred is to observe or measure behavior. The history teacher cannot tell if a student has learned a chronology of events unless the student can state the order of events orally, in a paper, or on an examination.

In our earlier discussion of the short and long-range purposes and goals of a speech, we mentioned that stating the purpose of your speech in behavioral terms increases the likelihood of being effective. Some behavioral purposes of informative speeches are: (1) to teach an audience *to recognize* differences or similarities between or among objects, persons, or events; (2) *to distinguish* among different things; (3) *to compare* items; (4) *to define* words, objects, or

Purpose = recognize differences
distinguish   state
compare
define wo

concepts; or (5) *to state* what they will know as a result of your speech. An informative speaker can say: "The immediate purpose of my speech is to have the audience restate at least two of the four reasons that I give for buying food at a discount market," or "The immediate purpose of my speech is to teach the audience to distinguish between a clerk-typist and a secretary," or "The immediate purpose of my speech is to enable the audience to recognize edible mushrooms." In each case, the purpose is stated in such a way that the speaker can determine whether or not the purpose has been accomplished by the speech. Once the informative speaker has decided on the specific purpose of addressing an audience, strategies for achieving that purpose must be selected. In other words, the speaker must decide how to adapt the purpose and materials of the speech to the particular audience.

Presenting Information to an Audience

The informative speaker who wants to relate to an audience should first review the sections in chapter 11 dealing with selecting and narrowing the topic, as well as the material about audience analysis. Then he or she will be ready to determine how to adapt the topic and purpose to a particular audience. Audience analysis should help you determine how much the audience already knows and how much you will have to tell them to engender understanding. Then you will have to decide how to generate information hunger, achieve information relevance, employ extrinsic motivation, and select content for your speech.

Information Hunger   *Rhetorical Question*

An informative speech will be more effective if you can generate *information hunger* in the audience. That is, the speaker can create a need for information in the audience. Information hunger is easiest to create when a speaker has analyzed the audience and has reason to believe that hunger for the information can be aroused. The audience does not have to possess prior interest in the topic, but indications of potential interest through audience analysis can help. Interest in the subject matter of a speech before listening to it is not significantly related to comprehension, but arousal of interest during the speech is related to how much the audience will comprehend.[1] Here, for example, are some rhetorical questions that could be used to introduce an informative speech and to arouse audience interest: Do you know how to protect yourself from skin cancer? Do you know how to save money on food? Can you repair your own stereo? Can you tell a good used car from a bad one? Depending on the audience, these rhetorical questions could be of interest to the audience.

Information Relevance Right Type and Time.

A second factor in relating an informative speech to an audience is *information relevance.* When selecting a topic for an informative speech, the speaker should carefully consider the relevance of the topic. Skin cancer might be a better topic in the summer when students are sunbathing than in the winter when they are not.

An audience might find a speech on tax laws dull; a speech on how the present tax laws cost you more than they cost the rich might be more relevant; and a speech on three ways to reduce your taxes might be the most salient. However, if your audience happens to be composed of eighteen to twenty-one year olds who have never paid taxes, none of the three topics might be relevant. Similarly, a speech on raising race horses, writing a textbook, or living on a pension would be informative but not relevant because of the financial status, occupation, or age of the listeners. The informative speaker, then, should exercise some care to select a topic that interests the audience.[2]

ANIMAL CRACKERS

Research indicates that people expose themselves first to information that is supportive or that fits in with what they already believe or know. It also indicates that people reject less supportive information first. So an audience's predisposition toward a topic can determine whether a voluntary audience will show up to hear a speech and whether a captive audience will listen.[3]

Extrinsic Motivation   *Resons outside of speech.*

A third factor in relating an informative speech to an audience is *extrinsic motivation.* An audience is more likely to listen to and to comprehend a speech if there are reasons outside the speech itself for concentrating on its content.[4] A teacher who tells students to listen carefully today because they will be tested at the end of the hour is using extrinsic motivation. A student can use extrinsic motivation at the beginning of a speech by telling an audience: "Careful attention to this informative speech will help you improve your grades on objective tests," or "Listening to this speech today will save you money on gasoline," or as one student said, "I will give each of you one dollar for listening to my speech today, and I will tell you how to turn it into five dollars by the end of the week."

Informative Content

A fourth factor in relating an informative speech to an audience is the selection of *informative content.* In chapter 11, we discussed research and the selection of evidence, and gave examples and illustrations to support our contentions. Here we will briefly examine some principles of learning and some research findings that can guide you in selecting your speech content.

The first finding is that audiences tend to remember and comprehend generalizations and main ideas better than details and specific facts.[5] The usual advice to speakers, that content should be limited to a relatively small number of main points and generalizations, seems to be well grounded. Specifically, public speakers are well advised to limit themselves to two to five main points or con-

Figure 14.2   *words at appropriate level*
Few Main points   *HUMOR?*

tentions in a speech. Even if the speech is very long, audiences are unlikely to remember a larger number of main points.

A second finding about content is that relatively simple words and concrete ideas are significantly easier to retain than more complex materials.[6] Long or abstruse words may dazzle an audience into thinking that you are intellectually gifted or verbally skilled, but it may also reduce understanding of the content. The best advice is to keep the ideas, and the words used to express them, at an appropriate level.

Humor can make a dull speech more interesting to an audience, but it does not seem to increase information retention.[7] The use of humor also improves the audience's perception of the character of the speaker, and it can increase a speaker's authoritativeness when a speech is dull, although not when it is interesting.

Early remarks about how the speech will meet the audience's needs can create anticipation and increase the chances that the audience will listen and understand.[8] Whatever topic you select, you should early in your speech reveal to the members of an audience how the topic is related to them. Unless you relate the topic to their needs, they may choose not to listen.

Figure 14.3

Another finding is that calling for overt audience response increases comprehension more than repetition. In a study of this subject, the overt responses that were invited were specific, "programmed" questions to which the appropriate overt responses were anticipated.[9] The results were consistent with other studies that show the virtue of active participation by an audience.

An informative speaker can ask for overt responses from the audience by having them perform the task being demonstrated (e.g., folding a paper airplane to demonstrate a principle of aerodynamics); by having them stand, raise hands, or move chairs to indicate affirmative understanding of the speaker's statements (e.g., stand up if you are over 25 years old); or by having them write answers that will indicate understanding of the informative speech (e.g., picture of four plants are drawn on the board and the audience members are instructed to iden- tify the plant that they believe is marijuana). Having an audience go through some overt motion provides feedback to the speaker, and can be rewarding and reinforcing for both speaker and listener.

Now that we have examined information hunger, information relevance, extrinsic motivation, and findings about content, you are ready to review some specific suggestions about organizing the informative speech.

Organizing the Informative Speech

Chapter 12 contains detailed information about the overall organization of speeches. Here we shall add suggestions based on studies that reveal specific ways that the informative speaker can help an audience to understand the con- tent of the speech. In general, the research supports the old saying that you should tell an audience what you are going to tell them, tell them, and then tell them what you told them. Petrie, in his studies of informative speaking, found that the use of transitions can increase an audience's comprehension.[10] That finding underlines the importance of building, into the organization of your in- formative speech, transitions between your introduction and body and between your body and conclusion. Other places for transitions include the moves from one point to another in your speech and into and out of visual aids.

In organizing your informative speech you should determine which ideas, points, or supporting materials are of greatest importance. Apparently, an audi- ence will understand the important points better if the speaker signals their im- portance by saying "Now get this," or "This is very important." Some redun- dancy, or planned repetition, can also help increase comprehension.[11] Some of that planned repetition can be included in the previews and reviews in your in- formative speech.[12] One researcher demonstrated that "advance organizers," or previews in written work, aided retention by providing the reader with key points prior to their presentation in a meaningful, but unfamiliar, passage.[13] Per- haps it is true in speaking as well as writing that listeners can more easily grasp information when they are invited to anticipate and to review both the organiza- tion and the content of a speech.

When you have completed a sentence outline or some other form of outline that includes everything that you plan to say, you should check your speech for informational *overload*. Overload is a special problem in the informative speech because speakers have a tendency to inundate the listeners with information. Just as some students believe that a longer paper is a better paper, some speakers think that the sheer quantity of information that they present in a speech makes it better. The most effective public speakers know that the quantity of material in a speech makes less difference than the quality of the material. They also know that listeners will pay more attention to carefully selected material that is well adapted to their needs. In a five-to-eight-minute informative speech, the speaker has only four to six minutes to actually present supporting materials; the remainder of the time is spent introducing the subject, making transitions, and making internal and final summaries. Your organizational plan should show you what material you intend to include in your speech. It can also be your final check on the quantity and quality of the information that you intend to present.

Prior Preparation: The Document

Another way of making sure that your speech is ready for delivery to an audience is to prepare a *document* in which you state your topic, your purpose, your organizational plan, and your sources. Additionally, there is a section about *obstacles*. In this section, the speaker is asked to identify characteristics of himself, the audience, the topic, the classroom, or the content of the speech that are likely to hamper the effectiveness of the presentation. Considering the factors that can reduce your effectiveness is a practical exercise. Such a document follows. The side notes point out the function of the points to be made in the speech.

Title:	**The Oil Depletion Allowance**
Behavioral statement of purpose:	*Purpose:* The audience should be able to define what percentage depletion means in relation to tax policy.
Speech of definition. Expectation from audience and a means of determining effectiveness.	The audience should be able to define "percentage depletion" and to state at least one way that it is related to tax policy.
	Obstacles
Speaker lists obstacles and how he is going to overcome them.	1. Credibility. I am a business major with special interest in taxation. That, added to the fact that my audience analysis indicates that the audience knows little or nothing about oil depletion allowances or taxation, should make me a credible source.
	2. Because of my audience's level of information, I shall have to explain percentage depletion in the simplest possible terms.
	3. Language. I must not make the speech sound like a lecture. I will try to be conversational and proper in my delivery by avoiding technical language as much as possible.
	4. Because the numbers and percentages are complex, I will simplify the presentation with visual aids that will make the information easier to remember.

Organization

Rhetorical questions to arouse audience interest. Active participation by class. Speaker creates a need to know: information hunger.
Overt statement of purpose and transition. Credibility established.

Introduction: How many students in this room own oil wells? Raise your hands. (Prediction: none.) How many of you have heard the term "oil depletion allowance?" (Prediction: a few hands.) How many of you know what it is? (Prediction: one or two at the most.)

My purpose today is to define the meaning of the term "oil depletion allowance" and to show you how that term relates to you. As a business major interested in taxation. . . .

Body

Definition, an informative purpose. Speaker develops a main point that he wants the audience to remember.

Subpoints to explain the term.
Visual aids.

Second main point divided into two parallel subheads.

I. "Percentage depletion" is a term used by the Internal Revenue Service to refer to a tax break for people who invest in a natural resource like oil.
   A. The laws of nature are related to our tax laws.
   B. The Internal Revenue Service has a means of calculating percentage depletion allowances. (Visual aid presented here to show method of calculation.)
II. Percentage depletion affects development of natural resources and our tax base.
   A. Depletion allowances encourage the exploration and development of oil fields in this country.
   B. Depletion allowances reduce tax income by giving a tax break to those wealthy enough to afford such investments.

Motivation for learning and comprehension. Review and repetition of purpose.

Conclusion: As citizens we should learn about our own tax laws and understand how they work. As taxpayers we should know and understand percentage depletions and how they relate to our tax laws.

Sources of Information

Sommerfeld, Ray M., Hershel M. Anderson, and Horace R. Brock. *An Introduction to Taxation.* New York: Harcourt Brace Jovanovich, Inc., 1972.

Smith, Dan Throop, and J. Keight Butters. *Taxable and Business Income.* New York: National Bureau of Economic Research, 1949.

A periodical published by the Independent Petroleum Association of America, "The Oil Producing Industry in Your State." 1974.

Oil and Gas Journal 72 (October 1974): 90–91.

This student did a particularly good job of selecting a topic that was appropriate to his own knowledge and interests. It may have been somewhat less appropriate for an audience of college students, many of whom do not pay taxes. He did, however, arouse their interest with a rhetorical question, audience participation, and visual aids. He adjusted the speech to the audience's level of knowledge, and he made certain that the audience recognized his credibility, both by stating his qualifications and demonstrating his knowledge of tax law. He also did his best to research the topic and to show the audience how this percentage depletion related to it. The speaker was relatively thorough in determining the obstacles that were likely to hamper the success of his speech. The speaker had a document that showed his plan for the informative speech.

The Informative Speech: An Example

Many aspects of an informative speech are not apparent in an outline. For that reason, a complete informative speech is included here so that you can examine the language, the transitions, the forms of support, and the statements that inform the audience about the speaker's expertise. The side notes explain what the speaker is attempting to accomplish.

Grade Inflation

Common ground as college students.	As students in this college, all of you have heard the term *inflation* used to refer to the reduced value of our money. But how many of you have heard of *grade inflation*? This term refers to the reduced value of college grades. It means that more people are getting higher grades for the same accomplishments that previously brought somewhat lower grades.
Defining a term by comparison. Rhetorical question to arouse interest.	
Description of credibility. Common ground.	I am a sophomore who earns better than a B+ average, and I am concerned that my grades and yours will not measure up when we graduate.
Research: reading and interviewing.	I learned about grade inflation through an article in the school newspaper and through an interview with the dean of academic affairs. These sources told me that one out of every three students here has a B average or better. They also told me that the grade point average has been rising every year for the last five years.
Quotes credible sources. Cites statistics as evidence.	
Active participation and identification of reference groups in the audience.	Just to demonstrate how high grade expectations are in this college, I would like all the students in this class who expect to get a B or better in this speech class to stand up. Now I want those students who have a cumulative grade point average of B or better to raise their hands. As you can see, grade inflation may have already hit this college. That is why I want to explore this topic of grade inflation with you today.
Transition to body.	
Forecast or preview of speech organization and content.	I want to look first at some evidence that grade inflation exists and second, at some causes. Last, I will demonstrate why grade inflation, like currency inflation, can have a negative effect on all of us.
Speaker gets audience to anticipate content.	Many of you may be thinking to yourselves, "So what?" So what if we are earning better grades than those before us? Our high school commencement speaker told us that we were the smartest generation in human history! That's why we earn such high grades.
Common ground, or co-orientation.	
Research through interview to establish authority and credibility.	I went to the director of testing and counseling to find out if students here are more intelligent than they were in the past. The news was disappointing. He said that the standardized test scores for entering freshmen had gone down during the same years that the grades went up. However, there were "extenuating circumstances" to explain the *inflation of grades,* as he termed it.
Evidence.	
Transition.	
Preview of organization and content.	In fact, there seem to be at least four main reasons why the evidence shows that intellectual potential was going down at the same time that grades were going up. One reason stated by the director was that the standardized test—called SAT—which is used to measure our capability as college students may not measure or evaluate what is being taught in our high schools and colleges today. That test was developed to evaluate our knowledge of standard fare, including history, English, social studies, and math; but today's high schooler takes a wider variety of specialized courses in everything from science fiction to elementary psychology to beginning bio-feedback.
Quotations from an interview. First main point.	
Evidence. Common ground.	

Second main point.	A second extenuating circumstance, besides the possible inappropriateness of the test used to measure our potentialities, is the adoption of alternative grading systems in many schools and colleges.
Evidence from and interview of another credible source.	Many students, according to the registrar in the Administration Building, can, and do, take courses pass/fail or satisfactory/unsatisfactory.
Reasoning from the evidence.	The alternative grading systems can reduce the number of low grades and make grade point averages look better than they used to look.
Third main point.	A third extenuating circumstance is that the rules for dropping, adding, and petitioning into and out of courses have become increasingly permissive so that, as the registrar says, "Even a not too bright student can now figure out how to avoid receiving a poor grade in a course."
Evidence from interview that the speaker did research.	
Fourth main point. Speaker suggests that the end of the speech is near. Quotations from another interviewed source.	A fourth and final extenuating circumstance is that college departments and divisions survive if they attract students and sometimes die if they do not. The head of the Language Arts Division told me in an interview that lower grades can result in fewer students signing up for a course.
Evidence and reasoning leading to a conclusion.	That results in less faculty, fewer courses, and less money for a department. These days, professors know that when they give grades, their own survival may depend on what they do with their power to grade or evaluate students. So professors, too, can contribute to grade inflation.
Repetition of the term.	Next time you hear the word "grade inflation," I hope you realize that the entrance tests, the new courses in the curriculum, the alternative grading systems and the drop-add procedures, and even the professors may be among the causes.
Transition. Review of main points.	
Application to listeners.	I hope that you also realize that more and more students nationally are getting the grades that used to be earned by the very few. Finally, I hope that you realize that when many students have high grades, it takes even higher ones to be the very best. Grade inflation, like economic inflation, devalues the currency used to evaluate you.

The speaker used a number of methods to help the audience comprehend and recall the message. The term *grade inflation* was repeated ten times in a short speech. The speaker previewed the main points, included one internal summary, and reviewed the main points. There were transitions into the body and into the conclusion. No visual aids were used, but audience participation, statistics, authoritative sources, reasoning, and evidence were all used. The speech was highly appropriate to a college audience since everyone in the room received grades and could be affected by grade inflation.

Summary

In this chapter, we examined the purpose of informative speaking, surveyed ways of relating information to an audience, and provided advice for organizing an informative speech. We suggested that a document, or plan, for an informative speech can help the speaker to anticipate obstacles, can provide an outline of organization, and can show how the speaker intends to employ informative strategies in the speech. We concluded with an example of an informative speech by a student. In the next chapter, we turn our attention to the persuasive speech.

New Terms

Informative speaking	Distinguish	Overt audience response
Cognitive change	Information hunger	Redundancy *planed rep*
Recognition	Rhetorical questions	Advance organizers
Comparison	Information relevance	Informational overload
Definition	Extrinsic motivation	Obstacles
Statement	Informative content	*Hamder*

Additional Readings

Arnold, Carrol C.; Ehninger, Douglas; and Gerber, John C. *The Speaker's Resource Book.* 2d ed. Chicago: Scott, Foresman and Company, 1966. *Numerous texts of speeches are given, with questions to help the student understand the techniques and strategies of the speakers. Also contains a short handbook on public speaking principles: delivery, topic selection, audience analysis, and research.*

Dickens, Milton, and McBath, James H. *Guidebook for Speech Communication.* New York: Harcourt Brace Jovanovich, Inc., 1973. *A workbook approach to the study of public speaking techniques. Contains numerous exercises to develop awareness and skills in presenting information to others.*

Hart, Roderick P.; Friedrich, Gustav W.; and Brooks, William. *Public Communication.* New York: Harper & Row, Publishers, 1975. Pages 178–206. *Informative speeches are discussed in detail, and barriers to the communication of ideas are examined. Contains advice on clarifying, intensifying, sequencing, and timing the presentation of factual information.*

Hasling, John. *The Message, The Speaker, The Audience.* New York: McGraw-Hill Book Company, 1971. *Quick and easy source of fundamental techniques of the informative public address. A discussion of organization, support, visual aids, and delivery as they apply to the presentation of information to audiences.*

Linkugel, Wil A., and Berg, David M. *A Time To Speak*. Belmont, Calif.: Wadsworth Publishing Co., Inc., 1970. *The skills of informative speaking are presented in a jargon-free style. The text is a bit superficial but contains interesting insights into the fundamentals of organizing and presenting your ideas.*

Swanson, Richard, and Marquardt, Charles. *On Communication: Listening, Reading, Speaking, and Writing*. Beverly Hills, Calif.: Glencoe Press, 1974. Chapter 6. *A brief explanation of informative speaking processes. Covers a large amount of material, though a bit superficial in explanations. A good review of important concepts and techniques.*

Verderber, Rudolph F. *The Challenge of Effective Speaking*. 3d ed. Belmont, Calif.: Wadsworth Publishing Co., Inc., 1976. Pages 123–68. *Verderber differentiates several types of informative speeches and discusses the techniques and strategies that are most effective for speeches of process, description, definition, and exposition. Clearly written, and oriented toward applying the principles to actual speaking.*

Notes

1. Charles R. Petrie, Jr., "Informative Speaking: A Summary and Bibliography of Related Research," *Speech Monographs* 30 (1963): 79–91.

2. See N. C. Cofer, *Verbal Learning and Verbal Behavior* (New York: McGraw-Hill Book Company, 1961).

3. Lawrence R. Wheeless, "The Effects of Attitude, Credibility, and Homophyly on Selective Exposure to Information," *Speech Monographs* 41 (1974): 329–38.

4. Charles R. Petrie, Jr. and Susan D. Carrel, "The Relationship of Motivation, Listening Capability, Initial Information, and Verbal Organization Ability to Lecture Comprehension and Retention," *Speech Monographs* 43 (1976): 187–94.

5. Petrie, p. 80.

6. Carole Ernest, "Listening Comprehension as a Function of Type of Material and Rate of Presentation," *Speech Monographs* 35 (1968): 154–58. See also, John A. Baird, "The Effects of Speech Summaries upon Audience Comprehension of Expository Speeches of Varying Quality and Complexity," *Central States Speech Journal* 25 (1974): 119–27.

7. Charles R. Gruner, "The Effect of Humor in Dull and Interesting Informative Speeches," *Central States Speech Journal* 21 (1970): 160–66.

8. Petrie, p. 84.

9. Charles O. Tucker, "An Application of Programmed Learning to Informative Speech," *Speech Monographs* 31 (1964): 142–52.

10. Petrie, p. 81.

11. See O. L. Pence, "Emotionally Loaded Argument: Its Effectiveness in Stimulating Recall," *Quarterly Journal of Speech* 40 (1954): 272–76.

12. Baird, pp. 119–27.

13. David Ausubel, "The Use of Advance Organizers in the Learning and Retention of Meaningful Material," *Journal of Educational Psychology* 51 (1960): 267–72.

15

The Persuasive Speech

An Application of the Principles of Public Communication

Objectives

After study of this chapter you should be able to do the following:

1. Define the persuasive speech
2. Identify and give examples of the purposes of the persuasive speech and write a statement of purpose to illustrate each
3. Suggest ways to adapt the persuasive speech to an audience
4. Discuss the impact of the sequence of arguments on opinion and the use of counter arguments for changing an audience's attitudes
5. Differentiate among the rhetoric of reason, refutation, and emotion; discuss the strategies that are available for each approach
6. Explain the purpose and value of the List of Inquiries for preparing a persuasive speech
7. Prepare and present a persuasive speech to your classroom audience; justify your selection of purpose, arguments, organization, and persuasive strategies

"You cannot convince a man against his will."

Samuel Johnson

"We are more easily persuaded, in general, by the reasons that we ourselves discover than by those which are given to us by others."

Pascal

"Information by itself almost never changes attitudes."

Karlins and Abelson

The purpose of informative speaking is to seek cognitive change through learning and comprehension so that the audience might know more than they did before the speech. The purpose of the persuasive speech is to alter the audience's *cognition* (what it knows), its *affective domain* (how it feels about what it knows), and ultimately its *behavior* (how it acts). Ordinarily such changes occur within a time span that varies with the depth of change and with the individual's readiness to change. An alcoholic may need twenty years of bad experiences and persuasive messages from family and friends before joining Alcoholics Anonymous; the same person might switch brands of soap as a result of a single persuasive message. In the public speaking classroom, you are bringing your persuasive message to a captive audience whose presence at your speech indicates nothing about its readiness to accept your message. Billy Graham can count on attracting relatively large numbers of people who are ready for religious renewal; you are speaking to people who need to be convinced that they should listen to your persuasive appeals.

As you prepare a persuasive speech, you should remember all of the things that you did for your informative speech. For both types of speeches, you have to select and limit topics, you have to determine your purpose, analyze your audience, seek and find supporting materials, organize your speech, and deliver it to an audience. You should not assume that the persuasive speech is entirely different from an informative speech; instead, you should build on what you have learned about the informative speech. In order to examine persuasive speaking, we will look first at the purposes of persuasive speeches.

The Purposes of Persuasive Speeches

Two purposes of persuasive speaking are of primary importance; they are also most frequently encountered. They are adoption and discontinuance.[1]

Adoption

When the speaker's purpose is to obtain *adoption,* the goal is to secure acceptance of a new idea, attitude, or belief and to influence the audience to demonstrate that acceptance by behavioral change. Adoption is the goal of much advertising: the advertiser wants the consumer to try a new soap, deodorant, coffee maker, perfume, or whiskey. Adoption is also the goal of speeches in which the persuader asks the audience to show more school spirit, be less materialistic, take classes more seriously, or use a bicycle instead of a car. These goals can be immediate, long-range or ultimate, or both. For example, a persuader whose ultimate goal is to have his audience switch from private cars to mass transportation might ask for a more narrow action—say, car pooling. The speaker whose ultimate behavioral or action goal is to enlist the audience in actively campaigning for welfare legislation might select, as an immediate purpose, eliminating some misconceptions about poverty-stricken people.

Discontinuance

A second goal of persuasion is *discontinuance,* convincing an audience that it should cease doing something. We ask an audience to quit smoking, to stop spending money on cosmetics, or to cease acting as if money is the key to happiness. When a persuasive speaker is asking for a large behavioral change in an audience, shorter-range purposes leading to the desired action may be necessary. The speaker whose ultimate goal is to convince the audience to drop out of college might first try to convince the audience that higher education takes too much time, costs too much money, takes too much effort, or requires too much conformity.

The focus of both the adoption and the discontinuance goals is on action, or behavior. Nothing short of behavioral change is satisfying to the persuader. The advertiser is not satisfied with your pleasant thoughts about a new brand of soap; the advertiser wants you to buy it. The evangelist is not satisfied with your warm and loving thoughts about others; the evangelist wants you to act better toward them. You may be unable to change an audience's behavior in a single persuasive speech, but it is important to keep in mind what you want your audience to do ultimately. Your persuasive speech is just one small contribution to ultimate change in the lives of other people. Your speech may inspire some individuals in your audience to seek additional information, to become less satisfied with their present position and, ultimately, to change both their attitudes and their behavior.

The ultimate goal can be either adoption or discontinuance; so can the immediate goal. A persuasive speaker may want first to convince an audience to discontinue its present behavior in order, later, to adopt new behavior suggested by the speaker. The speaker, for example, might argue that you should stop buying products from companies that finance silly soap operas on TV. The ultimate purpose may be to convince you to start buying from companies that support shows of artistic merit. Asking for too much change from an audience can make it resistant to change. The salesperson who tries too hard to sell can lose the sale. The public speaker who asks for too much from the audience too soon can end up with a boomerang effect: the audience will dislike the idea even more after the speech than it did before. Once you have decided on your topic, determined your immediate purpose and your ultimate goal, and analyzed your audience, you are ready to adapt your topic to the particular audience.

Relating the Persuasive Speech to the Audience

In chapter 14, "The Informative Speech," you were provided with some suggestions for adapting an informative speech to an audience. Because the persuasive

DOONESBURY   **by Garry Trudeau**

speech also imparts information, those suggestions are good ones for the persuasive speech as well. We know, for instance, that audiences are more easily persuaded by a speaker whom they perceive to be similar to themselves.[2] That is why the speaker who intends to persuade is encouraged to establish common ground with an audience. In informative speaking, repetition can improve the audience's comprehension of a message; in persuasive speaking, repetition of an appeal can help the change in attitude to persist longer. The repetition referred to here is a restatement of the persuasive appeal after an initial exposure to the persuasive message.[3] For example, if you have a second opportunity to persuade an audience, the repetition of your persuasive appeal will increase the length of time that the appeal will remain in the minds of the members of your audience.

Some additional suggestions are valuable to both informative and persuasive speakers. Opinion change in persuasive speaking, like comprehension in informative speaking, persists longer if the speaker requires active rather than passive participation from the audience.[4] Asking an audience to reply, to write, or to act in a certain way during the presentation are ways of obtaining active participation from the audience. Taking an audience through a detention home as you speak, instead of simply talking about detention homes, is another way of obtaining active participation from the audience.

When should your best arguments or information be presented first and when should they be presented last? Arguments and information presented first or early in a speech seem to have more impact in speeches on controversial issues, on topics with which the audience is not involved, on topics that the audience perceives as interesting, and on topics that are highly familiar to the audience. When the audience is involved, when topics are perceived as

LATER — INVOLVED
UNITIERESTING
UNFAMILIAR

[handwritten notes in top margin: "BOTH SIDES - audience disagrees HEAR OTHER SIDE SOON" / "ONE SIDE - FRIENDLY ONLY SIDE TO HEAR IMMEDIATE TEMP CHANGE"]

uninteresting, and when they are moderately unfamiliar to the audience, arguments and information seem to have more impact when they are presented later or last in a speech.[5]

When should the persuasive speaker present only one side of an issue? When should the persuasive speaker present both sides of an issue? A persuasive speaker should present one side of an issue when the audience is friendly, when the speaker's position is the only one the audience is likely to hear, and when the speaker is seeking immediate but temporary change of opinion. The persuasive speaker should present both sides or a number of sides when the audience initially disagrees with the speaker or when it is likely that the audience will hear other sides from other people.[6]

When should the persuasive speaker refute counterarguments? Should a persuasive speaker use familiar or novel arguments? Persuasive speakers should refute counterarguments before proceeding to their own if the audience is already familiar with the counterarguments. If you favor abortion and your audience is familiar with the arguments against that position, then you should refute those well-known arguments before proceeding to your own.[7] Original, novel, or new arguments tend to have more impact than arguments with which the audience is familiar. Persuasive speakers should use their minds, creativity, and research skills to find arguments that will have more impact than the ones with which the audience is already familiar.[8]

Although some research indicates that highly credibile speakers attain more attitude change when they ask for more,[9] the classroom persuader is advised to work toward more gradual change in an audience. The born-again Christian who tries to convert the class to his way of thinking may obtain less impressive results than a noted evangelist because of differences in both the speaker and the audience.

Now that you have received these suggestions about how much change to request, the use of novel arguments, the use of refutation, the placement of strong arguments, active participation, repetition, and on speaker-audience similarity, you are ready to consider specific strategies that you can employ in your persuasive speech.

Categories of Persuasive Strategies

Strategies are means for achieving a goal. If your goal is to get your audience to discontinue smoking, than you have to select strategies based on your audience analysis to achieve that goal. There are hundreds of possible strategies. Some of them will be more effective with your particular audience than others. The experienced persuader has a large repertoire of strategies that can be used to persuade a variety of audiences. To help you understand the idea of persuasive strategies, we will examine three types of strategies that can be employed in persuasive speeches. As you survey these strategies, you should keep in mind that persuasive speakers are flexible: they can adapt to an audience because they have many strategies to choose from. Rarely does a persuasive speaker use only emotional or only refutational arguments. A persuasive speech usually consists of a variety of appeals selected for and adapted to that particular audience. The categories of persuasive strategies that we will examine here include the rhetoric of reason, the rhetoric of refutation, and the rhetoric of emotion.

The Rhetoric of Reason   *LOGIC + CONSISTANCY*

One set of strategies employed in persuasive speeches is related to the speaker's and the audience's sense of logic and consistency. In this type of speech, speakers attempt to prove, by reasoning, that their persuasive propositions are acceptable. The rhetoric of reason includes a number of specific strategems.

If I Can Prove It, Then You Should Believe It   *PROOF BY RESEARCH*

The speaker who employs this stratagem tries to prove to the audience that the proposition being advanced is probable, true, or believable by providing evidence that the audience is likely to believe, respect, or accept. The speaker who argues that capital punishment deters murder could, for example, try to demonstrate that the rate of murder is lower in states with capital punishment than in states that impose life imprisonment or other less drastic punishments. The principle underlying this stratagem is that audiences should believe what can be proven, whether they like the results or not.

Unfortunately, audiences decide what constitutes proof for them, and they can decide not to believe a "proven" proposition. People do not always behave logically. Millions of people, for instance, take cures for cancer for which medical science cannot show any effectiveness. Millions of dollars are spent every year on cosmetics purported to forestall the effect of aging even though none of them actually have that effect. Still, proving a case to an audience is one method of persuading it to believe or to do something.

If You Are Consistent, Then You Will Do This

The speaker who uses this stratagem is appealing to an audience's or individual's sense of consistency. The stratagem works to the extent that people in the audience desire consistency. Fortunately, most people do.

The speaker might argue like this: If you believe that all people are created equal, then under the law all people, including blacks, gays, Jews, Italians, and women should have the same rights as whites, straights, Protestants, Swedes, and men. Another use of the appeal to consistency is to apply to a specific instance criteria about which the audience agrees. If the audience is consistent,

IF YOU BELIEVE THIS DO THIS

they may accept the specific instance that meets the criteria. For example, the speaker might argue: "We all agree that a person who is mayor of our city should be someone who has administrative experience in local government, has an appropriate educational background that will serve that person in the job, has demonstrable involvement in the community, and has the necessary skills to represent our city. John Jones meets these requirements. He has served two consecutive terms as alderman for the Second District; he graduated from the state university in both political science and law; he has spent the last fifteen years on city commissions, committees, and planning groups; and he demonstrated his ability to represent the city by securing over a million dollars in federal money for our parks."

The criteria-application pattern asks an audience to be consistent: if you believe in these criteria, then you will vote for the person who meets them. But, just as people are not always logical, people are not necessarily consistent. They may not vote for Jones because he is a Democrat and they are Republicans, even though he does meet the criteria.

The Rhetoric of Refutation

A second set of strategies employed in persuasive speeches is based on attacking or discrediting another person's evidence, logic, or credibility. While the rhetoric of reason focuses most often on the goals of adoption and continuance, the rhetoric of refutation concentrates most often on discontinuance and deterrence. In the classroom, the rhetoric of refutation comes into play in speeches that attack other ideas that are commonly believed even if they have not been formally presented. The rhetoric of refutation includes a number of stratagems.

Refuting the Evidence   The speaker who employs this stratagem attacks the supporting materials—the surveys, studies, testimonial evidence, and statistics—of the opponent. The tests of evidence cited in chapter 11 will provide ideas for refutation.

For example, take the argument for capital punishment just stated. Another speaker could attack the evidence by showing that comparing states with capital punishment with those with less severe punishments does not prove that death penalties deter murder. It might show, instead, that murder rates are more highly related to population, location, income level, and the number of large cities in a state than to the type of punishment dictated by state legislatures. The same strategies that are used to convince—such as logic and consistency—can be used to dissuade. The speaker who refutes can attack the logic and the consistency of the other speaker in an attempt to change the audience's perception of the issue, the problem, or the solution.

Discrediting the Source   The speaker who is attempting to deter or discontinue some belief, attitude, or behavior of the audience can do so by questioning the credibility of the opposing speaker or the opponent's sources. *Ad hominem* attacks, irrelevant attacks on a person, are taboo in most public speaking and debates, but attacks on the credibility of speakers and sources can be very effective.

Here is a good example of a brief refutation: A group of philosophers at a professional convention were listening to a scholar argue that the use of the

double negative is common in many cultures. He said that the double negative is understood as a positive in some cultures. (We have all heard the English teacher's admonition not to say, "I don't have no pencil," because two negatives make a positive.) But, in no culture, claimed the philosopher, do two positives make a negative. From the back of the room came an anguished "Yeah, yeah" which evoked laughter from the audience and humiliated the speaker. We can refute a speaker as unqualified, for overgeneralizing from his or her own experience, and for being unaware of other pertinent information about the issue. Similarly, we can refute the speaker's sources by using any of the methods reviewed in chapter 11 under testimonial evidence.

The Rhetoric of Emotion

As one writer said in a little rhyme about the role of emotion in persuasion:

> The creature man is best persuaded
> When heart, not mind, is inundated;
> Affect is what drives the will;
> Rationality keeps it still.[11]

The rhetoric of reason and the rhetoric of refutation are both more "reasonable" than the rhetoric of emotion. We can demonstrate on paper how both of those strategies work. Because emotion is more difficult to understand, less is written about it. However, our everyday experiences are a testimony to the impact and the long-lasting effect of emotion. Consider all that happened to you last week.

As a college student you were exposed to innumerable facts, arguments, exercises, and assignments, most of which are going to be tough to remember on the examinations. What emotional events happened in the last week? Did you have a dispute with someone near and dear to you? Did you become angry, show fear, act proud or happy over something that happened to you? We remember fear of a high place even when we forget the facts in our geology book; we remember the bitterness of unrequited love when we forget the information in our sociology book; we remember our pride in receiving an award when we forget why we received it. Our emotions are a powerful force on our behavior, a force that the persuader can learn to harness and control.

We shall name and explain some of the strategies that are commonly employed in persuasive speeches.

Showing the Wounds   Speakers using this stratagem indicate to the audience that they have earned the right to speak with authority on the subject. Sometimes the showing of the wounds is literal: the speaker speaks from a wheelchair, the speaker is black, the speaker has been mutilated in an automobile accident, the speaker lost a leg in the war. At other times, the showing of the wounds is figurative, and is revealed through self-disclosure: "I have five children," "I have had an abortion," "I have been married three times," "I have been a fire fighter for five years," "I have been raped," or "I earn $5,000 a year."

Fear and Trembling   A common stratagem for persuasive speakers is evoking fear in the attempt to induce the audience to conform. Even though many studies on appeals to fear exist, too little is known to make unqualified recommendations about their use in persuasive speeches. Janis and Feshbach examined three levels of appeals to fear in a communication on dental hygiene and found that the least threat was more effective than moderate threat, which was, in turn, more effective than strong appeals to fear.[12] Fredric Powell used strong and weak appeals to fear in a civil-defense communication that threatened loved ones, and found more changes of opinion when the threat was strong.[13] William J. McGuire theorized that a model which predicted high levels of initial concern (fear) would result in less compliance than one involving low levels of initial concern.[14] In other words, two forces function in appeals to fear: the more anxious people are, the more insecure they are, and thus the more likely they are to yield to the persuasive appeal; but, on the other hand, the more anxious people are, the more likely they are to be withdrawn and preoccupied, which causes them to be less susceptible to the persuasive attempt.[15] As these three experiments indicate, we know that appeals to fear are persuasive, but we do not know exactly which level of threat works best in which situation.

A recent experiment does provide some useful information. For twenty years, speakers were urged to provide some reassurance following a threat, to reduce some of the anxiety and to keep the listeners from becoming so anxious that the persuasive appeal was repressed or avoided. Current information on reassurance indicates that, although omitting reassurance does not influence the audience's ability to recall the facts in the speech, a speech with reassurance results in a greater shift of opinion than one without reassurance and the speaker who conveys reassurance is considered a better speaker than one who does not.[16] The message in this study seems to be that a speaker is well advised to include reassurance along with the appeal to fear—that is, the speaker should include information about how to reduce or avoid the threat.

The "Poor Me" Stratagem   This persuasive ploy is aimed at the audience's heart. The speaker encourages the audience to comply out of pity. This widely used stratagem was used in the Nazi war-crime trials ("We didn't know that those awful things were going on"), by General McArthur ("Old soldiers never die, they just fade away"), and by numerous Watergate defendants ("We didn't authorize them to do that"). In the classroom, the stratagem sounds like this: "My family was too poor to send me to a better place. I work my way through school. My wife works and my kids have paper routes." The political speaker says "I am no Rockefeller; I am no Kennedy. I have only your contributions to fight my way to a victory in November." Students are skilled in employing the poor me stratagem. All a teacher has to do is recall the hundreds of excuses for missed classes, missed speeches, and missed examinations.

The "I'm a Tender, Loving Human Being" Stratagem   Have you ever noticed how often male politicians list among their attributes the fact that they have wives and children? Have you ever noticed how often the family appears on the platform or television screen along with the candidate? The politician is demonstrating nonverbally that he is a tender, loving human being. I once heard a commencement speaker tell about a woman who had five children, two by Caesarean section. She contracted cancer when she was thirty-five and went through three operations to save her life. For a while, she was so distracted by her responsibilities and the threats to her life that she had to be placed in a mental hospital ward for rest and recovery. Now, because of her faith and her victories over death and destruction, she is a happy, healthy woman. "That woman," said the speaker, "is my wife."

The speaker, in a daring display of self-disclosure, managed to evoke a wave of sympathy and to show that he was a tender, loving human being. The stratagem is employed in classroom speeches by students who paint vivid pictures of their concern for their fellows, who talk of their close relationships with family and friends, and who enhance their credibility by exuding sincerity and trustworthiness. "I would rather take my own life than destroy the life of another," says the impassioned pacifist. "I have sympathy for the battered wife, but none in my heart for the man who beats her," states the feminist. "We cannot overlook the plight of the poor," says the aspiring politician. The student speaker has found, as others before him have found, that audiences respond to the person who is a tender, loving human being.

The "Imagine, if You Will" Stratagem   A skilled speaker knows that an audience with any imagination at all can fantasize a better world through word pictures. Martin Luther King, Jr. did it by revealing his view from the mountaintop; Jesus Christ did it by showing people through the ages what they could aspire to become; politicians talk about achieving a better world through "blood, sweat, and tears," about "a great society," or about "a world without war." Students in the classroom evoke imaginative pictures of what life would be like without a traditional marking system; with lower tuition fees and dormitory rates; with abortion on demand; without murder, war, inflation, or high taxes; or with high wages, shorter hours, full employment, and generous fringe benefits.

One researcher who studied students who were well- and ill-endowed in their richness of fantasy, or imagination, speculates that imaginative audiences may prefer less metaphorical language so that they can produce the rich imagery in their own minds. He also suggests that a speaker facing an imaginative group might have to contend with its ability to imagine the undesirable consequences of the persuader's proposal, a problem that the speaker could solve by imagining and refuting the possibly undesirable consequences of his proposition.[17] Unfor-

tunately, we do not have an easy way for the classroom speaker to assess the audience's level of imagination without using a questionnaire. A persuasive speaker can, however, have his audience "imagine, if you will" whatever consequence he sees for his persuasive proposal.

The persuasive speaker should keep in mind that one person's fact and reason can be another person's emotional appeal. A factual and rational approach to a speech on rape is an emotional experience to any woman in the audience who has faced the experience. Facts about abortion are emotional to some religious people. Unadorned information about water pollution can be emotional to the conservationist. Just as it is the audience that determines credibility, it is the audience, not the speaker, that determines whether a presentation is rational, emotional, or both.

An Example: A Student's Speech

Below is a persuasive speech delivered by a student. On the left are marginal notes that explain the function of each part of the outline. Notice the main arguments, the supporting materials, and the development of the speech.

Addiction!

Goal is discontinuance.
  Ultimate goal:
  Immediate purpose:

To convince my listeners to stop watching television.
To get my listeners to recognize the dangers of TV for children.

Introduction

Common ground.

I. Television and references to it are all around us.

Credibility through research.
Introduction of novel argument to arouse interest and to establish relevance to adult audience.

II. Most of us have never known a time when there was no TV.

III. There is much information available about the effect of television violence on children.

IV. What most of us do not know is that watching any type of television program can be harmful to children and adults.

Body

First main argument about problem.

I. Television is a major factor in the social and mental development of children.

Least offensive information presented early in speech.

A. Most children spend more time watching television than in any other activity except sleep.

1. Estimates of weekly viewing time of children range from 23 to 50 hours per week.

Statistics and conclusions based on statistics in support of the first argument. Strategy: rhetoric of reason.

2. That would mean that by the age of twenty, most people have watched between 24,000 and 52,000 hours of TV.

3. That would mean between 2½ and 6 years of TV viewing, 24 hours a day.

Logical inference based on the statistics.

B. Television has, for many children, replaced traditional childhood activities.

C. Television viewing has eliminated much of the normal interaction between parents and children.

The Metamorphosis

Nydegger/Die Weltwoche/Zurich

Second main argument
based on the purpose.

Supporting evidence for
second argument, from
outside sources.

Quote from an authority on
television.

A second subhead in
support of the second
argument.
Quotations from a source
summarizing research.

Information from a study
supporting second
argument.
Strategy: rhetoric of
reason.

II. Television viewing is potentially harmful to children,
    regardless of the content of the programs.
    A. TV serves many children and adults as a model
       of reality. Quote from Atkin, Murray, and
       Nayam's *TV and Social Behavior*.
       1. People tend to think that what is presented on
          TV is representative of the real world.
       2. The conflict between what is seen on TV and
          what is seen in life is unbearable for some
          children and adults. Quote from report to
          surgeon general.
    B. The new generation of television children is
       posing unexpected problems for school teachers.
       Quotes from *Newsweek* article.
       1. Nursery school teachers relate that children's
          play centers on TV fantasies.
       2. University of Southern California experiment
          involving 250 mentally gifted elementary
          children indicates that intensive viewing
          impairs all mental abilities except verbal skills.
       3. Many children cannot understand a simple
          story without visual illustrations.

Quote from an authority on TV.

An inference based on observation and reading.

A positive example used as contrast.

Third main argument. Movement toward solution. An example in detail to serve as a model.

Explanation of method.

Revelation of results.

How example overcomes problems depicted above through reading and interaction with parents.

Solution presented late in speech to reduce hostility. Behavioral change suggested. Careful not to ask for too much change.

Strategy: Rhetoric of emotion: ''Imagine if you will.''

4. Accustomed to seeing all problems solved in 30 to 60 minutes, children develop a low tolerance for the frustration of learning.

5. ''Educational'' programs such as *Sesame Street* and *The Electric Company* are causing elementary students to want to be entertained.

C. *Roots* and other such specials are rare examples of what television can and should be.

III. Even commercial television can be used as an educational tool.

A. Philadelphia's school system recently initiated a program which gives scripts of documentaries to children before air time.

1. The children read the script as they watch the program and discuss the show in class the next day.

2. Many students showed three years' improvement in reading skills on standardized tests.

B. Parents may view programs with children and discuss with their children the program's message and the values it contains.

IV. One way to eliminate television's ill effects is to reduce or stop television viewing. Another means would be to encourage the use of commercial TV as an educational tool. Present problems with TV could be reduced if there were better TV for children or no TV for children. Families could communicate and children could learn more and be entertained less. The solution is up to you as future parents.

Conclusion

Motivating statement

I. Television has an undeniable effect on children.

II. Since TV is here to stay, we need to learn how to live with it safely.

Sources

Atkin, Charles H., John P. Murray, and Oguz B. Nayam. *Television and Social Behavior.* Rockville, Md.: U.S. Department of Health, Education, and Welfare, 1971.

Blake, Richard A. ''Forget the Message, Worry about the Medium.'' *America,* No. 136 (March 26, 1977), 276–77.

Head, Sidney W. *Broadcasting in America.* Boston: Houghton Mifflin Company, 1976.

Rule, Elton H. ''Children's Television Viewing—the Parent's Role.'' *Vital Speeches* 43 (October 14, 1976): 24–26.

U.S. Health Service. *Television and Growing Up: The Impact of Televised Violence,* a report to the surgeon general. Washington, D.C., 1972.

Waters, Harry F. ''What Television Does to Kids.'' *Newsweek,* February 21, 1977, pp. 62–65.

Evaluating the Persuasive Speech: A List of Inquiries

Evaluating a persuasive speech is more difficult than evaluating an informative speech because of the large number of strategies that are possible and because the effect is less tangible. However, there are many questions that can help persuasive speakers to evaluate their own speeches or the speeches of others. The questions listed below are designed to help you find the areas of strength and weakness in your persuasive speech. They are the questions that you should ask about the source, the evidence, the organization, and other aspects of the speech.

The Source, or Speaker

1. Did the speaker indicate a basis for authority (personal commitment or involvement, research, major interest)?
2. Did the speaker buttress that authority with opinions, studies, surveys, and the authority of other experts?
3. Did the speaker appear to be knowledgeable about the issue or topic by providing relevant information, by anticipating alternatives or questions, and by avoiding elementary mistakes?

The Evidence

4. Were the personal experiences presented typical, generalizable, realistic, and relevant?
5. Were the studies and surveys authoritative, valid, reliable, objective, and generalizable?
6. Was the opinion from outside sources from credible, objective experts in their area of expertise; from professional studies and research?
7. Were the statistics from a reliable source, comparable with other known information, current, applicable, and interpreted so that listeners could understand them?
8. Were the speaker's inferences appropriate to the data presented? Were other inferences from the data equally sound?

The Organization

9. Did the speaker take the audience's attitudes and beliefs into account by building toward the less desirable propositions, by placing the more desirable arguments early, and by asking for an appropriate amount of change in the audience at the end?
10. Did the speaker repeat the persuasive proposition often enough so that the audience could not miss the intermediate purpose of the speech?
11. Did the speaker refute opposing arguments or ignore them? Which would have been more appropriate in this speech?
12. Did the audience understand the problem clearly before the speaker moved to solutions?

Other Factors

13. Did the speaker encourage active involvement of the audience?
14. Did the speaker present any new or novel arguments or approaches?
15. Did the speaker point out similarities between himself or herself and the audience?
16. Did the speaker explicitly state or strongly imply the attitude, belief, or behavior that was desired?
17. Did the speaker employ stratagems of reason, refutation, or emotion that were appropriate to the speaker, the audience, the topic, and the situation?
18. Could the audience clearly determine the speaker's ultimate behavioral goal (adoption or discontinuance)?

The answers to these questions can assist you, as a speaker, to assess your own persuasive speech; they can assist you as a critic to evaluate the speeches of others.

Summary

In this chapter, we reviewed the two goals of persuasion—adoption and discontinuance—and related them to the immediate purposes of a persuasive speech. We next examined a number of ways to relate the persuasive speech to an audience. Three categories of persuasive strategies were discussed: the rhetoric of reason, the rhetoric of refutation, and the rhetoric of emotion. Each category included a variety of stratagems such as the use of fear, appeals to consistency, and attacks on a source. We analyzed an outline of a persuasive speech, providing marginal notes that showed the function of each section of the speech. Finally, we summarized the chapter by including a list of inquiries, questions you can use to evaluate your own speech and the persuasive speeches of others.

New Terms

Persuasive speaking	Boomerang	Rhetoric of reason
Affective domain	Repetition	Rhetoric of refutation
Adoption	Active participation	Rhetoric of emotion
Discontinuance	Passive participation	Persuasive strategies
Immediate goal	Novel arguments	*Ad hominem* attacks
Ultimate goal	Refutation	Appeals to fear

Additional Readings

Arnold, Carrol C.; Ehninger, Douglas; and Gerber, John C. *The Speaker's Resource Book.* 2d ed. Chicago: Scott, Foresman and Company, 1966. *Persuasive speeches from politics, education, and religion illustrate principles of persuasive speaking. Each speech is followed by questions and analysis to help the student gain insight into the practical use of persuasive strategies.*

*Bem, Daryl J. *Beliefs, Attitudes, & Human Affairs.* Belmont, Calif.: Brooks/Cole Publishing Company, 1970. *A thorough discussion of the psychological, social, cognitive, and behavioral bases of attitude formation and maintenance. Information about attitudes is theoretical, but a good foundation is laid for making decisions about designing persuasive strategies and predicting audience response to persuasive messages.*

Cronkhite, Gary. *Persuasion: Speech and Behavioral Change.* New York: Bobbs-Merrill Co., Inc., 1969. *A thorough exploration of persuasive theories, techniques, and effects. Includes discussions of audience analysis, credibility, organization, and language as they relate to persuasive speaking. The classical theories of persuasion are examined.*

Ehninger, Douglas. *Influence, Belief, and Argument.* Glenview, Ill.: Scott, Foresman and Company, 1974. *Contains clear and precise definitions of types and uses of evidence as support for persuasive arguments, as well as fallacies of reasoning to avoid. Includes exercises designed to help you apply the concepts to your own speech assignments.*

Karlins, Marvin, and Abelson, Herbert I. *Persuasion: How Opinions and Attitudes Are Changed.* New York: Springer Publishing Co., Inc., 1970.

A summary of the research on persuasion, with emphasis on the effects of persuasion, the "sleeper effect," one-sided vs. two-sided messages, and the relation of information to persuasion. Each chapter contains questions that stimulate thinking about the decisions the speaker must make to prepare a successful persuasive message.

Larson, Charles U. *Persuasion: Reception and Responsibility.* Belmont, Calif.: Wadsworth Publishing Co., Inc., 1974. *Larson places persuasion into the context of our social structure and cultural environment and finds the psychological roots of persuasion in human needs. He also discusses ways in which a speaker can ethically adapt materials and arguments to meet those needs.*

Makay, John J., and Brown, William R. *The Rhetorical Dialogue: Contemporary Concepts and Cases.* Dubuque, Iowa: Wm. C. Brown Company Publishers, 1972. *Texts of famous speeches illustrate the discussion of evidence, reasoning, and organization. A good analysis of political, religious, and television speeches helps to clarify and explain the strategies employed by the speakers.*

Swanson, Richard, and Marquardt, Charles. *On Communication: Listening, Reading, Speaking, and Writing.* Beverly Hills, Calif.: Glencoe Press, 1974. Pages 118–40. *The authors discuss the nature of attitudes and the processes by which they are formed and maintained, reinforced, or changed. Credibility, reasoning, and emotions affect strategies for effecting attitudinal change. Includes a summary of Monroe's Motivated Sequence.*

*Indicates more advanced readings.

Notes

1. Adapted from Wallace Fotheringham, *Perspectives on Persuasion* (Boston: Allyn & Bacon, Inc., 1966), p. 33.
2. J. Mills and J. Jellison, "Effect on Opinion Change of Similarity between the Communicator and the Audience He Addresses," *Journal of Personality and Social Psychology* 9 (1968): 153–56.
3. T. Cook and C. Insko, "Persistence of Attitude Change as a Function of Conclusion Reexposure: A Laboratory-Field Experiment," *Journal of Personality and Social Psychology* 9 (1968): 322–28.
4. Cook and Insko, pp. 322–28.
5. R. L. Rosnow and E. Robinson, *Experiments in Persuasion* (New York: Academic Press, Inc., 1967), pp. 99–104.
6. Marvin Karlins and Herbert I. Abelson, *Persuasion: How Opinions and Attitudes Are Changed* (New York: Springer Publishing Co., Inc., 1970), p. 22 ff.
7. Marvin Karlins and Herbert I. Abelson, *Persuasion: How Opinions and Attitudes Are Changed,* 2nd ed., p. 22 ff. (New York: Springer Publishing Co., Inc., 1970)
8. D. Sears and J. Freedman, "Effects of Expected Familiarity with Arguments upon Opinion Change and Selective Exposure," *Journal of Personality and Social Psychology* 2 (1965): 420–26.
9. C. Hovland and H. Pritzker, "Extent of Opinion Change as a Function of Amount of Change Advocated," *Journal of Abnormal and Social Psychology* 54 (1957): 257–61.
11. Reprinted from Marvin Karlins and Herbert I. Abelson, *Persuasion: How Opinions and Attitudes Are Changed,* 2nd ed., p. 35. Copyright © 1970 by Springer Publishing Company, Inc., New York. Used by permission.
12. I. S. Janis and S. Feshbach, "Effects of Fear-Arousing Communications," *Journal of Abnormal and Social Psychology* 48 (1953): 78–92.
13. Fredric A. Powell, "The Effects of Anxiety-Arousing Messages when Related to Personal, Familial, and Impersonal Referents," *Speech Monographs* 32 (1965): 102–6.
14. William J. McGuire, "Effectiveness of Fear Appeals in Advertising," research proposal submitted to the American Advertising Foundation, 1963.
15. Rosnow and Robinson, p. 151.
16. Frances Cope and Don Richardson, "The Effects of Measuring Recommendations in a Fear-Arousing Speech," *Speech Monographs* 39 (1972): 148–50.
17. Dominic A. Infante, "Richness of Fantasy and Beliefs about Attempts to Refute a Proposal as Determinants of Attitude," *Speech Monographs* 42 (1975): 75–79.

Glossary

action view of communication
The view that communication occurs when one person sends a message to another.

active participation
Asking the audience to write, reply, or act in a certain way during the speech in order to demonstrate ideas, ascertain audience attitudes, or involve the audience in the topic.

active perception
The view that people select the stimuli they receive.

ad hominem attacks
Irrelevant attacks on a person who supports views different from the speaker's; a tabooed strategy.

adoption
Aimed at inducing an audience to accept a new idea, attitude, belief, or product and to demonstrate that acceptance by behavioral change; an action goal of the persuasive speech.

advance organizers
Previews of the forthcoming content.

affective domain
The way the audience feels about what it knows; the audience's emotions and attitudes about a topic.

anticlimactic organization
A method of organization in which the speaker presents the best or strongest arguments and evidence early in the speech.

appropriate self-disclosure
Self-disclosure that is appropriate to oneself, the other person, the topic, and the length and intimacy of the relationship.

arbitrary meaning
The meaning assigned to words by people; words have no inherent meaning.

arousal
Initiating and maintaining audience interest, focusing attention on the speaker, stating the specific purpose of the speech, and describing the speaker's qualifications; a function of the introduction.

articulation
The production of sounds; a component of enunciation.

attitude
A predisposition to respond favorably or unfavorably to some person, object, idea, or event.

attitudinal scales
A measure of attitudes that requires written responses to concepts on an interval scale usually ranging from "strongly favor" to "strongly disfavor."

audience adaptation
Adjusting the verbal and nonverbal elements of the speech on the basis of data derived from audience analysis.

audience analysis
The collection and interpretation of data on the demographics, attitudes, values, and beliefs of the audience obtained by observation, questionnaires, or interviews.

audience interest
The relevance and importance of the topic to an audience; sometimes related to the uniqueness of the topic.

audience knowledge
The amount of information the audience already has about the topic.

Barnlund's "six persons"
Each person involved in a two-person communication has three points of view: a view of herself or himself; a view of the other person; and a view of the other's perception of him or her.

belief
A conviction.

blind area
The quadrant of the Johari Window that illustrates the proportion of information about oneself that is known to others but not to oneself.

body
Part of the speech that contains the arguments, evidence, and main content of a speech.

body orientation
The degree to which a person's shoulders, legs, head, and torso are turned toward another person.

body position
The placement and arrangement of the body's extremities; the relationship of the

body to the horizontal and vertical
dimensions of space and the tenseness of
the orientation; includes posture.

boomerang effect
Occurs when the audience's attitudes
toward the speaker's position on a topic
become more negative during the speech.

brainstorming
Listing or naming as many ideas as a
group can in a limited period of time.

captive audience
An audience that did not choose to hear a
particular speaker or speech.

cause-effect organization
A method of organization in which the
speaker first explains the causes of an
event, problem, or issue, and then
discusses its consequences.

classification
The process of ordering stimuli into
meaningful groups or classes using
language to identify similarities and ignore
differences; abstraction.

clichés
Words or phrases that have lost their
meaning and effectiveness through
overuse.

climactic organization
A method of organization in which the
speaker presents the strongest or best
arguments and evidence last.

closed question
A question framed so that the possible
answers are specified or restricted; an
interview question.

closure
The organization of stimuli so that
information missing in the original is filled
in by the perceiver in order to provide the
appearance of a complete unit or whole.

code
Any systematic arrangement or
comprehensive collection of symbols,
letters, or words that have been given
arbitrary meanings and are used for
communication.

cognitive change
A change in what an audience knows or
understands about the speaker's topic; a
purpose of the informative speech.

common ground
The experience, ideas, or behavior that
the speaker shares with the audience.

communication
Making common; understanding and
sharing.

communication situation
The environment and context of a
communication, usually defined in terms
of the number of people involved and the
function of the communication.

comparative validation
Interpersonal communication in which
perception is compared with past
interpretations of similar stimuli.

comparison
A behavioral goal of the informative
speech in which the audience weighs the
relative values and characteristics of the
speech or its uses of objects, events, or
issues.

competence
The degree to which the speaker is
perceived as skilled, experienced,
qualified, authoritative, and informed; an
aspect of credibility.

comprehension
The understanding of the meaning of a
message; sometimes tested by retention.

conciliatory remarks
Compliments or commendations that a
speaker gives to an audience.

conclusion
The last part of the speech; a summary of
the major ideas designed to induce some
mental or behavioral change in an
audience.

concreteness
Specificity of expression; using words that
are not ambiguous or abstract.

connotative meaning
Individualized or personalized meaning;
the emotional content of words.

consensual validation
Communication with others in order to
achieve agreement, or consensus, about
what is perceived.

content
The evidence, illustrations, proof,
arguments, and examples that are used to
develop a speech topic.

co-orientation
The degree to which the speaker's values, beliefs, attitudes, and interests are shared with the audience.

creative perception
The view that meaning is imparted to stimuli by the perceiver rather than being an inherent property of the thing perceived.

credibility is earned
The view that credibility is not inherent in the speaker, but is perceived by the audience, based on the speaker's life, his experiences, and his accomplishments.

criteria-application pattern
A method of presenting arguments for a persuasive message in which the speaker establishes criteria that the audience will accept and then shows how the proposition meets the criteria; the pattern asks that the audience be consistent.

cultural differences
The influence on perception of stimuli by the environments and situations imposed by the culture.

cultural role
The pattern of behavior imposed upon a person by the culture of which the person is part.

culture and subculture
Groups or classes of people defined in terms of their heritage, traditions, social structure, and value systems. The meaning assigned to words differs among cultures and subcultures.

dating
A component skill of concreteness; identification and statement when an inference or observation was made.

decode
To assign meaning to a verbal code that we receive.

defensiveness
The act of protecting and supporting our ideas and attitudes against attack by others; induced by the feeling that the self and the validity of self-expression are threatened.

definition
A behavioral goal of the informative speech in which the audience is expected to be able to define a concept of the speech upon its completion.

delayed revelation
The postponement of the statement of purpose until late in the persuasive speech; used especially when the audience is initially opposed to the speaker's purpose.

demographic analysis
Collection and interpretation of data about the characteristics of people, excluding their attitudes and beliefs.

denotative meaning
An agreed-upon meaning of a word or phrase; a formal meaning determined by agreement within a society or culture.

description
A technique for improving or establishing credibility; the speaker objectively describes his or her accomplishments or credentials.

descriptive feedback
Describing to another person his or her nonverbal and verbal behavior; telling the other person your objective understanding of messages that you are receiving.

descriptiveness
The describing of observed behavior or phenomena instead of offering personal reactions or judgments.

designated leader
A person who is appointed or otherwise selected to be the leader of a small group; the person with the formal or agreed upon title, "leader."

Dewey's method of reflective thinking
A sequence of steps for organizing, defining, researching, and solving problems in groups.

discontinuance
Inducing an audience to stop doing something; a behavioral goal of the persuasive speech.

distinguish
The ability of an audience to differentiate the characteristics of events or objects; a behavioral goal of the informative speech.

double bind
The conflict caused by a difference between verbal and nonverbal messages.
dyadic communication
Communication between two persons.
dynamism
The degree to which the speaker is perceived as bold, active, energetic, strong, empathic, and assertive; an aspect of credibility.

egocentrism
The tendency to view oneself as the center of any exchange or activity; an overconcern with the presentation of oneself to others.
empathy
The ability to perceive another person's view of the world as though the view were your own.
employment interview
An interview for the purpose of screening job applicants or hiring a person.
encode
To put a message or thought into a code.
enunciation
The pronunciation and articulation of sounds and words; a vocal aspect of delivery.
euphemisms
Words or phrases that are considered inoffensive as compared to those that have vulgar or unacceptable connotations, e.g., *washroom* as a substitute for *toilet*.
evaluation
A kind of self-description that does not usually enhance credibility; speakers evaluate their own accomplishments, usually in a complimentary fashion.
experiential superiority
The attitude that our experiences are more important and valid than the experiences of others.
extemporaneous mode
A delivery style; the speech is carefully prepared and researched, but it appears to be spontaneous in its delivery.
extrinsic motivation
A method of making information relevant by providing the audience with reasons outside the speech itself for attending to its content.

eye contact
The way a speaker watches the audience; an aspect of bodily delivery.

fact question
A discussion question that deals with truth and falsity; concerns the occurrence, existence, or particular properties of something.
factual distractions
The tendency to listen to facts rather than main ideas; a barrier to listening.
fear appeals
A strategy of the rhetoric of emotions that attempts to create anxiety in the audience and then offers reassurance that the speaker's ideas will reduce the anxiety.
figure and ground
The organization of perception so that some stimuli are brought into focus and the rest become the background.
finale
The last statement made by the speaker; ideally, a clever, insightful, or memorable statement that concludes an informative speech or a visionary, rewarding, or motivating statement that concludes a persuasive speech.
fluency
The smoothness of delivery, the flow of words, and the absence of vocalized pauses; an aspect of vocal delivery.
forecast
An overview of the speech's organization; occurs in the introduction or early in the body of the speech.
forewarning, or preview
A transition that serves to advise the audience of the next main idea.
functions of communication
Survival of self and survival of society.
funnel approach
A method of organizing an interview so that broad, general, and open questions are asked first, becoming increasingly restrictive and narrower in scope.

gestures
The movements of head, arms, and hands to illustrate, emphasize, or signal ideas in the speech; an aspect of bodily delivery.

group
A small number of persons who share common interests or goals, who regularly engage in communication with each other, and who all contribute to the functioning of the group.

hearing
The physiological process by which sound is received by the ear.

heterogeneity
Characterizes an audience whose members differ widely.

hidden agenda
When the underlying goal of the communication is different than the stated goal; the underlying goal is the hidden agenda.

hidden area
The quadrant of the Johari Window that illustrates the proportion of information about oneself that is known to oneself but not to others.

homogeneity
Characterizes an audience whose members are similar.

I'm OK—you're OK
An expression of the view that self-growth comes through accepting and liking ourselves and others; a model of the relationship between our attitude toward ourselves and our attitude toward others.

immediate goal
The short-range change the persuasive speaker hopes the audience will adopt.

immediate purpose
The short-range, immediate goal that the speaker wishes to achieve.

impromptu mode
A delivery style; the speech is delivered without notes and without preparation.

indexing
A component of concreteness; identifying the uniqueness of objects, events, and people and stating that one's observations and inferences are specific rather than generalizable.

indirect sequencing
A method of organization in which the speaker first states the grounds for an argument or conclusion and then states the generalization or conclusion based on that information.

inferences
Conclusions drawn from observation.

inferential method
A method of audience analysis in which inferences or tentative conclusions are drawn about an audience on the basis of partial or incomplete information.

inflection
The patterns of alteration, or lack of alteration, in the pitch of a person's voice.

information hunger
The audience's need for the information contained in the speech.

information relevance
The importance, novelty, and usefulness of the topic and the information; a factor in adapting an informative speech to an audience.

informational interview
An interview for the purpose of collecting information, opinions, or data about a specific topic.

informational overload
Occurs when the quantity of information presented is greater than the audience can assimilate within the given time.

informative content
The evidence, examples, and illustrations cited in a speech that develop and support the main ideas.

informative speaking
A speech whose purpose is to get an audience to understand, learn, or change its behavior.

inherent meaning
The view that meaning is inherent in stimuli; hence, that perception is passive.

intelligibility
The degree to which sounds and words can be understood.

interactional view of communication
The view that communication occurs when communicators take turns encoding and decoding messages.

interpersonal communication
The process of sharing and understanding between oneself and at least one other person.

interpretation
The assignment of meaning to stimuli.

interviewing
Communication, usually between two persons, involving the asking and answering of questions for a predetermined purpose.

intimate self-disclosure
Disclosure of information that is highly personal and risky.

intrapersonal communication
The process of sharing and understanding within oneself.

intrinsic meaning
Meaning that is an inherent property in words. The invalid assumption is that there is a direct connection between symbols and reality.

introduction
The first part of the speech; its function is to arouse the audience and lead into the main ideas presented in the body.

inverted funnel approach
A method of organizing an interview so that closed questions are asked first, becoming increasingly general and unrestrictive.

involvement
The importance of the topic to the speaker; determined by the strength of the feelings the speaker has about the topic and the time and energy the speaker devotes to that subject area or topic.

Johari Window
A model of self-disclosure that indicates the proportion of information about oneself that is known and unknown to oneself, others, and both.

journal
A daily or periodic record of personal experience and impressions.

kinesics
The study of bodily movements, including posture, gestures, and facial expressions.

language distortion
The use of ambiguous or misleading language for the purpose of confusing others.

leader
Anyone who acts as a leader or is selected or designated the leader of a particular group.

leadership
Any behavior that helps to clarify or achieve a group's goals; influence.

leadership characteristics
Communication skills that have been identified with effective group discussion leaders; includes listening, knowledgeability of topic and group process, and ability to communicate ideas to others.

leadership functions
The behaviors needed to meet the task, social, and procedural needs of the group process.

leading question
A question that suggests the answer; a question worded so that there is only one acceptable answer.

limiting the topic
The process of reducing a general topic to a less abstract and more concrete topic.

listenability
The degree to which sounds and meaning can be easily ascertained by listeners; closely related to comprehension.

listening
The selective process of receiving and interpreting sounds.

manipulation
A controlled, planned communication for the purpose of influencing or controlling the behavior of others.

manuscript mode
A delivery style; the speech is written and is read verbatim.

Maslow's hierarchy of needs
A ranking order of physical, safety, social, self-esteem, and self-actualization needs. Maslow states that lower-order needs must be satisfied before higher-order needs.

mean, or average
The arithmetic sum of a series of numbers divided by the total number of items in the series.

meaning
What we share and understand in the process of communication; that which is felt to be the significance of something. A more accurate and useful descriptor of the object of communication than *message* or *thought*.

memorized mode
A delivery style; the speech is committed to memory either by rote or repeated delivery.

mental distraction
Communicating with ourselves while we are engaged in communication with others; a barrier to listening.

message
A unit containing verbal and nonverbal symbols, but in which meaning is not inherent.

mode
The most frequently recurring number in a series of numbers.

modes of delivery
Four styles of delivery that vary in the amount of preparation required and their degree of spontaneity.

movement
The speaker's use of the entire body; an aspect of physical delivery.

multisensory validation
The use of more than one sense to verify an interpretation.

needs
Physical, psychological, or social desires that motivate a person's behavior.

negative self-disclosure
Disclosure of information about oneself that tends to decrease our esteem in the eyes of others.

neutral question
A question that does not suggest any particular or preferred response or direction.

neutrality
Indifference to another person.

noise
Any interference in the encoding and decoding processes which lessens the fidelity of the message.

nonfluency
Delivery characteristics, usually vocal, that break the smooth and fluid delivery of the speech and are judged negatively by the audience.

nonverbal code
A code that consists of any symbols that are not words, including non-word vocalizations.

novel arguments
New and original evidence or reasoning that the audience has seldom or never heard; often has more impact than the repetition of familiar arguments.

objectics
The study of the human use of artifacts as cues; object language.

objective perception
The view that the perceiver is a nonevaluative recorder of stimuli.

observation
Active observation of the behavior and characteristics of an audience.

obstacles
The characteristics of the speaker, audience, topic, situation, or content of a speech that are likely to hamper the effectiveness of the presentation.

one-sided message
Presentation of the arguments and evidence that support only the speaker's position on a persuasive topic; used when the audience is generally friendly, when the audience will hear only the speaker's position, or when the speaker is seeking immediate but temporary opinion change.

open area
The quadrant of the Johari Window that illustrates the proportion of information about oneself that is known to oneself and others.

open question
A question that is broad in nature, generally unstructured in form, and that requires a rather lengthy response.

operational definition
An explanation of the meaning of words by describing the behavior, actions, or property that words signify.

organization
The structuring of stimuli into meaningful units or wholes.

organization: form
The outline, structure or design of a speech.

organization: function
The functions of the parts of the speech; how organization governs content.

overt audience response
The involvement of an audience with a topic through signalling or actual performance of a task.

paralanguage
The vocal or physical aspects of delivery that accompany the language used.

paraphrasing
Restating the other person's message by rephrasing the content or intent of the message.

passive participation
The nonbehavioral involvement of the audience in a persuasive speech; cognitive change.

passive perception
The view that perceivers are mere recorders of stimuli.

pause
The absence of vocal sound used for dramatic effect, transition, or emphasis of ideas; an aspect of vocal delivery.

percentage
The ratio or fraction of 100 represented by a specific number; obtained by dividing the number by 100.

perception
What a person sees, hears, smells, feels, or tastes; the process by which one comes to understand.

perceptual constancy
The invariable nature of the perception of a stimulus once it has been selected, organized, and interpreted by the perceiver.

personal inventory
A speaker's survey of his or her reading habits and behavior to discover what topics and subjects are of interest.

personal language
The language of the individual, which varies slightly from the agreed-upon meanings because of past experience and present condition. The meaning of words is personal and changeable.

personal space
The space between one person and another; the space a person controls and that moves with the person.

persuasive interview
An interview for the purpose of selling a particular idea, product or service.

persuasive speaking
A form of communication in which the speaker attempts to modify the audience's behavior by changing its perceptions, attitudes, beliefs, or values.

persuasive strategies
Means for achieving the goals of a persuasive speech.

physical distraction
Environmental stimuli that interfere with our focus on another person's message; a barrier to listening.

pitch
The highness or lowness of a speaker's voice; technically, the frequency of sound made by the vocal cords.

policy question
A type of discussion question that concerns future action.

positive self-disclosure
The expression of information about oneself that tends to increase our esteem in the eyes of others.

primary question
A question asked in an interview to introduce a new topic or a new area of a topic under discussion.

primary research
Firsthand research; the acquisition of information from personal experience, interviews, surveys, questionnaires, or experiment.

principle of division
In outlining, the content must be divisible into at least two parallel parts.

principle of parallel construction
In outlining, the verbal forms of the main heads, subheads, main points, and subpoints should be consistent and similar.

principle of subordination
In outlining, the main headings, subheadings, points, and subpoints should be distinguished from each other so the speaker can convey to the audience which items are of greater or lesser importance.

problem-and-solution pattern
A method of organization in which the speaker describes a problem and proposes a solution to that problem.

process
Action, change, exchange, and movement.

projection
The body's support of the voice that ensures that the most distant people in the room can hear what is said.

pronunciation
The conformance of the speaker's production of words with agreed-upon rules about the sounds of vowels and consonants, and for syllabic emphasis.

proximity
The organization of stimuli into meaningful units or wholes according to their perceived physical or psychological distance from each other.

public communication
The process of sharing and understanding between oneself and a large number of other people.

quality
The pleasant or unpleasant characteristics of a person's voice, including nasality, raspiness, and whininess; the timbre of the sounds produced by the vocal cords.

questionnaire
A method of obtaining information about an audience by asking written questions about its members' demographic characteristics or attitudes.

range
The highest and lowest numbers in a distribution.

rate
The speed of delivery, normally between 125 and 190 words per minute.

raw numbers
Exact numbers cited in measures of population, production, and other measures of quantity.

reciprocity
The sharing of information about themselves by two or more persons. Persons tend to be more comfortable about self-disclosure when others are also disclosing themselves.

recognition
The ability of an audience to identify the presence or absence of characteristics, properties, or elements of objects and events; a behavioral goal of the informative speech.

redundancy
Planned repetition of words, phrases, or ideas.

regionalisms
The use of different words for similar objects or ideas in different parts of the country.

reliability
The credibility of the source of specific information or evidence.

repetition
A restatement of the persuasive appeal after its initial presentation.

repetitive validation
Intrapersonal validation of observations of stimuli in order to ascertain the consistency with which one is interpreting them.

review and inspiration
The indication that the speech is near its conclusion by language, tone, nonverbal behavior, and summary and motivational statements.

review of exposition
A review of the main points of the speech which helps the audience focus on the overall purpose and content of the speech.

rhetoric of emotion
A speaker's appeals to the feelings and emotions of the audience in order to gain support for his ideas; a persuasive strategy.

rhetoric of reason
A speaker's attempts to prove by reasoning, logic, and consistency that a proposition is acceptable to the audience; a persuasive strategy.

rhetoric of refutation
A speaker's attempts to gain support for a proposition or idea by attacking or discrediting another person's evidence, logic, or credibility; a persuasive strategy.

rhetorical questions
Questions asked by the speaker to stimulate an audience's thinking, but to which no overt response is expected.

role
Behavior expected by others because of the social category in which a person is placed.

sample
The people who received a questionnaire or were interviewed; a large sample is usually more useful, generalizable, and valid than a small sample.

Sapir-Whorf hypothesis
The theory that our perception of reality is determined by our thought processes and that our thoughts are limited by our language; language shapes our perception of reality.

secondary question
A question asked in an interview to follow up or develop a primary question.

secondary research
Second-hand research; the acquisition of information from published sources.

selective attention
A focus on particular stimuli such that other stimuli are ignored.

selective exposure
The perception of stimuli that we wish to perceive and the ignoring of stimuli we do not wish to perceive.

selective retention
The recollection of information after selection, organization, and interpretation

have occurred; the mental categorization, storage, and retrieval of selected information.

self-awareness
The ability to consciously distinguish between one's self-image and one's self-esteem.

self-concept
A person's consciousness of his or her total, essential, and particular being; self-image and self-esteem.

self-consciousness
An excessive concern about self-esteem.

self-control
Our manipulative, strategic, and analytical responses to the demands and expectations of others and situations; unspontaneous self-expression.

self-disclosure
Intentional statements about oneself that impart information that the other person is unlikely to have.

self-esteem
Our attitudes and feelings toward our self-image; how well we like ourselves.

self-expression
Our open, genuine, and spontaneous response to people and situations.

self-focus
Developing a view of oneself from one's own perspective rather than through the eyes of others.

self-fulfilling prophecy
The self-image and self-esteem expected of one by others; the tendency to become what others expect us to become.

self-image
The sort of person we think we are; our own description of who we are and what we do.

self-improvement
The strengthening of the awareness of self; the development of clear goals for oneself; the development of self-esteem and self-expression.

self-praise
An evaluative, self-serving method of conveying the credentials of the speaker to an audience.

semantic distraction
Bits or units of information in the message that interfere with understanding the main

ideas or total meaning of the entire
message; a barrier to listening.

sharing
Interaction between oneself and others,
with the purpose of exchanging meaning.

similarity
A basis for organizing stimuli into
meaningful units by perceiving the
similarities among them.

sleeper effect
An increase in changes of opinion created
by a speaker with little credibility; caused
by the later separation of the content of
the message from its source.

small
The number of persons in a group
discussion: generally between three and
twenty, more often between four and
seven.

small group discussion
A discussion in a group of approximately
three to twenty persons who share
common interests or goals, who regularly
engage in communication with each other,
and who all contribute to the functioning
of the group.

social function
The function of a small group that meets
the needs of the members to belong to
something, to share pleasant
companionship, and to satisfy
interpersonal needs.

source credibility
The degree to which an audience
perceives a speaker as credible; based on
perceived competence, trustworthiness,
dynamism, and co-orientation.

spatial organization
A method of organization in which the
speaker explains where the parts of a
problem exist in space.

speech delivery
The behavior of the speaker; the manner
in which the verbal content of a message is
enhanced or diminished by nonverbal
vocal and physical behavior.

spontaneity
A voluntary, genuine reaction to feelings
and ideas; non-manipulative self-
expression.

statement
The ability of an audience to verbally list
the major ideas, reasons, or propositions
of the speech; a behavioral goal of the
informative speech.

statement of purpose
A statement in which the speaker tells the
audience what he or she wants the
audience to do, learn, or understand.

statistics
Numbers that summarize numerical
information or compare quantities.

status
The relative social position, reputation, or
importance of another person.

stereotypes
Categories into which we place other
persons.

stereotyping
The process of placing people and things
into categories or of basing judgments
about them on the categories into which
they fit rather than on their individual
characteristics.

strength of belief
The stability and importance of a belief
held by the audience; can be inferred from
the responses of its members to an
attitudinal scale.

subcultural differences
The influence on perception and behavior
of membership in a subgroup of a culture.

subjective perception
The view that perception is based on the
physiological and psychological
characteristics of the perceiver.

surveys and studies
Evidence consisting of questionnaires,
experimental findings, and interviews.

suspended judgments
Postponed evaluations of messages and
persons while we attempt to listen to them
empathically.

symbol
Something that stands for, or represents,
something else by association,
resemblance, or convention.

sympathy
A response to a situation that is the same
as another person's.

tactile communication
Communicating by touch.

task function
A function of a small group that exists to share information or solve important and difficult problems.

territoriality
The need to establish and maintain certain space as one's own; the control of space that is typically unmovable and separate from the person.

testimonial evidence
Written or oral statements of the experience of persons other than the speaker.

tests of evidence
The methods for evaluating information based on the qualifications of the source, the recency of the information, the completeness and accuracy of the information, and the generalizability of the evidence.

thought
The cognitive process by which meaning is assigned to our perceptions.

time-sequence pattern
A method of organization in which the speaker explains a sequence of events.

topical-sequence pattern
A method of organization in which the speaker emphasizes the major reasons why an audience should accept a certain point of view.

transactional view of communication
The view that communication is the simultaneous encoding and decoding of messages by more than one person.

transitions
Linkages between sections of the speech that help the speaker move smoothly from one idea to another. Principal transitions are forecasts, internal summaries, and statements of relationship.

trustworthiness
The degree to which the speaker is perceived as honest, fair, sincere, honorable, friendly, and kind; an aspect of credibility.

tunnel approach
A method of organizing an interview so that all questions are similar, e.g., all open or all closed.

ultimate goal
The long-range effect that the speaker hopes to have on the audience.

understanding
The perception and comprehension of the meaning of incoming stimuli, usually the verbal and nonverbal behavior of others.

unknown area
The quadrant of the Johari Window that illustrates the proportion of information about oneself that is unknown to oneself and others.

values
Deeply rooted beliefs that govern our attitudes; goals rather than the means of reaching them.

verbal
Anything associated with or pertaining to words.

verbal codes
A code that consists of words.

vocal cues
All the oral aspects of sound, excluding the words that we speak; part of paralanguage.

vocal variety
Vocal quality, intonation patterns, inflections of pitch, and syllabic duration; a lack of sameness or repetitious patterns in vocal delivery; an aspect of vocal delivery.

vocalized pauses
Breaks in fluency; the use of meaningless words or sounds to fill in silences.

volume
The loudness or softness of a person's voice.

voluntary audience
A collection of people who choose to listen to a particular speaker or speech.

words
Verbal symbols by which we codify and share our perceptions of reality.

References

Addis, B. R. "The Relationship of Physical Interpersonal Distance to Sex, Race, and Age." Master's thesis, University of Oklahoma, 1966.

Adler, Ronald, and Towne, Neil. *Looking Out/Looking In.* San Francisco: Rinehart Press, 1975.

Allport, Gordon W. *The Nature of Prejudice.* Garden City, N.Y.: Doubleday & Co., 1958.

"American Youth." *U.S. News and World Report,* July 18, 1977, p. 19.

Anastasi, Thomas E., Jr. *Communicating for Results.* Menlo Park, Calif.: Cummings Publishing Co., 1972.

Andersen, Kenneth, and Clevenger, Theodore, Jr. "A Summary of Experimental Research in Ethos." *Speech Monographs* 30 (1963):59–78.

Anderson, Jane. "Discover Yourself: Go Hiking Alone." Fort Wayne *Journal-Gazette,* March 21, 1976.

Argyle, Michael. *Social Interaction.* New York: Atherton Press, 1969.

Argyle, Michael, and Dean, Janet. "Eye-Contact, Distance, and Affiliation." *Sociometry* 28 (1965):289–304.

Aristotle. *Rhetoric.* Translated by W. Rhys Roberts. In *The Basic Works of Aristotle,* edited by Richard McKeon. New York: Random House, 1941.

Arnold, Carrol C.; Ehninger, Douglas; and Gerber, John C. *The Speaker's Resource Book.* 2d ed. Chicago: Scott, Foresman and Co., 1966.

Ausubel, David. "The Use of Advance Organizers in the Learning and Retention of Meaningful Material." *Journal of Educational Psychology* 51 (1960):267–72.

Bach, George R., and Wyden, Peter. *The Intimate Enemy: How to Fight Fair in Love and Marriage.* New York: Avon Books, 1968.

Baird, John A. "The Effects of Speech Summaries upon Audience Comprehension of Expository Speeches of Varying Quality and Complexity." *Central States Speech Journal* 25 (1974):119–27.

Barbour, John. "Edwin Newman Talks to Himself, but for a Good Reason." *Des Moines Sunday Register,* June 5, 1977.

Barnlund, Dean C. "Toward a Meaning Centered Philosophy of Communication." *Journal of Communication* 12 (1962):198–202.

———. "A Transactional Model of Communication." In *Foundations of Communication Theory,* edited by Kenneth K. Sereno and C. David Mortensen, pp. 98–101. New York: Harper & Row, Publishers, 1970.

Bateson, Gregory; Jackson, D. D.; Haley, J.; and Weakland, J. H. "Toward a Theory of Schizophrenia." *Behaviorial Science* 1 (1956):251–64.

Beach, Dale S. *Personnel: The Management of People at Work.* 3d ed. New York: Macmillan Publishing Co., 1975.

Becker, Samuel L. "New Approaches to Audience Analysis." In *Perspectives on Communication,* edited by Carl E. Larson and Frank E. X. Dance. Shorewood, Wis.: Helix Press, 1970.

Beebe, Steven A. "Eye Contact: A Nonverbal Determinant of Speaker Credibility." *Speech Teacher* 23 (1974):21–25.

Beighley, Kenneth C. "An Experimental Study of the Effect of Four Speech Variables on Listener Comprehension." *Speech Monographs* 19 (1952):249–58; and Kenneth C. Beighley "An Experimental Study of the Effect of Three Speech Variables on Listener Comprehension." *Speech Monographs* 21 (1954):248–53.

Bem, Daryl J. *Beliefs, Attitudes and Human Affairs.* Belmont, Calif.: Brooks/Cole Publishing Co., 1970.

Benson, George, and Chasin, Joseph. "Entry Level Positions." *Journal of College Placement* 37 (1976):76.

Berne, Eric. *Games People Play: The Psychology of Human Relationships.* New York: Grove Press, 1964.

———. *What Do You Say After You Say Hello?* New York: Grove Press, 1972.

Berquist, Goodwin F. *Speeches for Illustration and Example.* Chicago: Scott, Foresman and Co., 1965.

Bettinghaus, Erwin P. "The Operation of Congruity in an Oral Communication Situation." *Speech Monographs* 28 (1961):131–42.

———. *Persuasive Communication.* New York: Holt, Rinehart and Winston, 1968.

Bird, D. "Teaching Listening Comprehension." *Journal of Communication* 3 (1953):127–30.

———. "Have You Tried Listening?" *Journal of the American Dietetic Association* 30 (1954):225–30.

Birdwhistell, Ray L. *Kinesics and Context.* Philadelphia: University of Pennsylvania Press, 1970.

Black, John W. "A Study of Voice Merit." *Quarterly Journal of Speech* 28 (1942):67–74.

Black, John W., and Moore, Wilbur E. *Speech: Code, Meaning, and Communication.* New York: McGraw-Hill Book Co., 1955.

Blau, P. M. *Exchange and Power in Social Life.* New York: John Wiley & Sons, Inc., 1964.

Bochner, Arthur P., and Kelley, Clifford W. "Interpersonal Competence: Rationale, Philosophy, and Implementation of a Conceptual Framework." *Speech Teacher* 23 (1974):279–301.

Bormann, Ernest G., and Bormann, Nancy C. *Effective Small Group Communication.* 2d ed. Minneapolis: Burgess Publishing Co., 1976.

Bowlby, John. *Maternal Care and Mental Health.* Geneva: World Health Organization, 1951.

Bradley, Bert. *Speech Performance.* Dubuque, Iowa: Wm. C. Brown Company Publishers, 1967.

Brigance, William N. "How Fast Do We Talk?" *Quarterly Journal of Speech* 12 (1926):337–42.

Brilhart, John K. *Effective Group Discussion.* 3d ed. Dubuque, Iowa: Wm. C. Brown Company Publishers, 1978.

Brown, James I. "The Objective Measurement of Listening Ability." *Journal of Communication* 1 (May 1951):44–48.

Bruskin Report. "What Are Americans Afraid Of?" Vol. 53. 1973.

Burke, Kenneth. *Permanence and Change.* Los Altos, Calif.: Hermes Publications, 1954.

Carney, Clarke G., and McMahon, Sarah L. *Exploring Contemporary Male/Female Roles.* La Jolla, Calif.: University Associates, 1977.

Carroll, Lewis. *Alice's Adventures in Wonderland.* New York: Random House, 1965.

———. *Through the Looking Glass.* New York: Random House, 1965.

Cathcart, Robert S., and Samovar, Larry A. *Small Group Communication: A Reader.* 3d ed. Dubuque, Iowa: Wm. C. Brown Company Publishers, 1978.

Chaikin, A. L., and Derlega, V. J. "Variables Affecting the Appropriateness of Self-Disclosure." *Journal of Consulting and Clinical Psychology* 42 (1974):588–93.

Clevenger, Theodore, Jr. *Audience Analysis.* Indianapolis: Bobbs-Merrill Co., 1966.

Cobin, Martin. "Response to Eye-Contact." *Quarterly Journal of Speech* 48 (1962):415–18.

Cofer, N. C. *Verbal Learning and Verbal Behavior.* New York: McGraw-Hill Book Company, 1961.

Connolly, James E. *Public Speaking as Communication.* Minneapolis: Burgess Publishing Co., 1974.

Cook, T., and Insko, C. "Persistence of Attitude Change as a Function of Conclusion Reexposure: A Laboratory-Field Experiment." *Journal of Personality and Social Psychology* 9 (1968):322–28.

Cope, Frances, and Richardson, Don. "The Effects of Measuring Recommendations in a Fear-Arousing Speech." *Speech Monographs* 39 (1972):148–50.

Cozby, P. C. "Self-Disclosure, Reciprocity, and Liking." *Sociometry* 35 (1972):151–60.

———. "Self-Disclosure: A Literature Review." *Psychological Bulletin* 79 (1973):73–91.

Cronkhite, Gary. *Persuasion: Speech and Behavioral Change.* Indianapolis: Bobbs-Merrill Co., 1969.

Culbert, S. A. "Trainer Self-Disclosure and Member Growth in Two T-Groups." *Journal of Applied Behavioral Science* 4 (1968):47–73.

Davis, James H. *Group Performance.* Reading, Mass.: Addison-Wesley Publishing Co., 1969.

Desper, J. L. "Emotional Aspects of Speech and Language Development." *International Journal of Psychiatry and Neurology* 105 (1941):193–222.

DeVito, Joseph A.; Giattino, Jill; and Schon, T. D. *Articulation and Voice: Effective Communication.* Indianapolis: Bobbs-Merrill Co., 1975.

Dickens, Milton, and McBath, James H. *Guidebook for Speech Communication.* New York: Harcourt Brace Jovanovich, Inc., 1973.

Diehl, Charles F.; White, Richard C.; and Burk, Kenneth W. "Rate and Communication." *Speech Monographs* 26 (1959):229–32.

Duker, S. *Listening Bibliography.* New York: Scarecrow Press, 1964.

Duker, S., ed. *Listening: Readings.* New York: Scarecrow Press, 1966.

Dyer, Wayne. *Your Erroneous Zones.* New York: Avon Books, 1976.

Edwards, David C. *General Psychology.* 2d ed. New York: Macmillan Publishing Co., 1972.

Egan, Gerard. *Interpersonal Living: A Skills/Contract Approach to Human Relations Training in Groups.* Belmont, Calif.: Wadsworth Publishing Co., 1976.

Ehninger, Douglas. *Influence, Belief, and Argument.* Glenview, Ill.: Scott, Foresman and Co., 1974.

Eirlich, H. and Graeven, D. "Reciprocal Self-Disclosure in a Dyad." *Journal of Experimental Social Psychology* 7 (1971):389–400.

Ekman, Paul, and Friesen, Wallace V. "Head and Body Cues in the Judgment of Emotion: A Reformulation." *Perceptual and Motor Skills* 24 (1967):711–24.

———. *Unmasking the Face: A Guide to Recognizing Emotions from Facial Cues.* Englewood Cliffs, N. J.: Prentice-Hall, 1975.

Ellingsworth, Huber W., and Clevenger, Theodore, Jr. *Speech and Social Action: A Strategy of Oral Communication.* Englewood Cliffs, N. J.: Prentice-Hall, 1967.

Ernest, Carole. "Listening Comprehension as a Function of Type of Material and Rate of Presentation." *Speech Monographs* 35 (1968):154–58.

Fairbanks, Grant; Guttman, Newman; and Murray, Miron S. "Effects of Time Compression upon the Comprehension of Connected Speech." *Journal of Speech and Hearing Disorders* 22 (1957):10–19.

Fast, Julius. *Body Language.* New York: Pocket Books, 1970.

Fotheringham, Wallace. *Perspectives on Persuasion.* Boston: Allyn & Bacon, 1966.

Fraser, Alistair B. "Fata Morgana—The Grand Illusion." *Psychology Today* 9 (January, 1976):22.

Fromm, Eric. *The Art of Loving.* New York: Harper & Row, Publishers, 1956.

Gergen, Kenneth J. *The Concept of Self.* New York: Holt, Rinehart and Winston, 1971.

Gilbert, Shirley J., and Whiteneck, Gale G. "Toward A Multidimensional

Approach to the Study of Self-Disclosure." *Human Communication Research* 4 (1976):347–55.

Gilkinson, Howard, and Knower, Franklin H. "Individual Differences Among Students of Speech as Revealed by Psychological Tests—I." *Journal of Educational Psychology* 32 (1941):161–75.

Glasgow, George M. "A Semantic Index of Vocal Pitch." *Speech Monographs* 19 (1952):64–68.

Goffman, Erving. *The Presentation of Self in Everyday Life*. Garden City, N.Y.: Doubleday & Co., 1959.

Gordon, Chad, and Gergen, Kenneth J. *The Self in Social Interaction*. New York: John Wiley & Sons, 1968.

Gruner, Charles R. "The Effect of Humor in Dull and Interesting Informative Speeches." *Central States Speech Journal* 21 (1970)160–66.

Guardo, Carol J. "Personal Space in Children." *Child Development* 40 (1969):143–51.

Gundersen, D. F., and Hopper, Robert. "Relationships between Speech Delivery and Speech Effectiveness." *Speech Monographs* 43 (1976):158–65.

Hall, Edward T. *The Silent Language*. Greenwich, Conn.: Fawcett Publications, 1959.

————. "Proxemics—The Study of Man's Spatial Relations and Boundaries." *Man's Image in Medicine and Anthropology*. New York: International Universities Press, 1963.

Haney, William V. *Communication and Organizational Behavior*. Homewood, Ill.: Richard D. Irwin, 1967.

Hard, Roland J., and Brown, Bruce L. "Interpersonal Information Conveyed by the Content and Vocal Aspects of Speech." *Speech Monographs* 41 (1974):371–80.

Harms, L. S. "Listener Judgments of Status Cues in Speech." *Quarterly Journal of Speech* 47 (1961):164–69.

Harris, Thomas A. *I'm OK–You're OK: A Practical Guide to Transactional Analysis*. New York: Harper & Row, Publishers, 1969.

Hart, Roderick, P.; Friedrich, Gustav W.; and Brooks, William. *Public Communication*. New York: Harper & Row, Publishers, 1975.

Harwood, Kenneth A. "Listenability and Rate of Presentation." *Speech Monographs* 22 (1955):57–59

Hasling, John. *The Message, The Speaker, The Audience*. New York: McGraw-Hill Book Co., 1971.

Hastorf, Albert H.; Schneider, David J.; and Polefka, Judith. *Person Perception*. Reading, Mass.: Addison-Wesley Publishing Co., 1970.

Hayakawa, S. I. *Language in Thought and Action*. 3d ed. New York: Harcourt Brace Jovanovich, 1972.

Hayworth, Donald. "A Search for Facts on the Teaching of Public Speaking." *Quarterly Journal of Speech* 28 (1942):247–354.

"Headless." *Time*, July 18, 1977, p. 21.

Heath, Robert L. "Variability in Value System Priorities as Decision-Making Adaptation to Situational Differences." *Communication Monographs* 43 (1976):325–33.

Henrikson, Ernest H. "An Analysis of the Characteristics of Some 'Good' and 'Poor' Speakers." *Speech Monographs* 11 (1944):120–24.

Hertzler, Joyce O. *A Sociology of Language*. New York: Random House, 1965.

Hildebrandt, Herbert W., and Stevens, Walter. "Manuscript and Extemporaneous Delivery in Communicating Information." *Speech Monographs* 30 (1963):369–72.

Holtzman, Paul D. *The Psychology of Speaker's Audiences*. Glenview, Ill.: Scott, Foresman and Co., 1970.

Horrocks, John E., and Jackson, Dorothy W. *Self and Role: A Theory of Self-Process and Role Behavior*. Boston: Houghton Mifflin Co., 1972.

Hovland, Carl I.; Janis, Irving J.; and
Kelly, Harold H. "Credibility of the
Communicator." In *Dimensions in
Communication: Readings,* edited by
James H. Campbell and Hal W. Hepler.
Belmont, Calif.: Wadsworth Publishing
Co., 1970.

Hovland, Carl I. and Pritzker, H.
"Extent of Opinion Change as a
Function of Amount of Change
Advocated." *Journal of Abnormal and
Social Psychology* 54 (1957):257–61.

Hovland, Carl I., and Weiss, Walter.
"The Influence of Source Credibility on
Communicator Effectiveness." In
Experiments in Persuasion, edited by
Ralph Rosnow and Edward J. Robinson.
New York: Academic Press, 1967.

Infante, Dominic A. "Richness of
Fantasy and Beliefs about Attempts to
Refute a Proposal as Determinants of
Attitude." *Speech Monographs* 42
(1975):75–79.

Janis, I. S., and Feshbach, S. "Effects of
Fear-Arousing Communications."
*Journal of Abnormal and Social
Psychology* 48 (1953):78–92.

Johannsen, Richard L. *Ethics and
Persuasion.* New York: Random House,
1967.

Johnson, Wendell. *People in Quandaries.*
New York: Harper & Row, Publishers,
1946.

Jourard, Sidney. "Self-Disclosure and
Other Cathexis." *Journal of Abnormal
and Social Psychology* 59 (1959):428–31.

———. "Healthy Personality and Self-
Disclosure." In *The Self in Social
Interaction,* edited by Chad Gordon and
Kenneth J. Gergen. New York: John
Wiley & Sons, 1968.

———. *The Transparent Self.* 2d ed. New
York: Van Nostrand Reinhold Co.,
1971.

Jourard, Sidney, and Jaffe, P. "Influence
of an Interviewer's Disclosure on the
Self-Disclosing Behavior of
Interviewees." *Journal of Counseling
Psychology* 17 (1970):252–97.

Jourard, Sidney, and Landsman, M. J.
"Cognition, Cathexis, and the 'Dyadic
Effect' in Men's Self-Disclosing
Behavior." *Merrill-Palmer Quarterly of
Behavior and Development* 9 (1960):141–
48.

Jourard, Sidney, and Lasakow, Paul.
"Some Factors in Self-Disclosure."
*Journal of Abnormal and Social
Psychology* 51 (1958):91–98.

Jourard, Sidney, and Resnick, J. L.
"Some Effects on Self-Disclosure
Among College Women." *Journal of
Humanistic Psychology* 10 (1970):84–93.

Kafka, Franz. "Give It Up!" In *The
Complete Stories,* edited by Nathum N.
Glatzer. New York: Schocken Books,
1972.

Karlins, Marvin, and Abelson, Herbert I.
*Persuasion: How Opinions and Attitudes
Are Changed.* New York: Springer
Publishing Co., 1970.

Katz, Elihu. "On Reopening the Question
of Selectivity in Exposure to Mass
Communication." In *Speech
Communication Behavior: Perspectives
& Principles,* edited by Larry Baker and
Robert Kibler. Englewood Cliffs, N.J.:
Prentice-Hall, 1971.

Keller, Paul W. "Major Findings in
Listening in the Past Ten Years."
Journal of Communication 10 (March
1960):29–38.

Kiesler, C. A.; Kiesler, S.; and
Pallack, M. "The Effects of
Commitment on Future Interaction on
Reactions to Norm Violations." *Journal
of Personality* 35 (1967):585–99.

King, Robert G. *Forms of Public
Address.* Indianapolis: Bobbs-Merrill
Co, 1968.

Knapp, Mark L. *Nonverbal Communication in Human Interaction.* New York: Holt, Rinehart and Winston, 1972.

Korten, Frances F. "The Influence of Culture on the Perception of Persons." *International Journal of Psychology* 9 (1974):31–44.

Kramer, Cheris. "Folk-Linguistics: Wishy-Washy Mommy Talk." *Psychology Today,* June 1974, p. 82–85.

Kramer, Edward J. J., and Lewis, Thomas R. "Comparison of Visual and Nonvisual Listening." *Journal of Communication* 1 (1951):16–20.

Kramer, Ernest. "The Judgment of Personal Characteristics and Emotions from Nonverbal Properties of Speech." *Psychological Bulletin* 60 (1963):408–20.

Kruger, Arthur N. *Effective Speaking: A Complete Course.* New York: Van Nostrand Reinhold Co., 1970.

Laing, R. D. *Knots.* New York: Pantheon Books, Inc., 1971.

Laird, Charlton. *The Miracle of Language.* Greenwich, Conn.: Fawcett Publications, 1953.

Laird, Jess. *I Ain't Much Baby, but I'm All I've Got.* New York: Doubleday & Co., 1972.

Larson, Charles U. *Persuasion: Reception and Responsibility.* Belmont, Calif.: Wadsworth Publishing Co., 1974.

Lee, Irving J. *How to Talk With People.* New York: Harper & Row, Publishers, 1952.

Lee, Melvin; Zimbardo, Philip G.; and Bertholf, Minerva. "Shy Murderers." *Psychology Today* 11 (November 1977):148.

Levin, F. M., and Gergen K. "Revealingness, Ingratiation, and the Disclosure of Self." *Proceedings of the 77th Annual Convention,* American Psychological Association, 1969.

Levinger, G., and Senn, D. "Disclosure of Feelings in Marriage." *Merrill-Palmer Quarterly of Behavior and Development* 13 (1967):237–49.

Linkugel, Wil A., and Berg, David M. *A Time To Speak.* Belmont, Calif.: Wadsworth Publishing Co., 1970.

McCroskey, James C.; Larson, Carl E.; and Knapp, Mark L. *An Introduction to Interpersonal Communication.* Englewood Cliffs, N.J.: Prentice-Hall, 1971.

McCroskey, James C., and Wheeless, Lawrence R. *Introduction to Human Communication.* Boston: Allyn & Bacon, 1976.

McGuire, William J. "Effectiveness of Fear Appeals in Advertising." Research proposal submitted to the American Advertising Foundation, 1963.

Magill, Barbara A.; Murphy, Roger P.; and Feinberg, Lilian O. *Industrial Administration Survey Shows Need for Communication Study.* American Business Communication Association Bulletin, 1975.

Makay, John J., and Brown, William R. *The Rhetorical Dialogue: Contemporary Concepts and Cases.* Dubuque, Iowa: Wm. C. Brown Company Publishers, 1972.

Markgraf, B. "An Observational Study Determining the Amount of Time that Students in the Tenth and Twelfth Grades are Expected to Listen in the Classroom." Master's thesis, University of Wisconsin, 1957.

Mehrabian, Albert. "Communication Without Words." *Psychology Today,* September 1968, pp. 53–55.

———. *Silent Messages.* Belmont, Calif.: Wadsworth Publishing Co., 1971.

Mehrabian, Albert, and Kerris, Susan R. "Inference of Attitude from Nonverbal Communication in Two Channels." *Journal of Consulting Psychology* 31 (1967):248–52.

Mills, Glen E. *Message Preparation: Analysis and Structure.* Indianapolis: Bobbs-Merrill Co., 1966.

Mills, J., and Jellison, J. "Effect on Opinion Change of Similarity between the Communicator and the Audience He Addresses." *Journal of Personality and Social Psychology* 9 (1968):153–56.

Montagu, Ashley. *Touching: The Human Significance of the Skin.* New York: Harper & Row, Publishers, 1971.

Morris, Desmond. *The Naked Ape.* New York: Dell Publishing, Co., 1967.

Mortensen, C. David. "Communication Postulates." In *Messages,* edited by Jean Civikly. 2d ed. New York: Random House, 1977.

Morton, John, ed. *Biological and Social Factors in Psycholinguistics.* Urbana, Ill.: University of Illinois Press, 1970.

Newman, Edwin. *A Civil Tongue.* Indianapolis: Bobbs-Merrill Co., 1976.

Newman, Robert P., and Newman, Dale R. *Evidence.* Boston: Houghton Mifflin Co., 1969.

Nichols, Ralph, and Stevens, Leonard. "Listening to People." *Harvard Business Review* 35 (1957):no. 5.

Nolte, Dorothy Law. "Children Learn What They Live," 1954.

Oliver, Robert T.; Zelko, Harold P.; and Holtzman, Paul D. *Communicative Speaking and Listening.* 4th ed. New York: Holt, Rinehart and Winston, 1968.

Osborn, Alex F. *Applied Imagination: Principles and Procedures of Creative Thinking.* New York: Charles Scribner's Sons, 1953.

Pei, Mario. *The Story of Language.* New York: New American Library of World Literature, 1949.

Pence, O. L. "Emotionally Loaded Argument: Its Effectiveness in Stimulating Recall." *Quarterly Journal of Speech* 40 (1954):272–76.

Petrie, Charles R. "Informative Speaking: A Summary and Bibliography of Related Research." *Speech Monographs* 30 (1963):79–91.

Petrie, Charles R., Jr., and Carrel, Susan D. "The Relationship of

Motivation, Listening Capability, Initial Information, and Verbal Organization Ability to Lecture Comprehension and Retention." *Speech Monographs* 43 (1976):187–94.

Phelps, Lynn A., and DeWine, Sue. *Interpersonal Communication Journal.* New York: West Publishing Co., 1976.

"Playboy Interview: Abbie Hoffman." *Playboy,* May 1976, p. 64.

Powell, Fredric A. "The Effects of Anxiety-Arousing Messages when Related to Personal, Familial, and Impersonal Referents." *Speech Monographs* 32 (1965):102–6.

Powell, John. *The Secret of Staying in Love.* Niles, Ill: Argus Communications, 1974.

———. *Why Am I Afraid to Tell You Who I Am?* Niles, Ill.: Argus Communications, 1974.

———. *Fully Human, Fully Alive.* Niles, Ill.: Argus Communications, 1976.

Prather, Hugh. *Notes to Myself.* Moab, Utah: Real People Press, 1970.

Quinn, P. T. "Self-Disclosure as a Function of Degree of Acquaintance and Potential Power." Master's thesis, Ohio State University, 1965.

Rankin, Paul T. "Measurement of the Ability to Understand the Spoken Language." Ph. D. dissertation, University of Michigan, 1926, cited in *Dissertation Abstracts* 12 (1926):847.

———. "Listening Ability: Its Importance, Measurement, and Development." *Chicago Schools Journal* 12 (1930):177.

Renuk, James M. "A Medium for His Message." *Washington Post,* 1977.

Richmond, V. P., and Robertson, D. "Communication Apprehension as a Function of Being Raised in an Urban or Rural Environment." Monograph, West Virginia Northern Community College, 1976.

Robb, Stephen. "Fundamentals of Evidence and Argument." In *Modcom: Modules in Speech Communication.* Chicago: Science Research Associates, 1976.

Rogers, Carl R. *On Becoming a Person.* Boston: Houghton Mifflin Co., 1961.

———. *Freedom to Learn.* Columbus, Ohio: Charles E. Merrill Publishing Co., 1969.

Rogers, Carl E., and Farson, Richard E. "Active Listening." In *Readings in Interpersonal and Organizational Communication,* edited by Richard C. Huseman, Cal M. Logue, and Dwight L. Freshly. Boston: Holbrook Press, 1969.

Rokeach, Milton. *Beliefs, Attitudes, and Values.* San Francisco: Jossey-Bass Publishers, 1968.

Rosenfeld, Lawrence B., and Civikly, Jean M. *With Words Unspoken: The Nonverbal Experience.* New York: Holt, Rinehart and Winston, 1976.

Rosenthal, Robert, and Jacobson, Lenore. *Pygmalion in the Classroom: Teacher Expectation and Pupils' Intellectual Development.* New York: Holt, Rinehart and Winston, 1968.

Rosnow, Ralph L., and Robinson, Edward J. *Experiments in Persuasion.* New York: Academic Press, Inc., 1967.

Rubin, Zick. "The Rise and Fall of First Impressions." In *Interpersonal Communication in Action,* edited by Bobby R. Patton and Kim Griffin. 2d ed. Harper & Row, Publishers, 1977.

Schramm, Wilbur. "How Communication Works." In *The Processes and Effects of Mass Communication,* edited by Wilbur Schramm. Urbana, Ill.: University of Illinois Press, 1971.

Schutz, William. *Here Comes Everybody.* New York: Harper & Row, Publishers, 1971.

Sears, D., and Freedman, J. "Effects of Expected Familiarity with Arguments upon Opinion Change and Selective Exposure." *Journal of Personality and Social Psychology* 2 (1965):420–26.

Shapiro, Jeffrey G.; Krauss, Herbert H.; and Truax, Charles B. "Therapeutic Conditions of Disclosure beyond the Therapeutic Encounter." *Journal of Counseling Psychology* 16 (1969):290–94.

Sharp, Harry, Jr., and McClung, Thomas. "Effects of Organization on the Speaker's Ethos." *Speech Monographs* 33 (1966): 182–83.

Shaw, Marvin E. *Group Dynamics: The Psychology of Small Group Behavior.* New York: McGraw-Hill Book Co., 1971

Shostrum, Everett L. *Man, the Manipulator.* New York: Abingdon Press, 1967.

Smith, Raymond G. *Speech Communication: Theory and Models.* New York: Harper & Row, Publishers, 1970.

Sommer, Robert. "The Distance for Comfortable Conversation: A Further Study." *Sociometry* 25 (1962):111–16.

Stewart, Charles J., and Cash, William B. *Interviewing: Principles and Practices.* 2d ed. Dubuque, Iowa: Wm. C. Brown Company Publishers, 1978.

Swanson, Richard, and Marquardt, Charles. *On Communication: Listening, Reading, Speaking, and Writing.* Beverly Hills, Calif.: Glencoe Press, 1974.

Taylor, D. A. "Some Aspects of the Development of Interpersonal Relationships: Social Penetration Process." *Technical Report No. 1.* Center for Research on Social Behavior. University of Delaware, 1965.

Taylor, D. A., and Altman, I. "Intimacy Scaled Stimuli to Use in Studies of Interpersonal Relations." *Psychological Reports* 19 (1966):729–30.

Terris, Walter F. *Content and Organization of Speeches.* Dubuque, Iowa: Wm. C. Brown Company Publishers, 1968.

Thomas, Coramae, and Howard, C. Jeriel. *Contact: A Textbook in Applied*

Communications. Englewood Cliffs, N.J.: Prentice-Hall, 1970.

Thompson, Wayne N. *Quantitative Research in Public Address and Communication.* New York: Random House, 1967.

Thonssen, Lester, and Baird, A. Craig. "The Character of the Speaker." In *Readings in Speech,* edited by Haig A. Bosmajian. New York: Harper & Row, Publishers, 1971.

"Time of Reckoning for Student Deadbeats." *U.S. News and World Report,* July 18, 1977, p. 21.

"Tomorrow." *U.S. News and World Report,* July 18, 1977, p. 8.

Triandis, Harry C. "Cultural Influences upon Perception." In *Intercultural Communication: A Reader,* edited by Larry A. Samovar and Richard E. Porter. 2d ed. Belmont, Calif.: Wadsworth Publishing Co., 1976.

Tucker, Charles O. "An Application of Programmed Learning to Informative Speech." *Speech Monographs* 31 (1964):142–52.

Tuppen, Christopher J. S. "Dimensions of Communicator Credibility: An Oblique Solution." *Speech Monographs* 41 (1974):253–60.

Verderber, Rudolph F. *The Challenge of Effective Speaking.* 3d ed. Belmont, Calif.: Wadsworth Publishing Co., 1976.

Vohs, John L. "An Empirical Approach to the Concept of Attention." *Speech Monographs* 31 (1964):355–60.

Voor, John B., and Miller, Joseph M. "The Effect of Practice upon the Comprehension of Time-compressed Speech." *Speech Monographs* 32 (1965):452–54.

Voss, F. "The Relationships of Disclosure to Marital Satisfaction: An Exploratory Study." Master's thesis, University of Wisconsin, 1969.

Walter, Otis M. *Speaking to Inform and Persuade.* New York: Macmillan Publishing Co., 1966.

Weaver, Andrew T., and Ness, Ordean G. *An Introduction to Public Speaking.* New York: Odyssey Press, 1961.

Weinrauch, Donald J., and Swanda, John R., Jr. "Examining the Significance of Listening: An Exploratory Study of Contemporary Management." *Journal of Business Communication* 13 (Fall 1975):25–32.

Wenburg, John R., and Wilmot, William. *The Personal Communication Process.* New York: John Wiley & Sons, 1973.

West, Morris L. *The Shoes of the Fisherman.* New York: William Morrow & Co., 1963.

Wheeless, Lawrence R. "The Effects of Attitude, Credibility, and Homophily on Selective Exposure to Information." *Speech Monographs* 41 (1974):329–38.

Whorf, Benjamin Lee. "Science and Linguistics." In *Language, Thought and Reality,* edited by John B. Carroll. Cambridge, Mass.: M.I.T. Press, 1956.

Wiley, Ruth C. *The Self-Concept: A Critical Survey of Pertinent Research Literature.* Lincoln, Nebr.: University of Nebraska Press, 1961.

Wilt, Miriam E. "A Study of Teacher Awareness of Listening as a Factor in Elementary Education." *Journal of Educational Research* 43 (1950):626.

Winans, James A. "Conversing With an Audience." In *Selected Readings in Public Speaking,* edited by Jane Blankenship and Robert Wilhoit. Belmont, Calif.: Dickinson Publishing Co., 1968.

Woolbert, Charles. "The Effects of Various Modes of Public Reading." *Journal of Applied Psychology* 4 (1920):162–85.

Worthy, W.; Gary, A.; and Kahn, G. M. "Self-Disclosure as an Exchange Process." *Journal of Personality and Social Psychology* 13 (1969):59–63.

Zelko, Harold P., and Dance, Frank E. X. *Business and Professional Speech Communication.* New York: Holt, Rinehart and Winston, 1965.

Topics for Activities

Name Index

Subject Index

Articulation, 72
Attention, 231
  gaining and maintaining,
    231–35
Audience adaptation, 188, 225
  adapting supporting
    materials for, 227–28
  adapting your purpose for,
    226–27
  adapting yourself for, 188
  adapting your topic for,
    225–26
  adapting your verbal and
    nonverbal codes for, 188
Audience analysis
  audience attitudes, beliefs,
    values in, 181–83
  audience interest in topic in,
    179–81
  audience knowledge of topic
    in, 179–81
  captive and voluntary
    audiences in, 175–77
  demographic analysis in,
    177–79
  levels of, 174
  methods of, 183
    inference in, 184–86
    observation in, 183–84
    questionnaires in, 186

Barnlund's "six people," 5
Bodily movement, 67–68
Body of the speech, 235
  form of, 235
Boomerang effect, 291
Brainstorming, 160

Classification, 50–51
Clichés, 43–45, 55
Closure, 31
Clothing, 72–73
Code, 8, 40
  nonverbal, 8
  verbal, 8
Common ground, 200
Communication
  definition of, 3
  functions of, 10
  problems in, 12
  and self, 5
  situations, variety of, 6
Comparative validation, 35
Concreteness, 58–61
Connotative meaning, 48
Consensual validation, 34, 56

Dating, 58–59
Decode, 8, 40, 129
Defensiveness, 136

Delivery, 253–68
  articulation in, 262–63
  bodily aspects of, 264–67
  enunciation in, 262
  extemporaneous, 254
  eye contact in, 266–67
  fluency in, 263
  four modes of, 254
  gestures in, 264–67
  impromptu, 255
  manuscripts, use of, in, 254
  movement in, 267
  pause in, 259–61
  pitch in, 257–58
  pronunciation in, 262
  rate of, 258–59
  vocal aspects of, 256–64
  vocalized pauses in, 260
  vocal variety in, 264
  volume in, 261
Denotative meaning, 48
Descriptive feedback, 57–58,
  76, 77
Descriptiveness, 55–58
Double bind, 76

Egocentrism, 137
Empathy, 129–42
  improving our ability in,
    140–42
  interference with, 133–40
    defensiveness and, 136
    egocentrism and, 137
    experiential superiority
      and, 137
    factual distractions and,
      133
    mental distractions and,
      133, 134
    physical distractions and,
      133, 134–35
    semantic distractions and,
      133–34
    status and, 137–39
    stereotypes and, 137–39
Encode, 8, 40, 129
Enunciation, 72
Euphemisms, 42–45, 55
Evidence, 216–225
  types of, 220
    statistics, 223
    surveys and studies,
      220–21
    testimonial, 222
Experiential superiority, 137

Facial expression, 67–68
Fear of public speaking,
  173–74
Figure and ground, 31

Gestalt psychology, 29–32

Hidden agenda, 15

Index card, 219
Indexing, 59–60
Inferences, 56
Inflection, 72
Informative speech, 273–86
  document of the, 281–83
  extrinsic motivation and the,
    277
  information hunger and the,
    275
  information overload and
    the, 280–81
  information relevance and
    the, 276–77
  informative content and the,
    277–78
  obstacles in the, 281
  organizing the, 280–83
  purposes of the, 274–75
Intentional confusion
  avoidance of, 55
Interpersonal communication,
  6, 7, 81
Interviewing, 146–51
  definition of, 148
  organizing the interview, 151
    funnel approach, 151
  purposes of interviews, 152
  types of interviews, 152–56
    employment interviews,
      155–56
    informational interviews,
      152–53
    persuasive interviews,
      153–55
Intrapersonal communication,
  6, 81
Introduction of a speech,
  231–35
  purpose of, 231–35

Johari Window, 106–8
  blind area in the, 107
  hidden area in the, 107
  open area in the, 107
  unknown area in the, 107
Journal writing, 91–100

Kinesics, 67–68

335

338

page 74   DUNAGIN'S PEOPLE by Ralph Dunagin. 1975
           Sentinel Star. Courtesy of Field Newspaper Syndicate.

page 75   © 1956 United Feature Syndicate, Inc.

page 76   © King Features Syndicate, Inc. 1976

Chapter 5

page 83   Photograph by Peter Karas

page 84   Photograph by Jean-Claude Lejeune

page 87   Photograph courtesy of Wide World Photos

page 89   Photograph by David S. Strickler, Strix Pix

page 91   Photograph by Rick Smolan

page 93   Reprinted by permission of the Chicago Tribune-New
           York News Syndicate, Inc.

page 98   Photograph by David S. Strickler, Strix Pix

Chapter 6

page 105   CONCHY by James Childress. © Field Enterprises,
           Inc., 1975. Courtesy of Field Newspaper Syndicate.

page 106   Photograph by Jean-Claude Lejeune

page 108   Photograph by Rick Smolan

page 111   Reprinted by permission of the Chicago Tribune-New
           York News Syndicate, Inc.

pages 114 (*upper*)Photograph by Jean-Claude Lejeune
and 115

pages 114 (*lower*) Photograph by Jon Jacobson
and 115

page 118   Photograph by David S. Strickler, Strix Pix

Chapter 7

page 129   © 1975 United Feature Syndicate, Inc.

page 130   (*left*) Photograph by Nell Campbell, UFW Photo

page 130   (*right*) Photograph by Rick Smolan

page 134   Photograph by James L. Shaffer

page 138   © King Features Syndicate, Inc. 1976

page 141   Photograph by Jean-Claude Lejeune

Chapter 8

page 147   (*top*) THE WIZARD OF ID by permission of Johnny
           Hart and Field Enterprises, Inc.

page 147   (*middle*) Reprinted by permission of the Chicago
           Tribune-New York News Syndicate, Inc.

page 147   (*bottom*) © 1976 United Feature Syndicate, Inc.

340

Chapter 12

Chapter 13

Chapter 14

Chapter 15

(continued)